Florence Caddy

Footsteps of Jeanne d'Arc

A pilgrimage

Florence Caddy

Footsteps of Jeanne d'Arc
A pilgrimage

ISBN/EAN: 9783337289522

Printed in Europe, USA, Canada, Australia, Japan

Cover: Foto ©ninafisch / pixelio.de

More available books at **www.hansebooks.com**

FOOTSTEPS

OF

JEANNE D'ARC

A PILGRIMAGE

BY

MRS. FLORENCE CADDY.

'The life of Jeanne d'Arc is like a legend in the midst of history.'
WALLON.

IN ONE VOLUME.

LONDON:
HURST AND BLACKETT, PUBLISHERS,
13, GREAT MARLBOROUGH STREET.
1886.
All Rights Reserved.

CONTENTS.

INTRODUCTION.

BOOK I.
THE CALL.

CHAPTER		PAGE
I.	DOMREMY.—THE CHURCH	3
II.	JEANNE D'ARC'S COUNTRY AND HOME	23
III.	JOURNEY TO VAUCOULEURS	40
IV.	TOUL AND NANCY	60
V.	THROUGH THE HEART OF FRANCE	72
VI.	ARRIVAL AT CHINON	93

BOOK II.
THE TRIUMPH.

VII.	THE TRIAL AT POITIERS	123
VIII.	THE LOIRE	150
IX.	THE MAID OF ORLEANS	166
X.	A WONDERFUL WEEK.—JARGEAU AND PATAY	201
XI.	THE CORONATION AT RHEIMS	217

BOOK III.
THE TRAGEDY.

XII.	THE ABBEY OF ST. DENIS	249
XIII.	THE KING'S RETREAT.—CAMPAIGN ON THE UPPER LOIRE	279
XIV.	THE ROYAL IDOL BROKEN.—THE FOREST OF FONTAINEBLEAU	300
XV.	COMPIÈGNE	314
XVI.	THE PRISONER OF LE CROTOY	333
XVII.	JOURNEY TO ROUEN	346

APPENDIX . 365

INTRODUCTION.

'Through thy cornfields green, and sunny vines, oh, pleasant land of France.'

THE traveller from England in quest of scenes of excitement, or change from the bustle of too eager life, has just wearied himself over the plains of Belgium or the north of France without finding either the sublimity or the calm he sought. He has just settled himself down to a comfortable discontent until he shall reach Switzerland or Italy, or it may be the East, which will give him either the stir or the repose he craves, when he comes upon a gentle landscape of hill and dale, the cradle of two well-known rivers. If he can curb his impatience so far as to examine it more closely, this region will give him the elements of the change he needs, which he may find in no greater completeness if he travel further afield in search of stimulus or repose. More and more we are learning to feel that it matters little how far off we go; we cannot leave this earth whose distant parts we know so prosaically much about, and we cannot quit our own shell. The best part of our knowledge is that which makes our home more spacious, and peoples it with the soul-friends whom we have known by name from infancy, whom we should be glad to know more intimately, whom we would willingly turn from shadows into statues and pictures.

Here the dead level of the north of Europe first breaks into the outlying billows which Nature has tossed into the petrified tempest of the Alpine chain.

The stately front of Rheims has reminded the traveller by train of the heroine of the fifteenth century, and, with a pause of pity for her fate, he passes on to some other drift of thought—to the risks to man in woman's suffrage, possibly.

Before he dives deeper into this drift, it will do him no harm to rub up his recollections of Joan of Arc, and to try if all the histories he has read have given her equal personality with the myths of early fable, or the beings of fiction created out of smoke. Though he may have a strong opinion as to the nature of her spiritual claims, he may find his conception of her character dim and broken as a reflection upon the surface of a ruffled lake, and his liveliest impression of her produced after all by actual pictures.

He who remembers the late lamented Bastien Lepage's picture of Jeanne d'Arc,*—and who that has seen it does not remember it?—must want to probe deeper into that wonderful life, that whichever way you read it is full of mystery and glory.

Lepage, born in the department of the Meuse, natur-

---

* It was exhibited in the triennial exhibition at Ghent in 1880, the year it was painted. It was sent from New York to be exhibited at the collection of Bastien Lepage's works in Paris, 1885.

ally had keen feeling for this subject of Jeanne 'Arc, as well as love for the soft Meuse landscape. His picture is a great work in every respect. Jeanne stands under an apple-tree in a green orchard, in the bloom of a spring such as no one has more perfectly represented on canvas than Lepage. She has turned away her head thoughtfully, in reverent amazement and self-questioning from the vision, which is still visible, and wonderfully painted. Her cottage, surrounded by faithfully-studied trees, forms the background.

The face and figure of the girl are a marvel of mixed expression, one reads the drama of her life upon her countenance. She leans against the tree-stem as if all strength had left her, she is so completely in the spirit as to be taken out of herself; yet withal there is no tinge of the pre-Raffaellite ecstacy or asceticism. The vision is too real for inquiry: she accepts a destiny. Her dress, when at last we think of it, is brown with a lavender-coloured jacket laced in front, showing white linen. Her spinning-wheel stands near. The vision shines between the cottage and the trees in the exact situation marked by tradition, for the landscape is a copy of the actual scene. The mystic figures are those of a knight (St. Michael) in golden armour holding out a sword; a female saint, wreathed with roses, clasps her hands imploring, another kneels weeping. For all that it is most dreamlike and supernatural, the painting is full of a wonderful realism, and, like all Lepage's vigorous handling, the figure of Jeanne is actual and solid. It brings the real woman before us. I do not know if the figure is a portrait, but it is very like one of the young girls of Domremy.

It is difficult with words to vivify Jeanne's image as Lepage has done it in painting, yet I will try to do it if my reader will trace with me the path of her interesting life. I know the way, having travelled the red route in this map, nearly inch by inch: much of it on foot, nowhere in a hurry, sometimes alone, sometimes more gaily, accompanied by friends or by members of my family. I do not, however, propose to obtrude my personal narrative upon the reader. If I cannot place Jeanne before him, I can at least point out the things she saw, the surroundings among which she moved. I am setting before my readers the plain facts, just the things that they probably do not know, if they have browsed like giraffes among the higher branches of history, the poets and such-like. As a military leader studies the nature of his ground, I think much might be gained by treating history geographically. If I chatter too much the reader can shut me up and put me in his pocket.

We will just get upon our ground, and afterwards we will not travel much by train, which is a poor way of seeing the country. My purpose did not allow of my being hampered by any vehicle of my own, but a double tricycle is a capital conveyance for two who like to talk. These French roads are eminently good for the cyclist.

Leaving Châlons by the side of the long rows of poplars bordering its canal, parallel with the more prettily and naturally wooded banks of the Marne, which is pea-soup coloured here by the weir, where the fish leap up so numerously, we begin to enjoy the country. The light, friable soil is warm in colour, ranging from creamy white to golden gravel streaked with rich, foxy hues. The low land is marshy, the water willowy: the mellowing woods are flushed with autumn's crimson. The narrowing Marne becomes rapid between the hills, spreading again as they widen out. Amber trees rear their heads against the blue sky, banded with light. The train moves slowly over the partially-flooded meadows stocked with geese and herds of cattle, some tawny, some white, and some dove-coloured steers like the oxen in the south, all feeding among the autumn crocuses.

These hills are the Argonnes, eastern and western, made famous by Dumouriez as the Thermopylæ of France, and made classical by Thiers in his 'History of the Consulate and the Empire.' Here is red-roofed Loisy-sur-Marne among the vineyards in the chalk hills, and soon comes Vitry-le-François, with its pinnacled square tower and the red roofs of its church, which is also bristling with pinnacles, and the land levels itself again and the sun waxes hotter. Here is the full tide of vintage going on. Busy vintagers carry funnel-shaped baskets at their backs, full of purple grapes, and empty them into carts, while other men in blouses and women are breakfasting under the cherry and plum-trees. The hill slopes are all vineyarded, except where they rise crested with fir and beech and many-coloured trees. Clear young rilling rivers, with women washing linen in them, flow among this sweet Vosges landscape, and now we see the yellow Marne again. Now we get among the oolite hills and woods, richer than ever with colour in this pleasant hilly country of Val d'Osne, and as fully stocked with white cattle.

Here is Joinville, and here, if strong and able to enjoy a walk, I should advise the tourist to leave the train and strike across the hills by way of the old Roman amphitheatre at Grand, and drop upon the valley of the Meuse, halting for rest and thought at the retired and peaceful village of Domremy-la-Pucelle. Little luggage will be needed, no best clothes.

If circumstances are different and walking impracticable, he had better go on from Joinville to Bologne, where, while roaming about the fields between the trains, he will have the opportunity of feeling the southern force of the sun. Change into the train (northward) for Neufchâteau, and at Neufchâteau change again for Maxey-Domremy, and walk across the meadows, with streamlets in them, mind you, tributaries of the Vair, which it is not always easy to cross, to the birthplace of Jeanne d'Arc. Murray says 'it is a hot walk across fields to Domremy. Little to be seen there.' Let us go and look.

Peep at the little church and the outside of Jeanne d'Arc's house before putting up at the tiny Hotel de la Pucelle, where you will get fresh milk when madame has 'pulled the cow,' but where they will probably have nothing, raw nor cooked, in the house for your choice, except eggs, but they will forage for you among the farms and make you comfortable in their primitive way with goodwill and attention; and, having things better than luxury, one is happy, even though the basin one has to use for a footbath is about the size and inconvenience of a soup-plate.

There is another small inn further up the village,

neater but not so well situated. You can walk about there or sit on the bridge (of fifteen arches) watching the early moonlight playing on the Meuse while your room and supper are being prepared. They will probably fish the first course fresh from the Meuse for you, and slay for you a fowl, a barn-door mongrel, which they will serve like a frog lying on its back with a very long neck and pinions displayed; but, with sauce à la grand'faim, it is very good, and there are worse pleasures in life than waiting for and relishing a supper of this sort.

All the better if the place is primitive; it is so, and it carries you back four hundred years or more, to the time of Joan of Arc herself. One sees the very way in which she lived and was brought up. The girls who pass you leading their cows home from pasture, or carrying a pitchfork, do so with an air, a dignity of manner that bespeaks the countrywomen of a heroine.

The little Joans of Arc, some of them pretty, all neat and clean with their close white caps and azure grey pinafores, rush out of church or school, clattering their sabots, eager to play, yet still more anxious to stop and look at strangers with their wonderful clothes and paint-boxes. For a stranger is a novelty; the train truly brings many French pilgrims, but these sweep through Joan's cottage and the church, cross themselves, sneer at the statue in the grove, which certainly lends itself well to criticism, light their cigars, and are off again by the next train.

The place seems to have slept, no, not slept, but simply wrought and rested for four hundred years. There is time to enjoy oneself in it. The village clock outside remains stationary at eight for hours sometimes, until the verger remembers to wind it up again for evening church: the neighbouring parish clock at Greux has the same habit; but when they do tick one can usually hear it, the place is so quiet; and the striking is an event. Who ever heard St. Paul's clock tick, I wonder; except our country-cousins who climb up on purpose?

The Domremy church clock has a convenient practice of striking twice, in case you should have forgotten to count the first time. It has only one hand, for people here do not shave time to a quarter-of-an-hour or so; they leave a good margin of half-an-hour to catch a train in, and then foster patience; for the trains take a long time to crawl over a very little bit of way, stopping a long while at each station, after they have slackened the pace for half-a-mile before reaching it, for fear of collision with a train that has not yet started from Pagny-sur-Meuse, the junction. This gives the station-master time to cease weeding his cabbages and dress himself to receive passengers. It will be understood that there are no express trains, and the railway has not caused much change in the habits of the people.

This calm, easy life is soothing after our metropolitan hurry. Yes, one is really carried back four hundred and fifty years; simplicity of life, especially of the pastoral sort, and the natural features and by-paths of a rural landscape, are among the most immutable things that our earth knows.

Here in Lorraine too we are on the borders of a foreign land whose contiguity has taught both peoples warfare, as it did four centuries ago. Yet, for all that it has been so often the frontier of war, Nature rights herself and heals the wounds. We see Jeanne d'Arc's life and her surroundings just as plainly as we see her actual dwelling; indeed, they are less altered.

The wild flowers, charming, and several of them new to us, are the very same that Jeanne twined into garlands for the 'beautiful May;' the cloud-berries and the grapes grow where they then did; Jeanne's favourite vineyard haunt is still the 'vignoble de Jeanne d'Arc.' War may pass over the land again and again, but the peace of poverty remains to it,—that poverty which is industrious contentment; not squalor, not wretchedness, but perhaps the most blessed condition of any, the very condition of life which our Saviour sanctified by holding it here upon earth.

We ate our newly-beaten butter with our breakfast at what seemed the late hour of eight, reasonable enough at home, here it felt disgracefully idle.

The early church-service was over and the dense white mist, which makes the spiders' webs like patterns strung in pearls, was lifting over the hill ranges and melting in the blaze of day.

Again I seemed to see Jeanne d'Arc herself among the young women with their long sticks or whips, leading their cows with tinkling bells afield.

I pictured her in a tall, finely-formed girl with her head set with commanding poise upon her shoulders, who returned my gaze with another full of modesty and pride, as if she said, 'Yes, Jeanne was one of us.' Her head only covered with her crown of thick braided hair, her figure with a short skirt and blue-grey 'caraco;'

she needed no other adornment while she had her youth, strength, and beauty of health and fearlessness. She carried her pitchfork like a sceptre.

We learn more by getting hold of the personality of good and great people, than by merely reading of them at second-hand through those who have only sought them in dusty folios. 'Life is the best commentary upon abstract truth,' says Sir Emilius Bayley. 'Life brings truth home to us, shows us how others have fought and conquered.'

BOOK I.

THE CALL.

CHAPTER I.

DOMREMY.—THE CHURCH.

'J'avais treize ans ; c'était en été, vers midi, dans le jardin de mon père, et je n'avais pas jeuné la veille. J'entendis cette voix à ma droite, vers l'église, et j'en eus grand'peur.' ('I was thirteen ; it was in summer, towards midday, in my father's garden, and I had not fasted the day before. I heard this voice at my right hand, by the church, and I had great fear of it.')

Evidence of Jeanne d'Arc.

EPIPHANY morning of 1412 dawned, in the extreme east of France, with the maiden's birth who was to fill the whole realm with the radiance of faith, and revive hope in a crushed nation : her birth who raised all womanhood in her person, to whom succeeding generations of women have been able to point as an example of what the female sex, at its best, is capable in the lines of heroism, patriotism, and self-devotion. An Amazon without cruelty, a heroine who never lost her womanhood, a patriot who sought no self-advancement, a prophetess who proclaimed only the power of God. Ant. Astezan, of Asti in Piedmont, first secretary of the Duke of Orleans, who wrote in 1435, says Jeanne d'Arc was born at the Epiphany. He is a trustworthy authority, who had good means of being exact. Much of the supernatural in her story is the fruit of divers authors' imagination. Yet more marvellous is the truth.

Ten centuries of sleep were ended, and, heralded by this extraordinary girl, mankind rose to clear away an accumulation of injustices and wrongs, preparing the world for a new epoch, an aurora of dazzling inventions, discoveries, and results. The poets, Dante, Petrarch, Chaucer, led the way for the discoverers and experimentalists, Columbus and the printers; but the prophets and earliest reformers woke first, and, in homely phrase, opened the windows and lighted the fires, and let in the light of truth to show the path of duty. Among these was Jeanne d'Arc. We, who live in a time when the world's manhood is relapsing effete into its second childhood, with garrulity as its characteristic, can scarcely conceive the flood of awakened energy that was bursting, not only its night coverings, but all bounds of home and city, to rush impetuous through all distances.

The dark ages, the dispensation of martyrs, ended in a blaze of glorious light. One female figure closed it in, 'the light of ancient France.' She began that crusade of patriotism for freedom, that claim of independent nationality in Christendom, which has since been bequeathed from bleeding sire to son. This was the close of the Gothic age. Is the Renaissance that followed a mimicry of the past, or an earnest of the millennial glory? Probably both; as in all things earthly, good and evil grow together until the harvest.

Believers in Jeanne d'Arc's spiritual pretensions regard her as the culmination of the religious faith and superstition of her age, and all the dark ages, ere Dante and Columbus gave new eyes to Europe: a view certainly interesting to Hibbert lecturers.

I wish rather to show the human side of her character, believing that God works with us by human means, using natural causes, and that He chooses His human instruments in the same way, with deep reverence be it spoken, that a wise man chooses his colleagues, a skilled workman his tools, or a sagacious monarch his counsellors. It is a selection of the fittest for the work which He is to direct. The task required obedience and faith. Again the Lord sought these in a woman; again the woman's answer was according to the pure and good woman's nature: 'Behold the hand-maid of the Lord.'

But the task also needed strength of body, a body trained in the routine and endurance of pastoral life, united to the highest qualities of the soul, a receptiveness and steadfastness of mind incompatible with the overloaded and easily-upset brain, the mind driven about with every wind of doctrine blown upon it from every book. A woman was the best instrument for the purpose of closing the long war. The whole of Jeanne d'Arc's campaign shows that this work of liberating France was meant to be carried out without bloodshed: it was the unfaith and wavering of rulers brought on the battles that the blind brutality of men precipitated.

Wherever Jeanne was permitted to go forward in the way the spirit led her, towns capitulated and armies melted away at her approach. We know she was often frustrated; yet, for all the wilfulness of men, the Lord of hosts showed in a marked way His saving power. God knew His purpose of mercy would be unvalued, and chose a fit instrument for all contingencies in a strong, healthy human girl—yes, Chadband notwithstanding, a thoroughly human girl; no divinity, still less a monstrosity or walking miracle; no epileptic nor maniac dreamer, but a healthy mind in a perfectly developed frame; a firm, self-reliant character with steady nerves, subject to no hysterical hallucinations.

This is opposed to the general opinion of Jeanne d'Arc, but I hope to show it true from history and a careful view of the situations in which she was placed. Without claiming for her any of the Messianic attributes which Henri Martin—who, with singular inconsistency, seems to believe in little else of supernatural—almost blasphemously assigns to Jeanne d'Arc; again with deep reverence I dare to say, her short life showed how a woman may closely follow the Saviour, from working life through childhood and youth to martyrdom; mingling with all ranks, yet loving her brethren the most; usurping no high sphere, ambitious of no sovereignty, growing up in favour with God and man.

Hume, improving upon the Burgundian Monstrelet, and following Voltaire, says Jeanne was twenty-seven years old when she went to Chinon; all other authorities agree that she was only seventeen at that time, except a short biography of her, fuller of mistakes than facts, published in the *Guardian* in the last century as one of a series of 'Famous Women of the World,' which gives the date of her birth as 1407. The *Encyclopædia Britannica* blindly follows this so-called history of Jeanne almost word for word in its article on France.

'The middle ages,' says Henri Martin, 'developed two great types of womanhood, the ladylove and the ascetic Madonna.' Neither of these was Jeanne d'Arc. And Michelet, vividly describing the epoch, points out that 'the agricultural population, which now seems incapable even of the blindly ferocious impulse of the Jacquerie, brings forth Jeanne d'Arc.'

The village of Domremy—it is scarcely more than a hamlet—lies at the foot of a hill whose table-land, called the 'Haut Pays,' stretches away far westward, until it forms the first slopes of the Champagne vineyards. It is a little commune of one hundred and five houses, with two hundred and seventy-five inhabitants, whose numbers are annually decreasing. In 1856 they were three hundred and twenty souls: a loss of forty-five out of so small a population is a significant fact, especially when there is no apparent misery or unhealthiness to cause it. Do the towns really absorb the country population everywhere in like proportion? If so, it is time to change our teaching, and for our philosophers to persuade the world that it makes a bad bargain in exchanging every bodily comfort, all the beauty of life, for the gratification of having so many extra coins slip through the fingers on Saturday afternoon.

But I must not be coaxed away from following the footsteps of Jeanne d'Arc, or Jeannette, as she was baptized and always called in her own country, in her childhood's rambles, in the scenes of her earliest day-dreams, where she played and danced with her little sister Catherine, and her young friends Mengette and Hauviette, and worked and prayed in all the sweet piety of childhood. With them we will walk through the Bois Chesnu, where a chapel, a sort of temple of white stone, is newly built to the memory of the maid among the vineyards, interspersed with apple-trees, bordering on the woods where Jeanne heard holy voices in groves haunted by the relics of a pagan superstition. These glowing woods are now mellowing into autumn beneath the tinted hill-tops, known in old maps as the King's Forest, with trees turning to orange and purply brown; Jeanne's much-loved native woods, Nature's own cloistered churches, pierced in the diagonal sunshine with translucent hues of gold and flame and russet green.

The path turns downwards from the new white

temple across the mushroomed meadows to Coussey, a neighbouring village, large enough to boast a post-office and a *gendarmerie nationale;* where there is a statue of Jeanne d'Arc near the washing fountain, and also a pretty church, whose round-arched door, with dog-toothed mouldings, and three-storied Romanesque tower, remain as they existed in her time. These objects, and the coned towers of the château of Bourlimont on the hill beyond, form a pleasing picture, of which the only things unfamiliar to Jeanne would be her own statue and the zinc tricolour flag. One can figure to oneself the tall, well-formed maiden, 'moult belle, of great strength and power,' as all her neighbours witnessed of her, walking through these fields, fearless among the horned cattle browsing here, where great tawny bulls come to drink at the large pond which often floods the road. Fear is a form of emotion unknown in Jeanne d'Arc's country.

There is much cattle in these meadows, some black and white, some spotted like our Guernseys, less shapely elegant than the Alderneys, some dove-coloured or tawny, with dark velvet muzzles and deep-blue calm eyes, mildly inquiring. Jeanne calls them with that sweet voice of hers—a true woman's voice, say those who heard its mild, firm tones.

They are always ready to talk and tell all they know, these good people, now as in the time when messengers were sent round the countryside gathering up gossip of the heroine at the times of her trial and her rehabilitation, when, however, they heard nothing but good of her; or in Jeanne's own childhood, when these people of Coussey pointed to the villages of Happoncourt-au-Pied and Moncel on the hill-side, both famous for a siege in 1372, sustained against the people of Metz, in which men and women alike defended themselves victoriously. Doubtless Jeanne had heard of this; it was recent enough, and such exploits last long for talk.

M. Siméon Luce, in a valuable article on 'Jeanne d'Arc at Domremy' in the 'Revue des Deux Mondes,' May, 1885, points out how Jeanne grew up in a time of effervescence of public feeling in the valley, caused by the marriage of Jeanne de Joinville, the young French heiress of the lordships of Greux and Domremy, to a Lorraine noble, Henri d'Ogeviller. The villages held fast their nationality and their allegiance to the fleurs-de-lis, and declined to be transferred to the foreign suzerainté.

How these Coussey people gossip! This shows friendliness and leisure. We only gossip now by newspaper: society papers in our class, more sensational prints in a lower rank—both bad; ours, perhaps, the meanest and most frivolous, theirs more transpontine and vulgar. We cannot give up our gossip, though its friendliness is lost. Here white-haired men have time to laugh and chat. It should be thus. Life should not be so hard but that white-haired men in blouses can sit and rest and talk over old times with their old friends. The little maidens, having changed their grey felt slippers for sabots, come clattering out of school, yet pretending to hide from the boys, who have been for the last five minutes all agog for mischief, and all have a little merriment before supper-time.

The good 'route nationale,' leading from Coussey home to Domremy, lined with grey-stemmed poplars, brings forward from the distance the spires of foliage which group so well under the moonlight by the Meuse, where the bends and eddies of the puzzling network of rivers at Domremy give an appearance of islets, 'a mazy world of silvery enchantment,' its topography rendered still more perplexing by the vertical reflections of some of the tall stems in the water, and the oblique shadows of others on the grass; the play of half-luminous shade and glinting lights below emulating the translucent calm of heaven and her glittering stars. Among these tangled lights and shades sails the glory of the moon, dazzling and darkening, hiding and enhancing, outshining the lesser lights; as the broader current of the Meuse, sparkling like a silver riband with fringed edges, moves paramount among all these mill-streams and backwaters and rivulets which have no name beyond the hills among which they bubble forth.

Nature is full of play and laughter too, and we are in the middle of it standing on the bridge. The scene is just as pleasant by daylight, when kingfishers haunt these waters and gleam like sapphires among the sedges; the Meuse rustles sparkling over its weir beside the poplars in these meadows where the ducks live so happily, and geese and horses feed in the wide, woven-fenced fields between the river and the railway. The spiring groves of distant elm and poplar are thrown out by the white clouds above the pointed tourelles of the Prince de Bourlimont's château (the same family lived there in Jeanne d'Arc's time), before which rises the slope of the Bois Chesnu and the Vineyard of Jeanne d'Arc. Tufted trees and bushes with clumps of poplar fringe the right side of the meadows, lying like a Mesopotamia between the mill-stream and the Meuse.

These foreground meadows seem to be an island of the Meuse, though one is never sure of the topography hereabout, it is not apparent on the surface, its mystery has to be unravelled. The trees agreeably break the long line of hill of the Bois Chesnu, where the purple of distance disputes its colour with the gold of autumn foliage. Above the foreground sedges a little green orchard, the orchard of Bastien Lepage's well-known picture, lies between us and the first cottages of the village; their tiled roofs, grey with age, affording perches to the pigeons whose nests are in the church eaves. The white, rough-cast cottages reflect themselves in what looks from here like a third branch of the river, which one thinks may be the mill-stream, but one is not sure of it till afterwards. This little river is important in determining Jeanne's nationality, which has caused so many disputes among historians who know the map but not the place, and who cannot, for that reason, take into consideration the double political jurisdiction over this frontier land in the fifteenth century.

To the left and north of this rivulet, in the direction of Greux, it was Champagne, and of course France; to the right and southward, on the side of Neufchâteau, the land, belonging to the Duchy of Bar, was part of Lorraine. This latter, the more considerable portion of the village, contained the house and the church of the D'Arc family, and was of Lorraine nationality. But as this territory belonged to the Duchy of Bar, royal or 'mouvant,' of which the King of France was suzerain, the Dukes of Bar having been French vassals since the time of Philip the Fair, Jeanne was verily and truly the liege subject of the King of France.

René d'Anjou, Duke of Bar, married in 1419 the heiress of Charles, Duke of Lorraine. While retaining its rights, customs, and privileges, the Duchy of Bar followed the destinies of Lorraine. The new duke, being brother-in-law to the Dauphin, Charles VII., sympathised openly or at heart with the cause Jeanne d'Arc espoused; so that in no case can she be truly said to have acted against the cause of her country, her king, her feudal lord the Duke of Bar, nor the Archbishop of Rheims, of whose metropolitan church Domremy was a dependency.

This village was called Domremy-sur-Meuse to

distinguish it from Domremy-la-Canne and Domremy-aux-Bois, situated more to the northward. It is now known to the whole world as Domremy-la-Pucelle, named, as the Abbé Bourgaut, curé of the parish, says, from St. Remi, father of the French monarchy and the inspired maid who saved it from ruin.

The little watercourse that separates the two territories is called the Brook of the Three Fountains, from its triple spring at the west of Domremy. Since the beginning of the eighteenth century, its course has been altered; it now re-unites its waters, divided for a short space, and falls into the mill-stream very near the present bridge over the Meuse, almost in front of Jeanne d'Arc's house.

The hill of the Bois Chesnu ends at this point, sloping downward and away in graceful lines, opening up another hill behind Jeanne d'Arc's house, which is screened from us here by a grove of larches and spruce firs round the railed statue (bust), which is perhaps the worst that has ever been modelled of the Maid of Orleans, with its feathered head-dress and costume of the fashion of Louis XVIII.'s time, as libellous and contrary to fact as most of her so-called biographies.

The next object in the view is the church, its tiled roofs and gabled-ended tower surmounted by a plain stone cross of Calvary. To the left of the entrance-door is a bronze statue of the Maid kneeling, with one hand raised to heaven. It was executed by an artist of Lorraine, and placed here in 1860.

Beyond the church (we must now stand on the other side of the bridge) lies the main street of the village, with its cross road, called Rue de l'Isle, or Rue du Château de l'Isle, fronting a cluster of cottages abutting on the river. A cross here marks the head of the former bridge, a little below the present stone bridge. Here, on the opposite bank, stood formerly a chapel and an old fortified manor-house, where Jeanne d'Arc used sometimes to lead her cattle, to save them from marauding men-at-arms. One buttress only marks the site of these structures; the place is now overgrown with willows and poplars, between which we see the village of Maxey by the station, and the opposite hill-slopes beyond the meadows by the railway. This is all that the eye can see from the bridge in front of Jeanne d'Arc's home and church. The essence of the place is peace—peace and prayer.

Bear with me while I walk round the little parish church of Domremy, pencil in hand, describing each object in succession in the manner of a bailiff's inventory. It would be pleasanter, prettier writing to indulge at this opportunity with divergent (and easy) reflections on light and colour, radiance and art, and their power over the innocent mind of the young enthusiast. By plentiful words, by talk of columns and stained glass, of shrines, emblems, and pictures, I might give an idea of the humble parish church as a miniature cathedral. I might enlarge upon the power of all good and beautiful influences (which are of heaven) ; for, to one unaccustomed to the *wealth* of beauty, and susceptible of passions at once pure, soft, and elevated, their power is immense.

The prosaic inventory might rise into poetry by added angels' wings and lustrous hues. By throwing back everything into the past tense, I might make it seem that what is homely now and commonplace was glorious then, and conjure up an imaginary Jeanne moving in the midst of an imaginary combination of Flemish and Italian art in fourteenth-century glory, with heart and soul opened by these things to every lofty species of conviction.

Or I might urge the merely philosophic aspect of the question, and dissect the young, untried heroine's enthusiasm, analyse the food it grew upon, and make a metaphysical study of her inspiration. But to what end?

There is, after all, a higher poetry than full-sailed words in view of a simple peasant maid like Jeanne, who believed herself called to a great work outside her knowledge of life. The clearest outline, unadorned with flowers of rhetoric, is most becoming to the simple maiden, explaining the growth within her of a mental power of unusual sort, and its outcome in action.

The church is not now as it was then ; its very orientation has been altered, but parts remain, and the rest is of the same sort as the original ; the few differences are obvious, and relate to Jeanne d'Arc's history and memory. The importance of her parish church in her history is the influence it had in moulding her character, and the love she bore to the place of worship. She had a hunger for prayer and for the Holy Sacraments. Enthusiasm such as hers must necessarily be fed.

Turning to the right on entering the church, hollowed in the shortened shaft of a plain round column, we find the holy water stoup, the same which Jeanne d'Arc so often used; before this hang the three cords attached to the bells. Jeanne always loved the bells, and heard her 'Voices' more clearly when they were pealing,

Above the stand for the wax tapers is a modern oil painting of Jeanne d'Arc kneeling by a chair before her own latticed window. She wears the short skirt, white shift, and laced bodice of the country girls, a costume rather of tradition than of fact. The picture is interesting but artless, a circumstance explained when we hear that it is one of three given and painted by a man with much feeling for painting and enthusiasm for the subject of Jeanne d'Arc, but little or no technical instruction.

The coloured windows are modern, but doubtless there were stained-glass windows, and of finer colour, in Jeanne's time, filling her villagebred mind with awe of the subjects and admiration of the jewelled light. So much depends upon the feeling one brings to the contemplation of a picture, and how far removed one's mind is from a position of criticism. The first window seems to represent St. Elizabeth of Hungary, by her lap full of roses. Then comes a window to St. Margaret. Probably there always have been coloured windows painted with St. Margaret and St. Catherine, in whose names the church was dedicated. These images would have been Jeanne's delight, her jewels, her art gallery, her ideals of glory and beauty, companioning her through life from infancy, her spiritual friends. It needed no more than the affectionate feelings of an enthusiast to name the voices of duty and comfort after these two beloved beings. Her 'Voices' were a personification of her religion. These were the sweet names she knew; these saints had been holy women, the godly matrons whose example she was to follow.

In the turn of the transept hangs a sixteenth century painting of the conversion of St. Norbert; this picture and another, in the opposite transept, of the angels ministering to Jesus in the wilderness after his baptism and fasting, were brought from the Abbey of the Prémontrés at Mureau (Mira Vallis), which formerly received half of the tithes of Domremy. The ruins of this abbey are visible near Pargny, to the westward of the vale of the Saunelle. Below this painting stands upright the 'Pierre tombale des fils de la veuve Thiesselin, Marraine de Jeanne d'Arc.'

There is a window to the Madonna in this transept. It was this that first opened my eyes to the wrong orientation of the church. I find this in my note-book :—'I can't make it out that the sun shines more on and through these windows now at eleven o'clock.' Asking the reason of this, I found that the bulk of the original three-aisled romanesque church had been pulled down at the time the cemetery was removed in 1823 to a neighbouring hill-slope. The churchyard previously lay between the church and Jeanne d'Arc's house. This removal caused a great alteration of the sacred building, whose situation was almost reversed in consequence. The three altars of the chevet, or choir, thus became placed at the other extremity of the aisles. The tower was opened so as to present a doorway to the road, of which four unenriched buttresses form all the architectural adornment. Its square and massive form gives the idea of the tower having been formerly a fortress.

The good Abbé Bourgaut, curé of Domremy, slily suggests that its situation at Domremy has caused this supposition, as if everything in this country of the illustrious maiden warrior must needs partake of a warlike character. Many traces remain of the original structure of this church, and the restorations were carefully copied from the ancient model. The sites and chapels connected with the Maid of Orleans have been kept sacred and unaltered.

The altar of the transept is dedicated to 'Our Lady of Victory.' A second painting of Jeanne d'Arc, with a lamb by her side, weaving garlands with her companions, by the same self-taught painter, hangs above the stand of tapers.

Next comes the florid altar of the Virgin, in gilt and painted stone in the style of Louis XIV., and then the polygonal chancel of the high altar, placed within railings and flanked by coloured statues of St. Joseph and Notre Dame de Lourdes. The three modern-painted windows, given by Monsieur Dupont of Neufchâteau, have Jeanne d'Arc for their subject.

Numerous chaplets, banners, and other votive offerings are hung in the roofs of the chancel transepts and in all the vaulted arches. These were sent from all parts of France, and brought here by the Duchess de Chevreuse, in protest against the fête held on the 30th of May, 1877, in honour of Voltaire, Jeanne d'Arc's foulest traducer. Many other ornaments are placed here by pilgrims; they all relate to Jeanne d'Arc, and are therefore appropriate. They make the little whitewashed building gay.

The altar of the third aisle is dedicated to St. Nicolas, patron saint of Lorraine. Near this is a curious statue of St. Elophe in his cope, holding his head in his hands. The saint was martyred in the fourth century in this valley of the Vair. The remarkable sanctuary which encloses his tomb crowns the valley at the point where it joins the valley of the Meuse, nearly facing Domremy.

Railed in under the western transept window is the plain old octagonal baptismal font. Archæologists date this font from the twelfth century. In it the 'little Romée,' (for so Jeanne d'Arc was also surnamed, according to the old custom, after her mother Isabelle, or Zabillet, as they spelt it, Romée) was baptised by Messire Jean Minet, curé of Greux and Domremy. According to the ancient practice which subsisted till the council of Trent, she was presented by a crowd of sponsors. History has preserved the names of five godmothers and four godfathers, who almost all bore the name of Jean or Jeanne. The Maid in her turn held a neighbour's child, that of Gerardin, the Burgundian, for baptism at this font.

A third picture by the amateur aforesaid hangs above the font. It represents Jeanne beholding the vision of St. Catherine and St. Margaret. Near this is a statue of St. Remi, patron of the parish; the window above depicts the bishop, St. Remi, in the act of baptizing three young people in a tub. This is rather comical.

The confessional stands in its original position below the old picture, from Mureau, of Our Saviour with the ministering angels. The pulpit turns the aisle. The sun, streaming through the coloured window of St. Catherine, could not fail to bring up many thoughts concerning Jeanne and the heavenly light surrounding the appearance of 'her Voices,' her council, as she called them.

Last of all is a double window labelled, 'St. Remigius hujus parochiæ patro,' and 'Angelus puerorum custos,' done by Tremotte of Neufchâteau.

The chapel of the Du Lys family, relations of

Jeanne d'Arc, which is at the end of the southern aisle, has an altar to St. Michael and Jeanne d'Arc inscribed, 'Fille de Dieu, va! va! va!' A black tablet near the entrance-door of the church marks ' Chapelle de N.D. de Domremy, où Jeanne d'Arc priait.' The church is seated with old-fashioned benches, like those in an English country church. The arches of the vaulting are some of them round, some slightly ogival. The irregularities of the building are unusually interesting as affording a clue to its history, and testifying to the veneration felt by succeeding generations of her fellow-parishioners for the heroine of Domremy, their love and their poverty, giving precious offerings out of their small store.

Each year, in those middle ages, on the occasion of the fête of St. Remi, the curé would pronounce from the pulpit the panegyric of their patron saint, and describe with fervour the legend of the baptism of Clovis, with the story of the Sainte Ampoulle, the first anointing of a king of France, perhaps with all the marvellous circumstances added by Hincmar to the primitive narration. The wondrous tale would not be without its effect on the devout and impressionable child, who pondered all these things in her heart.

CHAPTER II.

JEANNE D'ARC'S COUNTRY AND HOME.

Bonne fille ; honnête, chaste, et sainte, parlant en toute simplicité, selon le précepte de l'Evangile : ' Oui, non ; cela est, cela n'est pas.' Sans manque. (A good girl ; virtuous, chaste, and pious, speaking in all simplicity, according to the precept of the Gospel : ' Yes, no ; it is, it is not.' Without fail.)
Evidence of Jeanne d'Arc's neighbours.

THE country-side in these north-western Vosges teems with memories of Jeanne. At Ceffonds, near Montiérender, where her statue crowns a public fountain, the actual house of her father is still shown. The family seems to have taken its name from the village of Arc-en-Barrois, situated on the Aujon, an affluent of the upper Aube, at twenty-six kilometres to the south-west of Chaumont. During the second half of the fourteenth century we find, in ancient records, many individuals of this name established along the valley of the Aube and its tributaries ; among them a canon of Troyes, the curé of Bar-sur-Seine, and the chaplain of the royal chapel of N.D. in Chaumont, and, lastly, Jacques d'Arc, father of Jeanne, born in 1375 at Ceffonds ; thus decisively fixing her paternal family in Champagne. In 1398 a lady belonging to this family, bearing also the name of Jeanne d'Arc, held the manor of Sarrey, a village near Chaumont. She married into the noble family of Saulx.

Jacques d'Arc figured in the first rank of the notables of his village, and in 1427 he was officially employed in maintaining the rights of the people of Domremy against certain exactions, before Baudricourt, Governor of Vaucouleurs. At Martigny testimony was gathered favourable to Jeanne's rehabilitation, in 1455, after her trial and condemnation in 1431. At Autreville a statue has been erected in her honour. Her godmother, Jeannette Thiesselin, was from Sionne; from Frébécourt, Etienne de Sionne, curé of Rouceux, another witness at the second trial, on which side it is needless to say, since all the evidence was warmly in her favour.

Jean Hordal (a descendant of Hauvy, niece of the Maid of Orleans, the daughter of Pierre d'Arc, who married Estienne Hordal) speaks of going for change of air, after his illness and the loss of three of his children, to Domremy, and then to 'Rup (Ruppes), Neufchâteau, La Motte et autres lieux où la dicte Pucelle avait hanté et frequenté.' Among her little pleasures and pilgrimages, Jeanne often visited the chapel of Notre Dame de Beauregard, built in the fourteenth or fifteenth century, which crowns the vine slopes above Maxey at the junction of the roads from Ruppes and Autreville.

In the shade of the aged elm, which covers the

threshold of this chapel with its branches, a wide landscape of beauty is visible. In the valley from Neufchâteau to Vaucouleurs one can count twenty villages, some nestling in the vale, some eyrie-perched on hills. The château and chapel of Bermont are on the opposite hill. Domremy lies low to the south-west.

From Beauregard one has a fine view of the sunset and wide-waving hills of the Vosges before they break into actual mountains. The turf on these breezy downs is decked with Alpine flowers, gentians and deep-rose pinks; harebells and many others rise elastic from the tread; one's foot and heart are both so light up here. Fruit-trees are planted all about among these slopes, giving the country the aspect of a garden in the spring, though its time of glory is the autumn. One should make a point of seeing these vine-lands in October, while the vintage is yet joyous and full of reward for toil.

One way back to Domremy is through Maxey and across the bridge over the Vair to Greux, a village larger and more prosperous than Domremy, which still, as in Jeanne d'Arc's time, 'makes one with Domremy. The principal church is at Greux.' These are Jeanne's words. Greux and Domremy are both exempt from tax: 'Néant à cause de la Pucelle.' The tax-collector's hand is stayed for love of her, long dead, whose good works follow her.

Charity never faileth, but 'charitable work is

not easy. Time, thought, rest, pleasure must be sacrificed to it. Deception and ingratitude must not discourage the giver.' Jeanne d'Arc gave to Domremy and to France the 'charity of ripe thoughts.' In those disturbed times even the secluded and humble village of Domremy became sometimes a theatre of war. Not only the childish play in which we hear of Jeanne's brothers taking part against the children of Maxey, who were furiously Burgundian. Her historian, Miss Parr, says Maxey (Marcey she calls it) was two leagues off.

This trifle shows the difficulty of writing history from books and maps only. It is a kilometre distant, about five furlongs. Village children cannot habitually meet to play at fighting from two leagues apart. Sometimes on the approach of a troop of partisans of the opposing faction there were skirmishes for the defence of their property and houses. Jeanne said she often helped to lead the cattle to the meadows, or to the fortified place called Château de L'Isle, 'for fear of the Burgundian foragers. After I reached years of discretion, I did not generally tend the cattle,' she continued.

These attacks had nothing to do with the English; this was the Burgundian frontier. But at one time came more than a skirmish, and all the inhabitants of Domremy fled to Neufchâteau, at a distance of eleven kilometres (about seven miles), driving their cattle before them. The Abbé Bourgaut, curé of Domremy, from whom in conversation I learnt most of the traditions concerning Jeanne connected with this part of the country, says it was when Jeanne was about ten years of age that she took refuge with her family at Neufchâteau. Wallon, in his book, —which is one of the best records of Jeanne's life that we possess,—puts the date in 1428, when Jeanne was sixteen years old. He also says it was after her first journey to Vaucouleurs to ask Baudricourt to send her to the service of the king. Every writer dates it differently.

It is likewise a disputed point whether the family stayed four days or a fortnight at Neufchâteau, where they took refuge with a good woman named La Rousse, the mistress of an inn, to whom Jeanne made herself very useful. A little maiden is often very handy at ten years old, but it is more likely Jeanne was sixteen, as she led to pasture the cattle her parents had brought there. It is from her stay here that the story arises that she was the servant at an inn. It seems, from her own declaration, that she was fifteen days servant at the inn at Neufchâteau.

Neufchâteau is a small, neat, insignificant town built on a hill crowned with church towers, and set in a hilly, arid landscape with rocky valleys and sparse verdure. It is a wholesome town, of 3,920 inhabitants, with gardens on its slopes, and pleasant views from the windows, in which blue pyramidal campanulas grow like flowery curtains. The school-children sing hymns, which echo down the quiet streets; men weave hempen cloth by hand, and are content to do it; and long carts piled high with grapes let fall their luscious load into the cellars beneath the houses, shooting down the piles of grapes as easily as we drop letters into the post. In the hill-country hereabout the grapes are sometimes frost-bitten; but they seem to make a very fair wine all the same. There are two churches dating from the eleventh century: St. Christophe, which has been restored, and St. Nicholas, re-consecrated in 1697, built above an early subterranean church. In the church on the top of the hill, where it rises abrupt and rocky from the valley, is a Calvary, with life-sized coloured figures, and two good pictures, one a Vandyke, the other a crucifixion of Caravaggio-like power and darkness. A replica of this is at Toul. None of these things, however, are very remarkable. The statue of Jeanne d'Arc is the most interesting object in the town.

Doubtless the family of Arc were glad to return home. Had it not been for their cattle, they might as safely have stayed at Domremy, for, by the appearance of Jeanne d'Arc's house and the few other cottages of that date that remain in the district, they were built as strong as little fortresses. Their homes were really their castles, as doubtless they had need to be. But the church had been set on fire by the marauders and greatly injured, to Jeanne's grief and pious indignation.

The house where Jeanne d'Arc was born, and where several members of her ennobled family of

Du Lys dwelt since her time, is, externally, a rough-cast cottage with a low, lean-to roof, forming a kind of half gable of broad span. The house is not quite straight in front, the elevation forming a slight, nearly imperceptible angle.

Michel Montaigne visiting the place in 1580, in the course of his journey to Italy, says of it, 'The front of the cottage where Jeanne d'Arc was born is all over painted with her deeds, but time has greatly injured the painting.'

No trace of this painting remains; but there are several ornamental additions made by Claude du Lys and others, which are interesting as relating to Jeanne d'Arc.

The cottage is set low in the ground: it has probably sunk in the course of ages, as other heavier buildings do. This cottage has sunk one step (about eight inches) within five centuries: had it been a church or castle, it would probably be deeper in the ground by this time. The low door has three escutcheons over it, and a shrined niche with a statue above them. The central shield bears the arms of France, with the legend in Gothic letters, with fleur-de-lys between,

Vive le Roy Loys.

The right-hand shield is charged with the bearings given by Charles VII. to the family of Jeanne d'Arc, two golden lilies in an azure field, between them is a sword sustaining a crown on its point. The shield to the left bears three ploughshares and a spur-rowel, the arms of Thiesselin, whose daughter married, in 1460, Claude du Lys, then proprietor of the house, grand-nephew of the Maid of Orleans. The top of the ogive is adorned with symbols of the pastoral work Jeanne followed before she bore arms: corn and the vine, with the device, -|- *Vive* -|- *labeur* -|- and the date: † *mil* † *iiii*^{o} † *iiii*^{xx} † *i* † (1481).

This Gothic niche was destined to receive the statue of cast metal, precisely similar to an image in stone, which is to be seen in the first room in the house, and which dates from the time of the maid's rehabilitation in 1456, if we may trust the account of it by Charles du Lys, Advocate-General at the Cour des Aides under Louis XIII. Tradition says that the statue (the stone image) was formerly coloured and gilt, and that it was placed in the parish church at Domremy. It was said to be sculptured by an artist of Lorraine from a young relative of the heroine, who bore so striking a resemblance to the Maid that she was called 'the little Jeanne.' The figure has many points of resemblance to the original statue formerly on the bridge of Orleans. They were possibly by the same hand. Instead of the 'cheveux rondiz' that the heroine wore, she is represented with her hair flowing over her shoulders and below the waist. The hands are joined in prayer. The face, seen in profile, has a certain calm beauty of expression, but, though pleasing, we are not to take it as an actual likeness of Jeanne d'Arc.

The lower windows of the house are small, as

was the necessary custom of those days, when war and rapine were the habit of the times. Interiors were then more gloomy, exteriors more forbidding. We have flowers and muslin now, instead of prison-like bars; life is gentler. The mullioned 'croisée' window above the kitchen belongs to the large garret, occupied as a bedroom by Claude du Lys, curé of Greux-Domremy in the first half of the sixteenth century. The dwelling-house consists, besides, of four rooms upon the ground-floor. One enters at once from the outer door upon the kitchen, the living-room of the family, and also, according to the general present custom in France in this rank of life, the bed-room of the parents of the family, the bed being curtained within an alcove.

Here Jeanne was born, and here she was brought up by her pious mother in habits of obedience, work, and prayer. Jeanne did not break her family ties in wilfulness; it was against her own will that she left her father and mother, but she bent her will submissive to a higher call, and made of these pure earthly affections a precious sacrifice. She loved more, not less, than others; but, her heart being greater, she was able to love the Lord better also.

The kitchen was warmed by the hearth, where Jeanne is said often to have slept on the floor when she had given up her own room to passing strangers or poor pilgrims; for in this house dwelt much of 'the charity that is in poor men's homes.'

The iron plaque in the fireplace bears the cross of Lorraine, 'fleur de lysée.' This is later than Jeanne's time, but they say the wooden bracket (poutre), to hang a lamp by the fireplace, is the same that was used by Jeanne and her family. The main beam of the kitchen roof still remains, notwithstanding the depredating knives of pilgrims, and there are the same two recesses for kitchen utensils. The statues and museum furniture of the room are interesting, and furnish and enliven the room, though they would perhaps suit the museum better. A reduced copy in bronze of the statue of Jeanne by the Princess Marie of Orleans was given to the cottage in 1843 by King Louis Philippe, her father. The princess superintended the making of this copy.

Jeanne's own inner room at the back of the house, now more than half underground, strikes chill and damp, though the baking-oven just outside the house warmed it periodically. The now paved floor was earthen in her time. Here are the self-same beams and the wardrobe-cupboard that she used, and the two small beams or sticks nailed in the roof-beam where she hung her clothes, her simple wardrobe. The tiny window is further shaded by the honeysuckle twining round the trees that now darken it, and the broad aristolochia leaves that embower this side of the garden. But what ecstatic light entered by this small aperture and filled Jeanne's soul? Little light can pierce this dense greenery now. Only the eastern sun of midsummer morning is focussed into a flame through the narrow opening.

Probably there was only a curtain between her room and the kitchen where her parents slept. The door is walled up leading to her brother's room, which is much more cheerful and better-lighted than Jeanne's; boys being made more of in France than girls. There were, however, three sons in the family, and only two girls, even if it is certain that Jeanne had the young sister who is mentioned as Catherine by some chroniclers. The fuchsias of the nuns who take care of the cottage are housed in the brothers' room now when cold weather sets in. Their roses, vines, and cabbages all grow together outside in well-cultivated mixed borders as pleasant as the more strict front garden, surrounded by spruce fir-trees, a garden of asters and carnations, rock anemones and pansies, and a fine scarlet pyracanthus, what country folks call candleberry myrtle, and the French call 'burning bush,' which seems to have set on fire the virginia creeper trailing up among the sculptured escutcheons of the front. The garden is watered by a branch of the Trois Fontaines, whose clear brook runs under a wooden bridge behind the house.

The venerable cottage is set back from the road between two houses, one of which contains in its salle de réception a museum of objects of interest relating to the heroine; the other is the village school, salle des filles, where three sisters of the 'congregation enseignante de la Providence' (de Portieux) direct the primary school. They also visit the sick of the village, and act as friendly guides to pilgrims who come to visit the illustrious cottage under their care. Of the three kind, good sisters here, the *supérieure* teaches the children and shows the museum, which has a bookcase full of literature relating to Jeanne d'Arc (Southey's poem is the only English book); the *inférieure* chops wood; while the *juste milieu* cleans the carrots for the soup. They sing the service sweetly in the church, leading their little choir; they do their marketing, and also make the place pleasant to strangers with their kindly talk. The *supérieure* gave us leave to sit in the garden in front of the house, where we sketched the portal, with its escutcheons, whose lost blazonry is outrivalled by the exquisite hues of the virginia creeper that trails among its sculptures. Here, before the railings which connect the buildings and protect the cottage, is the precise spot, so says the curé, Abbé Bourgaut, where Jeanne saw her first vision.

The church is close by—so near, that while on her knees, astonished and all trembling with awe and piety, she could hear the girls' voices singing in the village church. The nuns, however, describe the place where Jeanne saw her first vision, and others, as having been in the side garden in front of her own window. They picked me some pansies in remembrance of the spot. I incline to their view myself. I hardly think she would have knelt so conspicuously in front of the house, or the circumstance would have been more observed. Still, arrangements and growth of shrubs and other things may have been different. The tradition may have been handed down from her own account of it to her family.

For all its present seclusion, historians are wrong in supposing Domremy to have been in Jeanne d'Arc's time as isolated and retired as it has been in later years. The Roman road from Langres to Verdun, a high-road much traversed in the middle ages, passed directly through the village, and this was one of the most important routes between the great Burgundian dominions, whose heavy wine-carts moved by it from Burgundy to Flanders. By the same road arrived in Burgundy the cloths of Ghent and Ypres, besides the travellers and personages of importance who journeyed to and fro, and all this traffic passed immediately in front of the cottage of Jeanne d'Arc.

The railing defends the garden from the school-children, who remind one of the young Burgundians of Maxey in Jeanne's time. How the little Philistines rushed out of school, and daily fell upon us to see all there was to see—books and paint-boxes! How they were interested in the stranger ladies, and how they loved their Jeanne and their home, and, in their simple-hearted, child-like way, their church and their God! They turned away to admire a gay three-horsed wagonette full of eight highly fashionable pilgrims, whose wide-open minds were soon satisfied on all points connected with Jeanne d'Arc: they had read the latest histories, and knew everything already.

It was bliss to sit in the calm shade and scent of balsam fir-trees, surrounded by rock anemones and red roses, not full, but very sweet. The purling brook beside us, the hallowed house in front, above us the song of birds whistling good-night, while a waggoner cracked his whip in air as he drove his team of two horses and a bullock home. Women were going home with full hottes of grapes at their backs, carts passed piled high with root crops, and wine-carts with their great tubs of purple heaps; the cattle and the green hay, all were going home. We are accommodated with chairs and footstools by the sister, who is now gone out with her provision-basket on an errand of charity or necessity, perhaps both. The *supérieure*, after neatly preparing the vegetables, which were brought to her clean-washed, is reading and resting in her porch. How calmly she sits and waits while we work in the wreaths and tendrils among the sculpture! Hollyhocks, carnations supported by a light hoop between two canes, periwinkles, and trails of crisp fading aristolochia, with harebells in the grass, fill up the details, each adding a pleasure. The little church on the right hand walls us in with a sense of holy calm, shedding its mute welcome on us strangers and pilgrims.

This is enjoyment, sure, to anyone. Ah, what is it to a train and cab and telegraph-ridden Londoner? Few English pilgrims come here, however; the accommodation is poor. They say about ten English a year may come, which includes Americans, but they do not stop. Out of hundreds of pilgrims—I may say thousands, according to the visitors' book—I saw only one British name, a Scotch one, besides our own.

The Angelus is sounding, our landlady is plucking a duckling for our supper; there is time for an evening walk up the hill, a tough climb through a sweet wilderness of shrubbery to the gentian-studded downs on a yet unvisited hill to see the sunset. Everything grows so naturally and picturesquely hereabout. If people see a lovely wild rose-bush trail, all over scarlet hips, they leave it alone in its glory to refresh the next comer. Up through a yellowing hazy glade of silver birch, the woods behind their stems aflame with autumn, and the setting sun reflected on moist leaves, the early hunter's moon above.

A man, a carter, saluted us in German. He was glad when we answered him in the same language: he loved to pour forth in his native tongue. We soon knew all that man's history, the tale of his journey to America and his return.

They are an innocent and primitive people here, who have not heard much of England. Unlike Jeanne in that, they do not hate us, nor think ill of us: though Hordal, Jeanne's relative, relates, 'Et si en bonne compagnie j'ay ouy objecter aux Anglois, que Judas, le prototipe des traistres, estoit Anglois.' *

They take every stranger to be Alsacian, and

* 'And thus in good society I have heard it objected to the English, that Judas, the prototype of traitors, was an Englishman.'

they mostly accost them in German : not the people of Domremy village, they are entirely French, but the peasants on the roads and in the fields away to the eastward.

Life here takes us back a hundred years; and why not two, or three, or four? Yes, it is just about that time. 'Or more,' cries F——, who spies three truncated pillars or 'druidical monuments.' We make for them. Lo! They are sacks of potatoes filled and standing upright against the red sky. How many discoveries are mistakes : how many are merely acknowledgments of our (previous) ignorance.

Humbled by our archæological error, we work our way thoughtfully through the copse, among the purpling foliage laced with blackthorn stalks, hoary with grey lichen, and down to the village, where the people are playing pleasantly with their children by their supper fires, the younger men and girls standing on the doorsteps, chatting, or moving off in pairs towards the bridge.

If I have been lengthy in describing the church and Jeanne's home, it is because these had such a significant bearing on her after career. One must take into account the home influences, the earliest, the strongest, and always especially strong with the French people. What is so soothing as that mild monotony of daily life; that sweet half-tint on which our history is painted? 'What novelty is worth that sweet monotony where everything is known, and *loved* because it is known ?'

We learn to love Jeanne more, to understand her better, and the age which reared her, when we see her early life, in the common and everyday aspects which make up the sum of life: we are familiarised with the minutiæ of her people's ways, their belongings, their habits, wants, and wishes, as we tread her floors, and stand within the very walls of her home, by her fireside, or look forth from her windows. We think of her in her happy, peaceful life, her 'healthy human passion, without the morbid craving for the exceptional,' which makes young dressmakers and factory girls, and those whose lives are a sordid tunelessness, or, at best, a tune played only on one string, devour romance and live mentally in the midst of false creations without due preparation for the higher life, which is to come to us all some day. Because she lived excellently, working at well-doing, therefore the exceptional came to her, who was framed and bred strong enough to carry out exceptional work without fainting under it.

CHAPTER III.

JOURNEY TO VAUCOULEURS.

'Et qui est ton seigneur?' dit le sire de Nouillonpont. 'Le roi du ciel.' ('And who is thy lord?' said the master of Nouillonpont. 'The king of heaven.')

WE two pilgrims left Domremy at ten a.m. on October 12th, having a walk before us of twenty kilometres to Vaucouleurs (twelve miles and a half), with the train at hand to help us, if we pleased. The friendly villagers assembled in the road to say adieu. We had been there some days, and they knew we admired and loved their Jeanne. They forgot that the English destroyed her. Outside the village of Greux, the larger sister parish of Domremy, a hill-path to the left gave promise of a pleasanter walk to Vaucouleurs than the *route nationale*, besides passing directly by Bermont, formerly called Bellamont from its beautiful landscape, and Burey-la-Côte, scenes of much interest in the life of Jeanne d'Arc. Could anything be pleasanter than a forenoon walk through vineyards painted by October, with a few purple branches left hanging for the gleaner a trifle frost-bitten, perhaps, but sweet and good.

The delicious woods were enjoyed with the keen feeling of its being perhaps the last of the summer days, the one to be made the most of; the flowery fields were still dewy, and the air full of floating gossamer cobwebs : an atmosphere of fairy silver.

We took Jeanne's own direct path, by way of the old road to Verdun, which gives a lovely view over dear little Domremy nestling in its valley, with the copper-tipped hills bathed in the blueish film of morning mist fast vanishing in the sunshine, the sky full of white clouds, a Turner sky and most Turneresque landscape, with its poplars and boundless waves of distance. We have often cried out, 'How like the "Rivers of France" this place is!'

Even we felt a 'serrement du cœur' in leaving this peaceful nook, as if there were a hard world to be faced outside. Jeanne's heart must have ached, and needed all its high resolve when she gazed from these hills for this last time, when she had left her home never more to see that beloved little world.

We looked back fondly many times while skirting the potato-fields and colza crops, before descending into a beautiful woodland, all hill and dell, with glades embowering blue distances and mossy paths, and soft, still, dreamy foliage-screens of silver birch and yellow beech, with here and there a maple sapling glowing like the rosy cheek of a country child.

One is not long in discerning Jeanne's favourite chapel of Our Lady of Bermont, where she went almost every Saturday to pray, and enjoy herself with her young playmates, wreathing the altar with flowers which she was skilled in weaving. The young girls laughed at her devotion, even little Mengette, her own especial friend, made her blush by calling her 'too pious.'

Happy days these when the young girls could play in the woods together, drink at St. Thiebault's fountain, and together pray and give thanks for another week of gladsome life; then light their tapers in the chapel, emblems of the faith that lights the world and the love of warm hearts to God.

The statue of the Virgin in the chapel was the same that exists there at this day. A crowned figure less than life-size, carved in oak and painted, bearing a sceptre in the right hand, and in the other the infant Jesus, who holds a bird. There are four statues altogether in the chapel, surrounding an altar of stone and painted wood. Many of the objects here are of high antiquity; the wooden cross on the top of the arch above the image of St. Thiebaut is supposed to date from the twelfth century, and the cross at the gable of the chevet of the chapel is thought to be of the eleventh century. The Gothic inscription round the bell has never been deciphered. It runs thus, in thirteenth century characters:

⁂ a b e m r e i a d e a a r m a n g t

which ingenious readers have tortured into a motto of praise to Jeanne d'Arc, which would be a wonderful prophecy, considering it was inscribed two centuries before she was born.

Philip of Bergamo, who wrote in the reign of Charles VII., tells us that when Jeanne was about sixteen she took refuge in a chapel from a storm, and there saw the vision which first decidedly warned her of her mission, to which she replied that she was but a poor girl, incapable of leading an army. This chapel has been thought to be Bermont. Though it is more likely that the chapel where Jeanne took shelter was the one on the hill of the Bois Chesnu, rebuilt by Étienne Hordal and again destroyed by the Swedes when they invaded Lorraine, on whose site the new white temple has been built; yet it was at Bermont that Jeanne was filled with irresistible impulse to go forth to save her country and crown her king, so that she said afterwards, 'Since God commanded it, if I had had a hundred fathers and mothers, and been a king's daughter, had I been forced to wear away my feet to the knees, I must have gone.' She had no support from home for her resolution; public opinion, that of her little village, was all against the idea of her mission.

Yet at Bermont, with the memory of her childhood's happiness rushing over her in one great wave, when at one moment her whole life was reflected in it before her as she uttered her last prayer at the well-known altar, Jeanne must have needed all the supernatural strength given with the command, 'Fille Dé, va, va, va, I will be thine aid, go forth,' to carry her steps from her native village. This parting was twice repeated. She was very brave and strong in her faith to go forward again after her first repulse by Baudricourt at Vaucouleurs. She went on, strong in a heaven-sent strength, feeling an energy of life transcending grief and joy.

One need not go to America to see the autumn woods when such rapturous colour lies between us and Switzerland. The hill is quite a cathedral of splendour, fragrant with the incense of ripe autumn, gorgeous with its lines of scarlet, flame and purple, and flowered with pink skewerwood, mingled with rays of light and flashes and splashes of pure pale yellow flowerlike colour. The year is renewed into a second youth of colour, an afterglow more glorious than her early bloom.

We walk 'through verdurous glooms and winding mossy ways,' through ivied foregrounds, each miniature frond crying, 'Look at me more closely;' the emerald banks dappled with purple-veined ivy and strawberry-plants, telling of children's spring joys, and yellowing beech and crimson dogwood, Nature's own landscape painting, still moist with morning's mist, its colour heightened as is wetted jasper; one particularly lovely maple-tree with silver stem, is quite a rose among many other delicate maples. Each sweet dumb friend is another pang for Jeanne, whose affections had so twined round these things; and beyond this lay the sad thought that she was bringing sorrow into the lives of others—hardest of all sacrifices for the loving, unselfish heart.

Our way still lay through fields where our 'feet were soft in flowers,' then came a rough-hewn road. A path through somebody's back garden led us through the village of Goussaincourt and on to the high-seated village of Burey-la-Côte at two short leagues from Domremy, where lived Jeanne's maternal uncle Durand Laxart, who even last year had cheered her heart with belief in her mission when none else believed, and he took her to Vaucouleurs to see the governor.

Durand Laxart's house still exists. It looks very ancient, and has only a ground floor, sparingly ornamented in the pointed style of the fifteenth century, with an ogival portal and a trefoiled heading to the small window. Two large rounded archways allow the passage of carts to the back of the house. A little square-towered church, with its low, dark-grey steeple, points this village of Burey, which is visible on its hill-top for many miles.

Near where the path through the fields abuts on the high road, we spread our cloaks and reclined under a broad-branching plum-tree on a slope, enjoying the peace and beauty of the scene until we felt ready to take up our walk again. We could trace the winding road to Vaucouleurs for about four miles on, by its double line of trees as their shadows faded off in the distance curving down the broad hill slope. The hills and valleys are not so smiling as in the little nest of Domremy, which seems the choicest vale in all this country. The railroad is hidden by a long tunnel, and several tributaries to the Meuse flow in here. The plain seen in a peep between the two hills behind Burey-la-Côte looks like the sea in its far-off blueness. Nearer at hand are flocks of sheep, pigs, and goats, all herding together like happy families.

To the right in the valley proceeding northward is Maxey-sur-Vaise, where the heroine went several times to communicate to 'noble homme Geoffroy du Fay' her design of fighting the English. We passed through Maxey, a superior sort of village, with the Vaise flowing through it neatly embanked with stone. Sauvigny, the next station, is less important. We rested again near the sixth kilometre-stone out of Vaucouleurs, on a bank beneath a wayside chapel near the railway line.

The bank, sunny when we spread our cloaks upon it, was repose itself, with its canopy of soft-clouded sky, its prospect of violet hill-slopes, sunny meadows set with willows and tall poplars, and a near foreground of poppies, hare-bells, shepherd's purse, some pretty umbelliferæ and braided grasses. We lay in clover here, lapped in a sense of fine existence, and scorning wealth and capital cities: only feeling, as the train passed, leaving us behind, like Diogenes when he told Alexander to stand out of his light. It came between us and the willows. We wanted nothing of the train, but that it should not cast its smoke upon us; such very dirty smoke it is here in this eastern part of the network of the Chemin de Fer de l'Est, almost as bad as it is across the German frontier, where it seems the thickest and most poisonous of all coal-smoke. Otherwise the air here is perfect in its sweetness, coolness, and peace. Yet in this paradise of peace and ease, we looked back mentally to our little Domremy, with its moonlit river, as the sweetest spot of all.

We ate our chocolate, and looked down placidly on the slowly moving world, and into the wine-carts as they passed full to the brim of grapes. We had left the department of the Vosges, and, going northward, were now well within that of the Meuse. Many people carry guns about here, and there are plenty of sporting dogs.

A pleasant walk through park-like scenery brought us into Vaucouleurs by way of the Place Pétry; at the south-eastern corner of which the inhabitants of Vaucouleurs still point out the house of Henri le Royer, the wheelwright, who was Jeanne d'Arc's host during her stay in the town. The small house is unassuming, but not remarkable for any great appearance of antiquity.

Dining at Vaucouleurs that evening in the neat, unsophisticated Hôtel de Jeanne d'Arc, off omelette, cabbage, and the wine of the country, a shaggy, unkempt-looking personage in guise of an unsuccessful artist introduced himself by helping himself uninvited from our dish: his manner of solving the difficulties of natural selection where there is but one dish to choose from. He at once proceeded to draw us out. We had seen him previously in the town with something like a large sketch-book under his arm. His costume and *sans gêne* manners made us conclude he was a devotee of the Beautiful; but, no, he only sought the True. He was a scientific man, whose mission was to seek truth—truth only; and by trade—if I dare so to speak—he was a professional lecturer.

Besides being a philosopher and geographer, he was here holding a conference on hygiene at the Hôtel de Ville this night at eight. 'The entrance is gratuitous, and would you credit it, mesdames, Vaucouleurs has two thousand six hundred and ninety-five inhabitants' (which we afterwards found out to consist chiefly of babies), 'well, I shall feel myself fortunate if I have twenty listeners. The French are not like the English; you English' (a shaggy, sweeping bow) 'seek knowledge, but here even the vitally important subject of hygiene is disregarded; and yet it concerns us all.' He sighed, as he helped himself to cabbage. Friday in a small French town is a circumstance to sigh over.

Doubtless this neglect of the higher culture, etc., is one reason why Murray in his edition of 1864 does not mention Vaucouleurs at all, and in the latest edition it is only named.

'Are you of the province of Birmingehamme, mesdames?'

'No, we are from London.'

'Ah!' another shaggy bow recognises the superior style and breadth of the metropolitan mind—'ah! I have visited the most beautiful quarters of England. I took a tourist ticket to London; my fortune, unhappily, permitted me not to do more. I am historian also. I was writing the life of Cromvelle at the time, and I went to seek informations.'

'Indeed; and what did you see?'

'Oh, I visited the finest quarters; I saw the Faubourg de Berremingue'amme, and Veet'alle' (Whitehall), 'and Irving in " Charles I.," because I was making researches for my book on Cromvelle. I speak not English, but I read him.'

He finished our omelette. The talk naturally turned on Jeanne d'Arc. Doubtless we had heard of her. Yes, we were following her footsteps.

'I am at this moment writing a history of her life,' he continued. 'I have already covered eighteen and three-quarter kilogrammes of paper with materials I have already collected. It is to be in eleven volumes as high as this bottle,' —he helped himself. 'You are also making studies of her, doubtless, madame. Every elevated soul must,'—etc.

'Mine will not be such a monumental work as yours. We have just walked from her birthplace, Domremy, to-day.'

'Fifty kilometres! You English are wonderful people.'

'No, it is not so much as that; it is only twenty.'

'Pardon, it is fifty; I know it for certain.'

The mistress of the hotel smiled. She knew her man, we did not.

E

'And what did they show you?'

'Oh, everything.'

'But what? Did you see the house she was born in?'

'Certainly.'

'And the place where she tied up her cows?'

'No, we did not see that.'

'Then they showed you simply nothing. Who did you speak to about her?'

'The curé talked to us and lent us some books.'

'The curé he knows nothing. Bah! those curés,'—he shook his hair into wisps—'they admit no ideas; they are made up of antiquated prejudices. And their books, they are only legends, stories written for children. We seek truth, we others,'—drawing himself up and flinging aside the wisps,—'I have reached the profoundest depths of Jeanne's history. I have read through the *Mercury* from the fifteenth century, when it began, and there is only one complete copy now extant, and that is in Paris. Ah, nobody knows her veridical history. There are volumes to be told.'

'And yet it is such a little life.'

'A short life. It is true she died at nineteen years eight months and eight days and a half.' How accurate he was! 'Yet there is a huge volume to be written of her life after she was burnt'—a look of surprise on our part,—'yes, after her executioner saw her and asked her pardon.'

'Before her execution——'

'Pardon, madame, he asked it after her execution. He saw her. Was it a phantom he saw? Science forbids. Can two persons exactly resemble each other? It is not likely; so it must have been an effigy of Jeanne they burnt, while she escaped through a subterraneous passage. Yes, I have materials for more than eleven volumes, from the time when her father beat her for going to church instead of feeding the cows until her escape from the flames—et après—ah, vous verrez.'

Ah, he has so much to tell; he has exhausted Paris, but in Belgium there are countless unedited MSS., and he has not broken Belgian ground yet; but, so far as his studies have yet gone, he is convinced of La Rigaude having been really Jeanne, and that she lived to a good old age. About the subterranean passage—c'est positif—and that exonerates the English. Then it transpired that we had been to the wrong Domremy altogether; that Jeanne was born at a Domremy at fifty kilometres from here, 'là bas dans les Vosges.'

'But our Domremy was in the Vosges.'

'Ah, it is not the right one, and that is what the archbishop (?) found against her, that, being Lorrainaise, she fought against her sovereign, the King of England.'

I could not reconcile this with my previous reading, but I did not argue the point. This monsieur has, according to the habit of his rationalistic kind, denied all history and tradi-

tion, and is now proceeding to evolve a Joan of
Arc out of his moral consciousness. He has
found that all the world believes in the wrong
Domremy; he believes in one of the others for
reasons he has not yet edited. Disputing everything hitherto written, he has founded a Chinon
thirty leagues from here; not quite Château
Chinon—Schiller is wrong there: being a German, he must be wrong—altogether, he has drawn
everything from sources the most inedited and
profound; perhaps as profound as his researches
on Cromwell, as indubitable as Irving's acting
edition of Charles I.'s life. In this way there is
no end to the volumes one might write on the
subject of one short life. It was a mercy we had
found the real Vaucouleurs. He finished the last
handful of our cakes. Looking at his watch,

'Ah, I must hasten myself—I have a conference at the Town Hall to-night. Did I mention
it? I hope I shall have a greater success here
than I had at ——, when I conducted Madame la
Générale —to my lecture, and I awaited a tremendous fiasco.'

'Oh, I feel sure a lecture on so important a
subject will be well attended,' said I, soothingly.

'I hope I may have the pleasure of your assistance at my conference.'

I expected this. We had just walked about
thirteen miles, besides making some researches in
the town; still a lecture on hygiene might do us
good. He will accompany us—it is not far—and
give us reserved seats, and by frequent reference

to his watch we are given to understand there is no time to be lost. He loves the English. Was that young lady who had just gone to bring down my bonnet my daughter? Ah! une charmante demoiselle! Was madame a widow? He has the highest consideration for the English, and they return it fully.

'Indeed!'

Ah, yes. He met a lord of the Admiralty at Plombières who had £80,000 a year, who must have had £80,000 sterling a year, because he not only gave largely at one of his lectures, but he always drives four horses. Each horse costs twenty francs a day, so that the lord in question cannot on that basis of calculation have less than £80,000 a year, c'est positif.

'What is his name?'

He knows the name begins with a B and ends with an m; but, although he has his card among the three kilogrammes of visiting-cards that he has in his portmanteau, and all given to him in this tournée, he cannot recall the name for the moment, though he was so intimate. Thirteen hundred and four cards weigh a kilogramme, so he says. He is careful about accuracy in detail —the scientific mind is always so.

If he asks for my card to add to his collection, I must call myself Mrs. Smith of Great Britain, address, No. 6, Clapham Junction.

He was careful not to lose sight of his audience. We declined seats on the platform at the lecture, but he announced us about as distinguished foreigners, so that we were glad to get away as soon as the conference was over. Vaucouleurs does not seem to be of a scientific turn of mind, nor to care about hygiene; but the two first rows of seats gradually filled, and small boys crowded in at the back later on. State-paid lectures on hygiene are naturally less lively than those where the lecturers try to clear a profit, but his diagrams were very neat and good, and the audience woke up a little when the lecturer produced a large écorché picture, with opening leaves, displaying the organs of the body not usually exhibited. Like all men, he was most eloquent on the tight-lacing question, and weakest on the subject of tobacco. His lecture was dull, but moderately good.

We took care to be invisible next morning, and each time we caught sight of our philosopher lurking in corners in wait for us, we slipped out of a side-door and fled. He would be sure to mislead us in our search for traces of Jeanne d'Arc.

All this reads ludicrously, but philosophers of this sort are common enough. These artists think they can improve upon Nature, flatter the features of a character, arrange history better, and cover their want of anatomy by 'treatment.' This sketch is literal fact, shortened considerably, for our historian was very glib; and to what does it bring us? To more light?—oh, no; to an endless complexity of cobwebs. Is unbelief more profitable than faith? To me nothing is more marked than the utter barrenness of unbelief, which yet always accompanies the grossest credulity. They are not the most religious people who are gulled by tricks of spirit-rapping. Is materialism, realism, or what they like to call it, the safe guide to history? or does it make of it an inverted legend shorn of its beams and beauties, yet no nearer to the truth?

All the tinsel with which poetry has overlaid the story of Jeanne d'Arc reeks with verdigris when we approach the pure gold of truth, which is so clearly evidenced in buildings, distances, and geographical features, as well as in contemporary writings and law reports. Historical research is a veritable gold-washing of tradition.

Unbelief at Vaucouleurs is not confined to modern times. The Sire de Baudricourt, commandant of the castle, also could not believe in any wonder that lay outside his narrow comprehension. Some minds can only believe in their own experience. This is eminently provincial, yet not pastoral.

We need not attend to the legend of Jeanne's having recognised the commandant without having seen him before. This is said of her approach to every great man, and as all writers, including Shakespeare, affirm it, we may conclude that some one person, most probably Charles VII., attempted to deceive her by some juggling trick.

The truth and Jeanne's own good sense rejected all such extraneous miracle. Her power lay in her own conviction, and the natural ascendancy of a strong character over those more feeble and vacillating; and also the extraordinary fascination she exercised over all men and women with whom she came in contact. Superstition was a universal malady in those days, as unbelief is now. Baudricourt did not believe in Jeanne's mission; yet he was superstitious enough to have the young girl exorcised. It was not the first time he had seen Jeanne d'Arc. She had come at Ascension-tide in the previous year, in her coarse, red, peasant's dress, and he had sent her away in derision. But when she re-appeared before him, still in her peasant's garb, but with deeper conviction in her manner, and urged her mission to raise the siege of Orleans, and cause the dauphin to be crowned at Rheims: and when others round him began to talk of her, and to believe in her, this time he was not able to send her away unnoticed. There was something in all this, but whether of good or evil, who should say? If she had visions, whence came they? To clear up this point, Baudricourt came one day with the curé to the house of the wheelwright, where Jeanne was staying, and where she remained three weeks, helping his wife, spinning with her; dividing her time between household occupations and prayer in the church, or in the crypt, where she often prayed in the chapel of the Virgin. The curé, wearing his stole, prepared himself to exorcise the maiden, commanding her, if she were under the influence of an evil spell, to retire; if not, she was to approach. Jeanne approached the priest and knelt before him, and afterwards she told the commandant, who was still unsatisfied, of the popular prophecy that 'France should be lost by a woman and saved by a young girl.' This young girl was expected to spring from the marches of Lorraine. The woman was interpreted to be the wicked Isabeau de Bavière, the queen-dowager.

Time passed, the king's need was extreme, the people round Vaucouleurs were eager that Jeanne should go forward to save France according to her promise. Two gentlemen who offered to conduct her to the dauphin, also undertook to defray the expenses of the journey. One of them was Jean de Novelonpont, or Nouillonpont (on the frontier names are curiously confused in their spelling), surnamed Jean de Metz, a man of mature years, who held a royal office at Vaucouleurs. (Martin wrongly calls him 'un jeune bourgeois.') The other was a young esquire, Bertrand de Poulengy.

The people of Vaucouleurs equipped her with what she required, the military dress of the period, and they aided her uncle to buy her a horse. An old tapestry wrought in her time, and now in the museum at Orleans, represents Jeanne riding to Chinon on a sorrel-coloured horse, and wearing a red hood with an aigrette. Only Monstrelet says she was used to horse-riding. A marginal note to his work made by a commentator in Charles VII.'s or Louis XI.'s time, rectifies the assertion saying, 'ne james n'avoit veu cheval, au moyns pour monter dessus.' This would be the case with the peasant girls of Domremy now, they lead the cattle to the fields, but they have nothing to do with the horses, which are only used for draught. The habits of peasant life, being founded on necessities, do not change readily. Jeanne herself said she had never ridden on horseback. She had hitherto made her journeys on foot.

Jeanne knew nothing of feminine disabilities; she had to go, and she went. Schiller makes his Jeanne, a thoroughly German Johanna, give vent to a fine soliloquy on quitting her peasant condition and beginning a public career. The reality is that she felt all that Schiller describes, but said nothing about it (she was not given to much talking), but she went forth bravely with self-renunciation to do what the Lord commanded her in the way prescribed. The Voices told her to go to Baudricourt at Vaucouleurs; therefore she did not set out instead to walk to Chinon, begging her bread and falling into ill-repute by the way.

The church of Vaucouleurs is modern renaissance, with ceilings and spandrils painted in the Italian style. One walks up the flight of steps outside to the left of it to see what was once the crypt of the chapel where Jeanne d'Arc prayed. Very little remains of this; but two trefoiled windows and a small door explain its situation. The crypt is no longer a crypt, but the most exposed object on the hill-side. Its position shows that the chapel of the castle most probably stood above it; at the back of it, among reddening sumach and tangled vegetation, are vestiges of what was once finely-cut gothic sculpture. Several paths and flights of steps wind about among the ruins of the castle, held for the king by the Sire de Baudricourt, who continued unshakingly faithful to his king. As punishment for this fidelity, the Duke of Bedford sequestrated his lands at Chaumont. Vaucouleurs had become quite a Castle Dangerous.

Of this once important frontier fortress little but the fine site remains, and only traces of walls. It was well situated for a citadel, commanding, though at no great height, a view of the valley of the Meuse, and a wide reach of neighbouring country. It was one of the few towns north of the Loire that held out for Charles the dauphin. The castle and town of Vaucouleurs had to sustain the first shock of the Anglo-Burgundian bands.

Down in the town, not far from the railway station, there are several round towers of smoothly cut stone, forming part of the former town wall, which is now used as the back of a street of small houses. The town is well-situated on the Meuse, in the midst of a fertile flowery valley; hence its name, vallée des couleurs, vallis colorum.

CHAPTER IV.

TOUL AND NANCY.

' Et que vous a dit la voix ?'
' Elle m'a dit de répondre hardiment, et que Dieu m'aiderait.'
(' And what did the voice tell you ?'
' It told me to answer boldly, and that God would help me.')
Jeanne d'Arc's Interrogatory at Rouen.

THE fame of Jeanne's visions spread and reached the ears of the Duke of Lorraine, lying sick in his palace at Nancy. She must come to visit him and work his cure. There was time to spare, since, notwithstanding the pressing need of France and Jeanne's desire to set out on her great mission, Robert de Baudricourt could not make up his mind to send her to the dauphin, and a man who is afraid of facing a responsibility has always time to deliberate. This was a preparation to Jeanne for the harder trials of patience she would meet by-and-by, when she found greater people deliberate when they should be acting.

'What are you doing here, ma mie?' said Jean de Novelonpont, going to see her at the wheelwright's. 'Must the king be driven from the kingdom—must we all become English?'

Among the consequences of the treaty of Troyes was the occupation of Champagne by the invaders. The castle and town of Vaucouleurs was in fact the last shred of French territory that Charles had been able to retain in the eastern extremity of his kingdom. This is the point of the question put by Jean de Novelonpont, 'Why are you delaying, ma mie—are we all to become English?'

'I am come here, to the king's house'—Vaucouleurs was a royal town—'to speak to Robert de Baudricourt to take me or send me to the king. But he cares not for me nor for my words. And yet, before mid-Lent, I must be before the king, even should I wear my feet to the knees; for no one in the world, neither kings, dukes, nor the King of Scotland's daughter, none other can recover the kingdom of France. He has no help but in me; and truly I had much rather spin by my poor mother's side, for this is not my condition of life. But I must go and I must act, because my Lord wills it.'

'Who is your Lord?'

'He is God.'

The brave soldier, taking her hands between his own, swore by his faith that, God helping, he would conduct her to the king, and asked her when she would set out.

'To-day rather than to-morrow—to-morrow rather than later,' she replied.

This call of the Duke of Lorraine seemed to open another door of hope to Jeanne. He might do for her what Baudricourt refused or delayed, or he might send his son-in-law, Réné of Anjou, who was well affected to the cause, to accompany her into France. She would neglect nothing that might compass her object. She furnished herself with a safe conduct and went to Nancy. Jean de Metz (Novelonpont) accompanied her and her uncle to Toul, and she continued her journey to the duke with her uncle, Durand Laxart.

This was not the first time Jeanne had been at Toul. She had gone there the year before to deny before the diocesan officials a pretended promise of marriage with a man whom her parents encouraged, thus hoping to keep her at home and put all ideas of war and visions out of her head. It is taken for granted by Monsieur Siméon Luce that this young man became acquainted with Jeanne during her short sojourn at Neufchâteau. She appeared personally before the judge and made him believe her word. Vaucouleurs and the villages in its vicinity, although French, it appears were subject to the spiritual jurisdiction of the Bishop of Toul, which was a free city of the German empire, added to France in 1552.

This was Jeanne's first experience of ecclesiastical law.

Jeanne, in her first journey to Toul, did not pass through Vaucouleurs, but followed the ridge of the Roman road that runs from Toul to Langres. Part of this road still remains, and is visible near Domremy.

From Vaucouleurs there are two roads to Toul: one is the present route nationale by Blénod-lès-Toul, the other lies through the Bois du Chanois and the Bois du Domgermain. The forest road is that probably followed by Jeanne, as it is shorter. The railway to Toul passes by the junction at Pagny, where it crosses the Meuse and enters the valley of the Moselle, which has here the appearance of a canal. The towers of Toul look fine from a distance, but the town seems sad in being too near a foreign frontier. They are strengthening the already strong fortifications. The dirty town is tightly packed within its walls, giving it a decidedly mediæval aspect. The streets are tortuous and intricate; one is glad to find rest for the eye in the graceful, flamboyant cloister of St. Gengoult, resembling the cloisters of Westminster Abbey, enclosing a garden of bays, pomegranates, and oleanders. There is some fine old glass in the church. It is impossible to get a good view of this double-towered church, the town is so crowded round it. The only open space in the city is in front of the cathedral, which is also twin-towered, and a fine building.

This was the first cathedral Jeanne ever saw, an inferior Rheims, as moonlight unto sunlight; but still there is enough resemblance to have struck her forcibly on entering Rheims. After Domremy, breathing the spirit of peace and pastoral simplicity, it strikes a grisly contrast to enter this Bellona-like place, all bristling with war and eager for revenge. Beyond the cathedral lie the barracks and the especially military quarter. Drawbridges lead through the fortifications to the bridges over the canal, which here is islanded and broad.

The walk from Toul to Nancy is twenty-four kilometres, about fifteen miles, and when one once commits oneself to the road one must walk all the way, as no horse or carriage can now be obtained between the two towns, and there is no direct railway. Jeanne went there on foot with her uncle, as Jean de Metz had left them at Toul. The road was not so good then as it is now, as one can judge by portions of the old road visible as one gets into the hilly country about Nancy.

The way lies across the Moselle bridge. The view of the double-towered cathedral, with the traceried crowns, embosomed in trees and doubly reflected in the canal and the Moselle, is delightful when the mist lifts itself above a rounded but lofty hill, a spur of the Vosges. The road is charming as it drops into the suburb of Daumartin-les-Toul, with its Italian bell-tower and church, the cathedral remaining long in sight after the bastions have sunk in distance, as one ascends the hill to Gondreville. The way becomes even prettier on gaining the high champaign-land, where the high-road lies for many kilometres through a wood, the Bois de Hayes, which is cleared for about a hundred yards on either side of the road.

Hunting often goes on in this wood, and a sort

of battue-shooting. It is enchanting to hear the huntsmen winding their horns so prettily and frequently, or sometimes musically whistling the tune, while others within the wood are shouting and the dogs baying. Wolves are numerous in the recesses of the wood, but one seldom sees larger game than a hare scampering across the road. The hunters on battue days stand behind the trees with their guns cocked, ready to fire at anything that the dogs may turn out of the wood. This seems as patient work as fishing.

The road, in October, is a path of gold, lying beneath a vegetable cloister of alternate sycamore and poplar, the sycamores making the road dense with their falling leaves, mostly yellow, but often scarlet, green, and gold, like zonal geraniums. These trees, shorter than the poplars, fill the intervening spaces with their dropping amber, beautiful to walk under as a laburnum grove. One cannot tire of such a road in the brisk autumn weather, though it is a sparsely inhabited region. It was less beautiful when Jeanne d'Arc passed here in the middle of February, 1429.

Between Toul and Nancy there are only two tiny villages besides Gondreville, which is somewhat more important, and a half-way posting-house with empty stables. But the ground lies very high, and one can hear the distant chime of many village church bells on a Sunday, harmonizing with the hunters' chorus within the wood, for on a Sunday especially the air is musical with these latter sounds.

At the Poste Velaine, just half-way betwixt Toul and Nancy, the character of the road changes, and the landscape becomes more broken and picturesque in the peeps seen among the gathering mists. At present the road is carried across the valleys by two fine lofty viaducts lined with ash-trees : the old road lies green below, and even this has a low viaduct, which was probably not there when Jeanne and her uncle journeyed to Nancy.

The sick Duke of Lorraine had tried all human (and other) means to be healed, but that of leading a good life. Jeanne pointed out to him the only permanent cure. She told him he ruled himself ill, and would only amend by his own efforts, and counselled him to take back his good wife.

The common sense of a clear and pious mind was enough to show her this. She pretended to work no miraculous cures; she declared she knew nothing concerning his malady; but she unfolded to him her patriotic object, hoping the duke might be moved to aid her. If he would let his son-in-law command some men-at-arms to convoy her through France, she would heartily pray God to grant him health. Jeanne herself, while fully persuaded of her Divine mission, always used the plain good sense God had given her to help her forward in the way pointed out to her.

Michelet says, and truly, 'The originality of the Pucelle which ensured her success did not so much consist in her valour or her visions, as in her good sense.' Through all her enthusiasm the girl saw the question and how it was to be solved.

The duke had no mind to forward her ends; there were political difficulties in the way of this, but towards herself he showed respect and consideration. He bade her a gracious farewell, and supplied her with a small sum of money and a horse. Charles of Lorraine is said to have given her 'four franks at parting,' which she sent to her parents by her uncle. All this showed she had demeaned herself in a modest and decorous manner towards him, and that her unwelcome advice had not been couched in offensive language.

So ended a trial of faith for Jeanne; but she was not cast down. Had He not promised to be with her?—He whose archangel said, 'Fille Dé, va, va, va. Je serai à ton aide.'

The gay, bright town of Nancy has always been pretty, though it has no great architectural interest; a curious thing, as the town would seem to have always gone with the fashion. But it looks too new, and the old things have too much of the Renaissance character to have been seen by our Jeanne.

Murray calls the church of St. Epvre 'old, but much altered.' It looks modern in every stone. It is like a conservatory for light, being all over-coloured modern windows; really too gay not to be startling, but with every detail perfectly, exquisitely, and expensively carried out. The large aisle and clerestory windows are all of them sheets of dazzling colour. There is scarcely any wall left, all is rainbow glass. This has a most curious effect. Grey-tinted angels fill the spandrils, and the necessarily few wall decorations are everywhere equally well-executed, strictly in the selected period of pure decorated Gothic; but all breathes the very spirit of Nancy, gay, modern, bright, and pretty. 'La plus jolie ville de France' looks like a pretty young married lady decked in her new trousseau.

But the palace of the Dukes of Lorraine, a two-floored building with high-peaked roofs and dormers and tourelles, still remains, though not unaltered. The present building is for the most part flamboyant Gothic of the sixteenth century. The portal and gate-house are delightful. There are also several remains of the ancient walls and city gates. One of these, with a portcullis and a triple gateway is highly picturesque. These old walls are being levelled, which seems a pity; yet Nancy, the gracious lady in robes of peace, is happier-looking than Toul, the armed soldier. Its gilt gates and filagree fences are better suited to its gay disposition than old walls and bastions.

Nancy is frivolous and careless as ever. (They even sing out of tune in the churches.) There is nothing to compel one to anything but pleasure, one lives in a sweet dream of confectioners' shops, and Nancy's principal manufacture of pretty embroidery. The inns all look like limited liability companies' asylums; and oh, the pompousness and imprisonment of it all after little free-hearted Domremy!

Nancy cherishes no storied past; even the student subsides into a relish of the shops, the fashions, and the relief of there being nothing worth drawing or writing about, no goading conscience to egg him on to spoil a holiday; nothing 'early pointed,' or, if Gothic, of a viciously debased period, quite beneath an enlightened modern to care about; no objects of interest, no works of art.

Isabey, the painter, indeed presented a collection of his paintings to the town, and the town knows nothing of their whereabouts. Even a diligent quest may fail to discover their locality. The old concierge at the palace of the Dukes of Lorraine looks quite thankful that he has not got them to take care of and exhibit. The academy (or college), the Hôtel de Ville, and the Musée Lorrain resolutely repudiate the soft impeachment. We should disbelieve the guide-books which affirm their existence had we not once had a similar experience at Douai, where a search for Memling's paintings was equally bewildering to all the municipal authorities; where no one understood such an inquiry at all. No one had ever heard of Hemling—Memling?—no, nor any such name. They only knew the modern pictures in the churches, which cost, oh! ever so many francs. Where after a game of hide-and-seek, being passed on through every public building, from the museum to St. Pierre, and thence to Notre Dame, Hans Hemling's magnificent altarpiece was at length discovered in a dusty, uncared-for condition in the sacristy.

'Ma foi, c'est bien joli,' said a young workman, coming forward likewise to view a novelty. This seemed to us uneducated praise or faint appreciation.

Foiled in her hope of help from the great nobles, Jeanne d'Arc turned to God alone for encouragement. St. Nicholas-du-Port, a famous shrine in those days, where Jeanne took the opportunity, before leaving Nancy, to make a pilgrimage, is only two leagues out of the town. It is the first station on the line to Forbach and the Rhine. Alas, directly the frontier is crossed, the mutual hatred of two great nations, both of them leaders of a high civilization, is manifest in every petty detail. There is small thought of saints and saintly ways here, no care for pilgrimages, nor even forms of politeness.

The air is defiled with the dirtiest smoke of the dirtiest coal to be found anywhere; and hearts are blackened with international animosity. The very music is a war-cry. The 'Marseillaise' is hissed between the gnashing teeth on the crowded railway platforms. Patriotism is a defiance. 'Vive la France' is uttered bitterly and with flashing eyes, and answered with contempt. Both nations are seen at their worst and meanest. The good-hearted men of the Fatherland are petty tyrants here, full of rough insolence, insensible to the cruelty of trampling on a fallen foe. 'Pesche,' say they rudely as they hurry the swarming passengers into the crowded carriages of the market trains. 'Pesche,' their rough and ready way of saying 'dépêchez-vous,' to a people accustomed to the ceremonious politeness of 'Montez en voiture, s'il vous plait, messieurs et 'dames.'

The contrast of their manner is great when compared with their kindliness and attention to ourselves directly we are discovered to be English.

The days of chivalry are over, and war no longer carries the palliatives which made a condition of warfare endurable in former days. Let us hope that before long civilization may be able to perfect itself into peace.

CHAPTER V.

THROUGH THE HEART OF FRANCE.

'Allez donc, allez, et advienne que pourra!' ('Go, then, go, and let come of it what may!')
Robert de Baudricourt to Jeanne d'Arc.

FROM St. Nicholas-du-Port Jeanne returned to Vaucouleurs again to wait upon the good pleasure of her superiors. Faith must always be wrapped in patience. She was ready to work. News had come of the defeat of Rouvray (? so it is asserted). It must have travelled quickly, as Lent had begun, Ash-Wednesday was the 9th February, and the 'Battle of Herrings' was fought early in Lent. Again Jeanne pressed the commandant to send her to the dauphin's aid.

The well-known secret of eloquence is to be in earnest. Enthusiasm warms even unbelief with its own fire. Jeanne was certain of her mission, and so could impart its faith to those who could not read her credentials; who had never felt the glow of inspiration. Baudricourt, convinced or weary, troubled by her importunity, at length gave his consent to her departure on the 13th of

February, the first Sunday in Lent. This requires
explanation. Tradition says she warned him of a
pressing danger to France on the very day of
Rouvray; this is difficult to reconcile with his
disbelief in her word. Ill news travels fast, but
tidings of the defeat of Rouvray could scarcely
have reached Vaucouleurs by the 13th of February.
These more probably came in the further interval of
preparation for Jeanne's departure, and the date may
have coincided with her most pressing entreaty.
It is most likely a message from Chinon gave
sanction to Jeanne's journey. Now she was really
able to prepare to go : to set forth as succour to
the dauphin : a forlorn hope, looked upon by the
great as was the ark that Noah built to save the
remnant of a lost and wilful world. This little
seed of a great army comprised Jeanne and her
two friends, Jean de Metz, knight, and Bertrand
de Poulengy, squire, with their two servants, and
Colet de Vienne, the king's messenger, and
Richard the Archer. But it was not an army that
she sought at Vaucouleurs, it was leave to act, to
carry out what seemed a wild scheme. The late
Lord Lytton said ' nothing ever so inspires human
daring as the fond belief that it is the agent of a
Divine Wisdom.' One finds in ' fanaticism the
spot out of the world by which to move the world.
The prudent man may direct a state ; but it is the
enthusiast who regenerates—or ruins it.'

On Wednesday, the 23rd of February, Jeanne
set out for Chinon, a ride of one hundred and fifty
leagues, with five great rivers to cross, through the

heart of France, a country for the most part in the hands of the enemy, to meet the true heir to the throne, and cheer him by God's promises. The little troop travelled by the shortest way, as the crow flies, as nearly as the nature of the ground permitted. There was need of haste, for the cause was at its last gasp. On the morrow of her departure from Vaucouleurs, leaving Domremy on the left, she halted at the Abbey of St. Urbain (Haute Marne), which is at twenty-eight miles distance, in the straight line, which cannot therefore be reckoned practically as less than a thirty miles' ride. They ran the risk of many dangers. The men-at-arms of the marches of the Loire were reputed, with the Bretons, the greatest robbers the world produced. Their habits of brigandage, and of burning and pillaging the country became proverbial. There were four adventurers, the brothers Du Fay, who never ceased to ravage this part of the country. Perpetual skirmishes were likewise going on between the two great parties, Armagnac and Burgundian. Received at St. Urbain for the night with her little escort, she had the encouragement of hearing mass before recommencing her long and perilous ride. Portions of this abbey are still standing, and the village which grew up under the shadow of its walls is only a few kilomètres from the stations of Donjeux and Joinville.

Passing between Sionne and Midrevaux, they took the road to Grand, abutting on the left bank of the Saunelle. At Grand are the remains of a Gallo-

Roman town and vast amphitheatre, whose elliptic curve is traceable among heaps of grass-grown ruin. One portico remains standing. Grand was the scene of martyrdom of many noble victims under Julian the Apostate. The place was doubtless familiar to Jeanne d'Arc, who must at least have known the sepulchre of St. Libaire, the virgin martyr.

But thoughts of martyrdom were far removed from the heroic maiden, full of strength, with happiness rising in her like the spring sap rising in the woods around; achievement before her, after so long waiting; in all the joy of action; in the saddle with victory calling her on. It was a fine moment of expansion, of hope enjoyed, worth a lifetime of fulfilment. The sweet vivid dreams of youth were shared at any rate by the younger of her companions. It needed this sympathy to complete the enjoyment, for 'what but youth can echo back the soul of youth—all the music of its wild vanities and romantic follies.'

But no love-dreams mingled with Jeanne's gladness. Nowhere do we read that Bertrand de Poulengy was more to her than the staid old knight, Jean de Metz, who risked his lands and office for his trust in this chance of France's deliverance. Jeanne's life is not one of a succession of novels, as our English history has been called. It has no love romance—it is a tragic poem.

Throughout the whole campaign, notwithstanding her male attire and her military bearing, no one thought of Jeanne as other than a military leader, a public character of ideal interest. Her own conduct was so good and pure, while thrown entirely among men, that the halo of holiness, rather than romance, around her was held sacred by the chivalry of that time. Her foes maligned her, but it was left to the age when chivalry was extinct absolutely to insult her, notwithstanding the pretended modesty of her enemies concerning her apparel. As for the English, it was the supposed witch they shuddered at; as a woman, they even admired her. It shows the extent to which womanly influence may be carried that she purified the whole French camp.

Miss Parr says Bertrand de Poulengy was six years older than Jean de Metz; but no contemporary author is an authority for this. Petitot says De Poulengy was the younger of her two guides, and this is the general idea. Poulengy defrayed the expenses of the route. Lebrun de Charmettes says her brother, Pierre d'Arc, went with her from Vaucouleurs to Chinon, though he admits no deposition says so; indeed, all evidence from after-date writings is against it. De Metz and Poulengy avow that at first they felt much doubt and fear. Some of the party, when daunted by the perils of the journey, wished to put her in prison (dans quelque geôle). Lenglet du Fresnoy's translator makes it, 'throw her down a quarry,' connecting, I presume, the ideas of geôle and géologie. Being an error, of course other writers fall into it. One legendary historian makes quite a melodramatic passage concerning the wild quarries where it was proposed to throw Jeanne over the cliff and return from the foolish and hazardous expedition.

The land was bubbling with the February watersprings, and bursting with the first promise of buds, as the little cavalcade rode through these woods and broken ground, on the 24th of February; crossing the Marne above Joinville, set picturesquely in its rocky hills and vineyards; a beautiful country, where Jeanne could not yet feel entirely among strangers. These hills were also wellknown to her, at least in outline, for she was still not far from home. The breeze rustling among the crisp unshed brown leaves of the beech-trees in these high-seated forests; the rushing rivers among the lofty rocks, and the lowing of the cattle were all sounds familiar to her from infancy. Only the yellow Marne had replaced the clear green Meuse in this the next-door valley. The Ornain and the Saulx played and sparkled like her own brooks at Domremy. They slept on the ground in their armour by their horses.

From St. Urbain to Bar-sur-Aube is twenty-eight miles (in a direct line). They did not enter the town, but forded the river at a short distance above the walls. Most likely they halted for the night of February the 24th at some sheltered nook in the recesses of Mont St. Germaine, before arriving near the town which is situated on the right bank of the river. They would not care to ford the stream in the evening, for in February it is still early dusk, and fords are liable to become treacherous with the thaw. They may have supped on some of the good Aube trout, or have sent one of their number into the town to procure supplies. They were seven hungry persons to be catered for.

Bar-sur-Aube is now a town of 4,780 inhabitants. A chapel on its stone bridge marks the place where Charles VII. (Jeanne's dauphin) caused the revolted Bastard of Bourbon to be broken on the wheel and his body sewn in a sack and cast into the river. This was ten years after Jeanne d'Arc's death. Though not easily roused to the more generous passions, Charles was fully capable of revenge. The church of St. Pierre at Bar is very ancient, and deep sunken in the earth.

Friday's ride of about twenty-five miles to Bar-sur-Seine was over easier ground, and by using caution, they could follow the direct road. They were in an enemy's country, and of course wished to evade observation, being too few to defend themselves against numbers; still they were enough to overpower any small marauding party, being, in the strength of their resolution, equal to any ten men who might seek to hinder their passage. The country hereabouts loses its mountainous character, but its outlines are pleasing and picturesque. The Seine is here quite a young river, and the ford presents no great difficulty. Bar is now merely a quiet country town with a pretty church.

The necessity of providing supplies must have been embarrassing, as their little force would scarcely dare approach the bourgades or fortified villages; and in those unsettled times there were few outlying farms or detached dwellings which might have furnished them with what they needed for money or for love. Of course the castles and monasteries were the usual resource for travellers in those days, but they dared not venture near the castles, nor do they seem to have approached any monastery after leaving St. Urbain. The grass just springing made it comparatively easy to provide for their horses. On Saturday, the 26th of February, they took the Tonnerre road; presumably so, for no details are given of this part of their course. The high road from Bar-sur-Seine is by Les Riceys, but the road by Chaource and Coussegrey is the most direct, and Berriat Saint Prix thinks they followed this path. They would have passed near Tonnerre, but we cannot suppose in any case that they mounted the hill on which Tonnerre stands, crowned with the church of St. Pierre on its lofty platform of rock. The pleasant lime-tree avenues of Tonnerre would hardly then have rejoiced the travellers with their shade, even had this journey been in summer, though the lime lives to an immense age. They may have refreshed themselves at the old Roman spring, Fons Dionysi, as it is supposed to be from its modern name of

La Fontaine Fosse Dionne. Jeanne rarely touched wine; her habitual drink was water. They crossed the Seraing near Chablis, about twelve miles from Auxerre. By rising early on the morning of Sunday, the 27th, they would have reached Auxerre in time to hear the bells chiming for high mass. For the first time Jeanne refused to be led by her guides, but insisted on a halt that she might attend service in the cathedral. 'If we could hear mass,' she said, 'we should do well.'

She told them to have no fear, her heavenly guides would let them come to no harm. They had to cross the Yonne, and it seemed more reasonable to divide themselves and enter the town, which is on the left bank, by the bridge, than to risk fording the river swollen by the first spring floods. The attendants could buy provisions while the Maid was at mass, and they might set off again while they still had daylight before them for a long journey. Their horses, after two or three hours' rest and a good feed, would be fresh for another start. On examining coolly the Maid's suggestions, we always find a wonderful vein of practical intention in them; no romantic folly ever mars the details of her great plan. Here spiritually protected and unrecognised, though the fame of her mission was already pretty well dispersed throughout the country, which made her travelling all the more dangerous, Jeanne worshipped in the great cathedral. In all other respects in this long journey she let herself be led by her guides. God preserved her alike from treachery and from the enemy. The grand bulk of the lofty cathedral rising above the houses and buildings of the town, a large city, now of over twelve thousand inhabitants, and overtopping the other large churches, presented an irresistible attraction to Jeanne d'Arc. Great must have been the fearful pleasure of joining in the service. Internally this church, built in 1213, rivals even Coutances. It is built over a yet earlier church, date 1005, whose crypt lies beneath the choir. Jeanne must have seen, too, the curious painting at the end of the crypt of the White Horse of the Apocalypse, with its rider; its date is near the end of the twelfth century. The external traceries of this splendid cathedral are of the finest, boldest style, in high relief, and in some parts quite detached from the wall. The richly coloured glass must have been a marvel of magnificence to our shepherdess, and the splendid doors and rose windows, which are especially fine at Auxerre, must, in their gorgeous beauty, have given rise to emotions such as we can scarcely conceive. Perhaps an imaginative child's first sight of a transformation scene at a theatre is the nearest parallel we have to this luxury of æsthetic emotion in one so unsophisticated and susceptible as Jeanne. The Lady Chapel of this church is remarkably elegant. The ancient walls of Auxerre are now levelled and made into boulevards, and the moat planted in gardens shaded by acacias and vines. The ivied towers remain to form delightful foreground features of a highly pleasing landscape.

Jeanne incurred greater risk in entering Auxerre than perhaps she understood. The town had suffered too severely from the English in 1359 and afterwards, to allow them to afford shelter to professed enemies of that power. Even in the successful progress of the king towards Rheims, four months later, it was with the utmost difficulty that Charles could obtain the least concession from the timid inhabitants of Auxerre.

Refreshed in every way, that afternoon saw the little party well on their way towards the Loire; but whether by the Bleneau or the Toucy road cannot be ascertained, as, sleeping in the fields, it is not said near what villages they stopped, and towns are scarce hereabout. The high road lies near Toucy, Fargeau, St. Sauveur, and St. Amand. Going by Courson and the pools of Entrains, one turns to the right at Bleneau on the Loing, and strikes across westward to Gien, by way of woods and pools. It is difficult even at this day to say which road has the greatest advantages; then probably it was only between disadvantages one could choose, as at that time there was no high road between Auxerre and Gien. The ancient churches show that small towns or villages existed then, and paths of communication must have lain between them, if only for markets and purposes of barter. From Auxerre to Gien is forty-four miles direct; of course, considerably more when allowing for deviations of the road. It is only when we come upon the Roman roads, of which, however, there are many in France, that we can measure Jeanne's journeys with any degree of exactness; though the tracks most frequently followed the present lines. A line of road is one of the most permanent geographical outlines. It changes its course less frequently than a river, and walls are not to be compared with it for durability. The wall of China is the great exception, but then the Tartars have no roads.

At length they looked over the vale of the Loire, beyond which lived their friends. Monday night, the 28th of February, brought them to Gien, high-seated on its hill above the Loire, round the base of which the town now nestles. The red-brick castle, with its high-pitched lead roof with many pinnacles and flèches, and its tall, peaked church tower, then, as now, crested the height above the bridge, the deep-arched, heavily-buttressed bridge of unequal arches which rises to an angle of 140° in the centre. One now walks from the train to the town by the side of vine-yarded hill-slopes.

Gien was chosen for their passage of the Loire, being one of the few towns on the river faithful to the dauphin. There was, however, the doubt as to whether on their arrival it still belonged to France. They would have made guarded inquiries at Auxerre and later on, but information was difficult for them to come by without exciting suspicion, and events moved quickly in those times of war. Was Gien, at that moment, in the hands of the enemy? Upon this would depend the difficulty of the passage of the Loire. Were it a friendly town, it would be passed by the bridge; that is if there was a bridge at all; in which case it would be the same bridge that is at present standing, altered to its present form when the newly-built bridge of Blois was so greatly admired in Louis XV.'s time. If Gien were in the hands of the enemy, they must have passed it by a ferry and a ford—a matter easy enough, if under the eyes of friends in the castle above, but otherwise a fearful risk.

Oh, joy! it yet belonged to their friends. Gien is said to be the first French town Jeanne passed on the route. Doubtless she rendered thanks for her safe arrival in the valley of the Loire at the high-seated church of St. Étienne on the hill overlooking the river. Its old square, heavily-buttressed tower remains, though the nave is modern. One goes up many steps, in two or three long flights, to reach the church from the embankment road by the Loire, turning off on the right to the old castle, which is now the prefecture. The promenade beyond the church commands a fine view, with long reaches of the Loire, flowing by the Orleans she was to save. The Orleanais soon learned of the Maid's approach; she is very likely to have sent them a message from Gien. Jeanne had quite the modern idea of saving time by at once preparing for her next step by letter or by message.

Gien is now a dull little town of five thousand

five hundred inhabitants, of the same family as Blois, and many of the towns on the Loire; the conformation of the ground, and therefore their arrangement, is so similar, as is the waywardness of the river, that spoiled child among streams. It can be reckoned upon in its fits of passion, though not controlled. 'Quel torrent révolutionnaire que cette Loire!' exclaimed the demagogue on seeing the sand-banks brought forward and left dry by its current. Other people have also had reflections on the Loire. The engineer thinks he has perfected mechanism, which he says is merely educating the forces of Nature as we train our own strength for use. Yet he vainly tries to curb this river and make it a useful water-power and water-way. Did Barrère the democrat reflect upon the uselessness of an impetuous people when he only taught them to be self-willed?

Gien is proud of its potteries and enlivened by their smoke. Clothes beaten and washed in the Loire by women is the second active industry. This goes on always. Jeanne left the shelving hills and vineyards on the north bank, crossed the Loire, passed the Celtic tumulus called 'Motte du Leon,' then away through the poplared levels of the southern bank. Leaving to the northward the river flowing towards Jargeau and Orleans, scenes of her future triumphs, she rode across the then desolate district of La Sologne, by way of Romorantin on the Sauldre; though the little party seem to have avoided the towns even here in friendly country. Sleeping as they did out of doors, every night making this more endurable as the weather and the climate grew milder, this plan was swifter and safer; for even here, or perhaps especially here, past Gien in the country nominally obedient to Charles VII., there reigned 'toutes pilleries et roberies.'

This part of France is now a great meat producing country. There is veal and pork in abundance, and the new line of rail recently opened, from Romorantin to Blois, is especially useful to the farmers. The land, though well-cultivated in parts, is not naturally fertile, for all the splendour of crimson clover that the summer traveller sees. There are numerous fir plantations among the remains of ancient forest land. In winter it reveals itself as still the sad and sandy Sologne.

From Gien to Romorantin it is fifty miles direct. I shall not describe Romorantin here, as Jeanne only passed by it on this journey, and in later times she often had occasion to pass through the town. Indeed there is very little to describe, only two market places, side by side, and some pretty walks by the Sauldre. She followed the Sauldre from Selles-St.-Denis to Romorantin, thence by Salbris to Selles-sur-Cher. Murray, until his very latest edition, does not even mention the place at all.

From Romorantin to Selles-sur-Cher the country has still the same arid character, but on crossing the Cher, the horizon soon breaks into hills and undulating forests. The old but insignificant town of Selles is only of note as a radius for excursions to sundry fine castles in its neighbourhood.

Leaving Selles, one soon arrives at high-seated St. Aignan, with its octagonal battlemented tower and its fine romanesque church, with admixture of early pointed. The present château of St. Aignan is well kept up, with fine gardens beautifully laid out and thrown open to the townspeople. A tall mass of ruined wall represents much of St. Aignan's ancient splendour. In these more peaceful times, instead of lying close-packed and unwholesome within walls, it has a flourishing suburb of tile-roofed houses of hewn-stone, with artichoke gable-ends; and on the hills the tile or plank-roofed huts of vine-dressers, looking most habitable and comfortable, are set in vineyards where the earth is ridged high, almost like walls, to plant new vines.

The scenery is pretty, with a blue distance which in some dips looks like the sea in its intensity of azure, and a deep dell full of tall forest trees, by way of which one comes out upon a pleasant woodland, with broad oaks in the more open country, and a foreground of blue columbine, white orchis, and abundance of the most delicate little forget-me-nots imaginable, of an exquisite hue of blue. These gems of colour adorned Jeanne's triumphant return journey in May; but even now the wilder, unploughed portions of the ground were smiling with primroses and celandines.

This is the light friable soil that chokes the Loire with its drift. Buttercups stand so thick among the corn that the ridge furrows are yellow with them.

Tourists seldom or never come here. There is no railway in these parts. It exists in its primitive simplicity much as Jeanne d'Arc saw it in her travels, and her peasant eyes were not too much engaged with things supernatural, or the affairs of state, to note these things of earth. Dove-coloured oxen are harrowing on these undulating slopes, and the fields are girt about with forests, just as they must have been four hundred and fifty years ago. Many of these oaks must Jeanne have looked upon, and ridden under their branches. Her path would have skirted this Bois de la Laudière.

The village of Montrésor boasts an inn with the sign of Jeanne d'Arc, although no one now seems to know anything of the passage of the heroine. Yet she rode by here several times in her triumphant days when following the court. Chemillé has a romanesque church and the usual domical stone well-roofs.

From here the ground again rises into moorland with heather, gorse, and brambles; a brisk, cheery country, with crisp, fresh fine air and windy blue sky. Though not yet out in blossom when Jeanne passed on the 1st of March, this southern province of Berri was already wreathing itself with spring. We plunge down hill into the woods again. These are the woods and hills that gather the rain to fill the Indre and Cher. The road by the village of Chemillé lies in a white, winding line at the foot of some broken tufa slopes studded with birch and fir, bordered by golden meadows on the left, and crosses (now by a bridge) a rush-grown rivulet, with water-lilies roofing in its stream, before it again climbs the hill. The villages in the vales have high-pitched gables, spired tourelles, and peaked stone roofs, sometimes pyramidal, a survival apparently of old times.

Again we are on high champaign-land, with corn and vineyards, where kites soaring overhead pounce down upon the game, heedless of the vinedressers at work among the vines. This cultivated region is bounded by an oak forest, which is still so dense that on neither side can daylight be seen through its intricacies. Much of ancient travelling must have been done through these vegetable tunnels. It was a common proverb, says Richer, 'Que les Anglois, par leur puissance, avaient fait venir les bois en France.' The English are not directly responsible for this fine forest, but industry was so suspended by the war that there were not hands left sufficient to keep Nature in subjection. This forest is only pierced by the road, and landmarked by the obelisk near the 'Maison forestière de Beauchêne.' Here and there towers up a monarch beech, but for the most part it is a fine oak forest with undergrowth of beeches, fern, and broom. The deeply-ridged grey freckled stems of the oaks are a contrast to the satiny smoothness of the beech. The oaks grow tall, through being so close together, in the fashion of all French trees, which makes the timber better available for building purposes than our large-bolled, spreading trees. Like the old Romans, the French are builders and road-makers before all things

People here never seem weary of planting. The noble forest of Beauchêne gradually melts into the open, lessening into dense oak plantations with green alleys through them, and fir-clad slopes led up to by hedges lined with apple-trees. Here we are at a village, Genillé, with the tall, Romanesque spired tower of Beaulieu to the left. The abbey church of Beaulieu, built in the first years of the eleventh century and consecrated in 1007 under Pope John XVIII. This carries the imagination back into the gloom of the dark ages, when art had only dawned in western architecture. The stone, four-sided roofed cottage on the hill to the left, 'built very long ago,' as they say here, looks like the domestic architecture of almost as early a date, when strength and durability were the first of qualities in all things made for use.

It is a fair scene, this of the river Indre and its poplar meadows, with the view of the castle of Loches; but it is no longer unknown beauty here. Historical interest and the picturesque attract tourists and artists, and the law of cause and effect has given them a convenient railway from Tours.

Jeanne d'Arc doubtless left Loches on the right hand, and pressed onwards towards Chinon; but she must have gazed up with even keener interest than do the artists at the terribly beautiful group of towers and gates and lofty walls. Her king loved the place. Its towers were not yet imbrued with the crimes of Louis Onze. These and the tales of Agnes Sorel and her too tender heart were of a later day. She lived, and was beautiful, but the world knew little of her yet. Jeanne d'Arc was born in 1412, Agnes Sorel in 1400. It is said Charles never saw Agnes till 1431, after the death of Jeanne d'Arc, though this appears doubtful.

Loches will be more particularized by-and-by when Jeanne comes to stay in the town; at present we will pass it by with merely an upward glance as Jeanne d'Arc did, yet hoping to see it more nearly, for Loches is all over picturesque charms within and without the fortress walls. It is well seen from the opposite side of the Indre, where nightingales and frogs formerly gave the concert that is now replaced by the modern music of the military band and the railway whistle.

Even Jeanne must have drawn bridle a moment to view the scene before crossing the 'amber meadow.' It glows with the intense yellow formed by afternoon sunshine upon kingcups, marsh marigolds, and waterflags. Beyond this, coming from the Beaulieu road, lies a belt of purple hills, on the nearest of which rise the tall square donjon of Loches Castle and the two octagonal stone spires of the church of St. Ours, above a portcullised gateway. Below these lie the woods and the marsh with tall poplars standing black against the sinking sun.

Jeanne and her party hastened on; it was not wholesome to halt for the night in these low-lying meadows, they would find drier lodging among the tufa crags of the further slopes rising still westward. There is a tradition of bandits wishing to attack and rob her party somewhere hereabout (some authors say at L'Ile Bouchard), near the journey's end. It is hinted that La Tremouille, Charles's chief adviser, was a party to the affair, as he was jealous of every rising influence. If so, he would have done the work more effectually. I acquit him of this; he has enough to answer for.

CHAPTER VI.

ARRIVAL AT CHINON.

'Je te dis de la part de Messire que tu es vray héritier de France et fils du Roy.' ('I tell thee on the part of our Lord that thou art the true inheritor of France and son of the king.')
Jeanne d'Arc to Charles the Dauphin.

THE court was not at Loches. The dauphin often resided there, and might have been there now, as there was no daily court circular published all over the country to inform everybody of the royal movements. It was worth while passing near Loches to see if the royal standard were raised on the castle, even if it had not lain directly on the road to Chinon. Taking the right path instead of the left at the forest of Manthelau, Jeanne's little escort pressed on by way of Villeperdue, a village too small to be marked on most maps, but where there is a roadside railway station on the way to Ste. Maure on the new line by Port-de-Piles from Tours. The present communal road leads from Loches north-westward by Dolus, Tauxigny on the Echaudon, the large villages of Branchs and Sorigny, striking south-westward to Villeperdue, and again southward to Ste. Katherine de Fierbois.

Though now truly answering to its name, Villeperdue, the lost town, this place has its oral history. It was the site of a famous Roman villa formerly, called Villa Peurerà—at least so the good nuns, the sisters of the hamlet, spell it, and they are the guardians of all knowledge that is not lodged in the curé. In its ruins, or on its site, were built the prisons of the Mussulmans; for this country was overrun by the Moors, before they were beaten by Charles Martel on the plains near by. It belonged to the Duke of Anjou, so they say; but one cannot find out which line of Anjou, nor if it was Plantagenet land.

Did Jeanne see it as I see it now, arriving at the village while the moon was early in the blue sky, a cusped streak of gold, a broken ring? Did she see the fruit-trees, farms, and golden pastures, and hear the doves cooing, wild birds trilling, and men rejoicing in this 'pays de rire et de rien faire'? Nature was then as copious as now, we have not added one to her inventions. It is said of this rich Touraine that 'Nature does everything in this country, and man does nothing.' It is less clean and inviting than Normandy, it is also more primitive; that is, it carries one back to the middle-ages better.

It is a pleasant ride among fields of clover and buttercups 'growing lush in juicy stalks,' meadows watered by the Manse, across which is a viaduct of fifteen arches at Villeperdue, and on through winding parish lanes, shaded by occasional avenues of oak to Ste. Katherine de Fierbois. Murray calls it a mile or two, which is an error. It is a good six kilometres, and one has no choice but to walk the distance, which Joanne's guidebook asserts is nine kilometres. Murray says there is an omnibus from Villeperdue to St. Katherine. This is the most considerable error of the three: there is really no more omnibus than there was in Jeanne d'Arc's day.

The road passes between the poor little church of Villeperdue, sliced off at the gable and with a penthouse western porch, and the château of Boisbera, a perfect moated grange, with four round turrets and a full, square moat, with boat and drawbridges complete, and frogs croaking and leaping out of the forget-me-nots into the yellow iris tufts.

Further on, in a pool of yellow water-lilies and tall bulrush stems, where blue dragon-flies skim the sunny water, and much life is skippant and jumpant, the frogs are thick as leaves in Vallombrosa. They look like leaves until they splash and leap; then these green and yellow caperers look up at you and swell, and add their bass to the shrill orchestra of grasshoppers, those violins of the fields. The land all round is a well-wooded plain.

The light, delicate spire visible to the left is that of Ste. Katherine de Fierbois, where Jeanne found her famous sword, usually termed 'l'épée miraculeuse.' It was the age of legends of marvellous swords, they fitted well into chivalric poems. With the winding of the road the spire next appears on the right: it looks prettier than the church towers we have latterly seen; for the churches since Beaulieu have been architecturally insignificant, with plain, low, square towers, and funnel-shaped slate spires. Hereabouts the Moor was stayed by Charles Martel; here came Jeanne d'Arc. No one comes here now; it has no special attraction of scenery. Yet it is a pleasant land and a goodly. Historians following each other speak of Ste. Katherine as a famous pilgrimage. It is called a pilgrimage now in Joanne's guide-book, yet it is not famous, or at least, not frequented.

Doubtless Jeanne chose to halt here and wait for the return of her messenger to the dauphin, because the village bore the name of St. Katherine, her patroness.

Colet de Vienne, the king's messenger, rode forward with a letter, in which Jeanne asked permission to seek the dauphin at Chinon, and detailed to him her mission, a letter which threw Charles and his court into a great state of agitation and confliction. Jeanne meanwhile halted on Friday night, and stayed all through Saturday, the 5th of March, at Ste. Katherine, her soul thirsting for God's comfort. The name seemed to bring her so near the presence of her Voices: that music which cheered her and made her forget her fatigues. She attended divine service three times on the same day. This implies a day's halt, for consideration, doubtless, and the preparation of her letter, as well as for the despatch of the courier to Chinon, at twenty miles distant, and his return, which could not in any case be before Saturday evening. They had also to rest the tired horses.

From Vaucouleurs to Ste. Katherine is two hundred and seventy-seven miles direct as the crow flies, measured according to the scale of the map, without allowance for hills or obstructions.

Wednesday, Feb. 23th.—Vaucouleurs to St. Urbain, twenty-eight miles.

Thursday, Feb. 24th.—St. Urbain to Bar-sur-Aube, twenty-eight miles.

Friday, Feb. 25th.—Bar-sur-Aube to Bar-sur-Seine. (Bar-sur-Aube to Auxerre is sixty-two miles direct, map measurement.)

Saturday, Feb. 26th.—Bar-sur-Seine to Chaource, on the road to Auxerre.

Sunday, Feb. 27th.—Halt of half-a-day at Auxerre; they rode on towards Gien.

Monday, Feb. 28th.—Gien, by the Bleneau or Toucy road? (Auxerre to Gien is forty-four miles direct.)

Tuesday, March 1st.—Crossed the Loire, took the road by the Sauldre river by Salbris.

Wednesday, March 2nd.—Salbris to Romorantin. (Gien to Romorantin is fifty miles.)

Thursday, March 3rd.—Passed Selles-sur-Cher and St. Aignan.

Friday, March 4th.—Passed Loches and arrived at Ste. Katherine de Fierbois.

Saturday, March 5th.—Rested at Ste. Katherine. (Romorantin to Ste. Katherine is sixty miles direct, it is more by the communal roads.)

Sunday, March 6th.—Rode to Chinon.

H

These distances are measured to the entrance of each town; one must reckon about a mile for the breadth of the towns. (The kilometre-stones always reckon distances from the 'Place' or centre of the town.) This is averaging over thirty miles a day as the crow flies. Of course much allowance must be made for obstructions on the route, hills, forests, watercourses, rivers, and necessary deviations. This on good modern roads would bring it to at least five miles a day more. In the tracks of that time the calculation should be greater. Three hundred and thirty miles is a moderate computation of the actual distance. Truly the horses would need rest. According to Jeanne's guide, Jean de Novelonpont (de Metz), they had made in eleven days one hundred and fifty leagues, approximately, or indeed well-nigh exactly so according to my calculation, remembering that the French league is 2·72° English statute miles.

'But the souvenirs of Novelonpont,' Henry Martin says, 'are not exact (fidèles), the journey lasted twenty days.' Martin gives no data for this, and I should like to know a better authority for the length of the journey than he who made it.

'L'avant-dernier continuateur de Guillaume de Nangis'* gives the date of the 6th of March for Jeanne's arrival at Chinon, calling it the day following her arrival at Ste. Katherine. This might be so, supposing she arrived at early morning at Ste. Katherine; but we know she

* 'Procès,' t. iv., p. 303.

spent the whole day there, and heard mass three times.

Leaving Vaucouleurs on February 23rd, and arriving at Chinon on the 6th of March, as seems to be certain, she must have arrived at Ste. Katherine on the evening of the 4th of March, or, at the very latest, the early morning of the 5th, as we must allow for her courier's return from Chinon with the answer to her letter, even supposing it to be answered without delay, since one cannot reckon it at less than a day's hard riding from Ste. Katherine to Chinon and back; with a fresh horse for the return journey. And this corresponds with the eleven days of Jean de Metz. An eleven days' ride through a disturbed country at a time when its roads, such as they were in those days, were at their worst, the frost thawed and the paths not yet dried by the sun and wind of March, was no small feat for a peasant girl who had never been used to horseback. In all this long ride Jeanne showed a firm fearlessness which gave her companions confidence. They traversed the several provinces unimpeded, as if the country were at peace, without let or hindrance and without meeting any troops. Now they seemed at their journey's end, and now came the usual indecision (though not on the part of Jeanne) about what to do when they arrived, which seems so small a point at the beginning of a long road. Then we think the thing is to reach the journey's end—and that is all. Jeanie Deans found the difficulties after arrival the greatest, so did Jeanne d'Arc.

One gets to know the country well in riding or in walking across it. It is a thin line that one walks through, but the eye covers an average range of twenty-five miles on either side, and the slowness of the pace leaves one time to observe it carefully. Tradition says the church of Ste. Katherine was founded by Charles Martel in the eighth century. It was rebuilt by Charles VII. and Louis XI. The present church of Ste. Katherine de Fierbois is decorated Gothic of the flamboyant period, with what appears at a distance a bottle-shaped spire; which is really a wooden steeple, with flying buttresses. It has crockets, finials, and an elaborate west front. All the portals are crocketed and pinnacled, and yet it is little more than an ordinary village church. It is very well taken care of, and sets a good example to country churchwardens.

A tablet relates how the vaulted roof of the chapel in the southern aisle, having been totally destroyed by the fall of its surmounting gable, the workmen of the parish, responding to the appeal of their pastor, Monsieur l'Abbé Maubois, gratuitously restored this roof, for which the materials were given by the Marquis de Lussac. This work was done with so much zeal that it was executed in the eight days preceding the feast of Christmas, 1858.

A modern painted window in this aisle represents St. Katherine, and beneath her picture one of the vision appearing to Jeanne d'Arc, with the inscription : 'Ici Jeanne d'Arc fit prendre son épée en 1429 pour sauver la France. Souvenir du 10 Mai, 1879.'* Here was found the famous sword 'marked with five crosses, lying in a vault,' which Jeanne d'Arc sent for before she went to raise the siege of Orleans. It was found behind, or within, the tomb said to be that of Charles Martel. Though legend has gathered round this sword, yet Jeanne is not responsible for that. The sword might easily have been seen by her during the day she spent in the church : or she may possibly not have seen the sword, but priests at Ste. Katherine may have told her of it. The tomb and the supposed position of the sword were where the present high altar stands. The whole church has a vaulted roof of white stone. The holy water stoup is of an early period. It is a deep oval stone dish set on a low, round pillar. There is no statue of Jeanne here nor in the village. A cross stands in the 'place' in front of the church. The whiteness of the stone gives a brand-new appearance to all buildings hereabout. A new-looking house near the church is really a very old one. It has a crocketed portal with wyverns, shields, and other decorations, some of which have been carefully restored in the original style. Little is to be learnt from the people here concerning Jeanne d'Arc. Nobody seems able to understand why anyone should come to Ste. Katherine. The good souls evidently have no idea of tourists or pilgrims. An intelligent lad of

* 'Here Jeanne d'Arc took her sword in 1429 in order to save France.'

seventeen, from whom I inquired the way out of Ste. Katherine, wondered who on earth could have directed me from Tours to Chinon by way of Villeperdue and Ste. Katherine! He considered it an immense loss of time and money. Had he known all, he would have thought me mad.

There is no carriage, neither horse nor cart for hire at the 'Jeanne d'Arc' inn, whose walls are hung with such flaring prints of the heroine that it is no wonder they do not venerate her here. The crockery also depicts the story of Jeanne d'Arc, and how she hewed the English army in pieces at the battle of Patay. It seems as if Jeanne d'Arc and ourselves were the only strangers who had ever found their way to Ste. Katherine. We must walk on to Ste. Maure.

The place abounds chiefly in deficiencies; no omelette—they are saving all the eggs hereabout for sitting: no post-cards—they are out of them, as they are out of most things at the general shop: no curé—he had gone to Tours to meet the archbishop—indeed, we met him driving a dog-cart at a good pace upon our road: no convenience for washing, so we went outside and pumped upon our hands. But pilgrimage has its alleviations; they have andouilles, for those who are able to eat them, and the white wine of the country is refreshing and pleasant.

We sat on a well under a willow at the cross roads till some one should pass of whom we might ask the way to Ste. Maure; but everyone was at siesta. To the left of the straight, scorching high road is the Château de Comarque, of which the photographs bear an inscription, remarkable for its inexactitude: 'Château Comacre (or Comarque) near Ste. Maure, belonging to Monsieur le Marquis de Lussac, remarkable for the chapel of St. Cath. de Fierbois, where Jeanne d'Arc went to seek the sword which was deposited on the tomb of Charles Martel, in order to lay siege to Orleans.'

This is liable to mislead a pilgrim to suppose that the chapel of the sword is in the Château de Comarque, a modern Gothic château, built in 1850. The traditions concerning Jeanne d'Arc are as vague and inaccurate as those connected with Charles Martel. The unsophisticated people have not localised the sites; thus the spot where Charles slew Abderahmen is waved to as everywhere within twenty kilometres, at an angle under 180° of horizon. At least, one is not disturbed by the fictions and vulgarisms that crowd round more sacred localities in the Holy Land.

The supposed ambush laid for Jeanne as a test of her mission has been located between this place and L'Ile Bouchard. I regard this ambush as a myth.

Later on we found a turfy bank in the fretted shadows of some pollard willows, growing deep in grass in undulating ground, near a sort of viaduct, or bridge, over a poplar dell. Here we rested, looking up at the intense blue zenith, sung to by the birds and played to by the æolian harp in the poplar-trees.

But Jeanne was no longer weary here; she had

just been sent for by the king; her hope had culminated in fulfilment. A determined will carries victory with it. Thus Jeanne came from Vaucouleurs. The first stage of her mission was achieved. Now came the tests of truth; and the task of conquering Charles's dread of ridicule. In one sense ridicule is the test of truth: truth meets with ridicule and vanquishes it, with the hammer-logic of an accomplished fact. As it was in the days of Noah, so it always is in the outset of any high promise, any great truth. It is only falsehood that is run after by the multitude.

It is six kilometres to Ste. Maure, where there are conveyances to be had to the railways (some cross-lines are within reach of Ste. Maure by omnibus), or to the Dolmen of Ste. Maure not far from Bommiers. From Ste. Maure to L'Ile Bouchard, still following Jeanne's route, it is a pleasant drive of about ten miles through undulating country of well-watered park-like scenery with golden-brown oak-trees, where chalk-burning is the principal industry besides agriculture. The river Vienne flowing through the valley, spreading here and there into the appearance of a lake, reflects the poplars on its banks. Oak-trees line the roads, and walnuts and other fruit-trees are numerous. The people go bare-foot; wooden shoes are the luxurious exception; yet they look well-fed, well-housed, and well-to-do.

L'Ile Bouchard has a double bridge over the Vienne, which here forms an island. The town was doubtless in former days nothing but a fortified island. The walls have only been partially destroyed, and there are the ruins of a castle. It is an old-world place, with winding streets just wide enough to admit a carriage between the house-fronts. There are few foot-paths. The interesting church, always the apex of the people's culture, has a flamboyant hexagonal tower, a crocketed stone spire, and elaborate romanesque doorways. The chancel is early-pointed.

Here one can take the train to Chinon, but it is not too far for a drive. Jeanne d'Arc perhaps thought it an easy day's journey from St. Katherine to Chinon, but it is the very utmost if her courier could have gone and returned in the same day with her letter. He must have started at daybreak.

There is a delightful old cruciform romanesque church between l'Ile Bouchard and Sazilly. The Villa Anceiensi of the Latin records of Jeanne's trials, where her mother is said to have lived during the procès of her rehabilitation, was Auché, a village between Chinon and l'Ile Bouchard. The approach to Chinon is not imposing; the castle does not look so high-seated as it really is.

Jeanne was at length at Chinon. The king was at his last gasp: drowning, he clung to a straw. Still, for fear of ridicule, that terror of weak minds, he dreaded to receive her whom the enthusiastic common people reckoned as an angel. Truly she was to him an angel, the messenger sent from heaven to serve him in his dire need. But could God really have sent him such a simple instrument, a mere shepherdess, who could not read or write, nor speak the French language correctly? He would have had more faith in the magical sword of Fierbois, and far more in a chest of treasure.

Jeanne could speak to the point; she had intelligence equal to her courage, and she was being educated all this while. Jeanne saw the world; this was her university, the different grades of society she mingled with, the different 'forms' of her school. Fear of the Lord had given her principles, a happy home-life had established them in love, like apples of gold set in pictures of silver. Law she learnt first at Toul, then at Poitiers, last at Rouen. Manners she learnt in courts; she also learnt to loathe their vacillation and their faithlessness, first at Nancy, then at Chinon, then at Saint Denis. Against law, courts, and treachery were her hardest battles. Actual combat was easier. She was a being d'élite; acting of her own free will, Jeanne gave herself into the hands of God, eager to do His will, patient while He should bring it to pass, knowing that the wrath (or hurry) of man worketh not the righteousness of God.

Two days more to wait, while the court was deliberating or disputing whether she should be seen by Charles or not. It was the last hope of the people of Orleans; their deputies were at Chinon awaiting the king's decision. Ecclesiastics and others came to examine her, but she would only deliver her actual message to the king himself. Jeanne carried a letter—cold enough, doubtless—from the governor of Vaucouleurs, and, better than this, the warm witness of the companions of her journey, who averred themselves more fully settled in their belief in her mission since their more intimate knowledge of her character.

Where was she all this time, since she was not admitted into the actual castle of Chinon? Most writers, led by Berriat Saint Prix, speak of her being detained in the Château de Coudrai, seven miles off. This is far to go for what is nearer at hand. Within the walls of the fortress, though apart from the castle itself, is a strong, habitable tower called the Tour de Coudrai, where tradition has always said that Jeanne was kept safe, but hidden, until the time she was admitted to see the king. This is one of the mistakes that are at once cleared up to the satisfaction of one's mind at the sight of the places. Seven miles off is too far and too inconvenient for the hourly messages and conversations that are implied in the history of these two days.

The way up to the castle from the town is by a sort of paved gutter rather than a lane, then up a good many steps, where there are dwellings in the thickness of the old walls; poor people have burrowed here, as all through this province they are used to the idea of excavating dwellings in the calcareous tufa.

There is a fine view of the winding river Vienne and the surrounding landscape from the bridge leading across to the donjon. Many of these castles near the Loire are magnificently situated; their windows command views which show fine taste on the part of the monarchs who loved these residences. Chinon was a favourite abode of our Henry II. and Cœur de Lion. Both their tombs are near by at Fontevrault.

A portcullis entrance admits one to a garden of red roses within the loop-holed walls. The view traced from left to right includes a twin-towered church, the town seated on its islands, with a suspension-bridge and a double stone bridge over the two branches of the river. A romanesque church, with a stone spire, lies immediately below the castle, which is surrounded by the townspeoples' gardens lying deep below the walls. The castle is built of the abundant white stone of the country, like everything else; even the cottages are built of this fair, hewn stone. This whiteness makes the ruins appear more ghostly, especially by moonlight, though it detracts from their picturesqueness by day.

One is mercifully allowed to wander about alone in the labyrinth of these grass-grown walls, thick with poppies and bugloss, wild oats and mignonette, 'creatures whose office it is to abate the grief of ruin by their gentleness.'

The former royal apartments are comprised in the principal mass of the ruins. Though now no floors remain, nothing but the grass-grown ground, sometimes paved, sometimes cellared with dungeons, one can trace on the walls of the first floor as it was formerly, the deeply embrasured fireplace, with columned chimney-breast, of the room where, as the tablet says, Jeanne d'Arc came to recognise Charles VII., and another plainer fireplace below this and slightly to the right, which warmed the room beneath. The joist holes are also visible. The lower room has a narrow window overlooking the river, skewed into the thickness of the wall.

Some of the other rooms are less ruinous than these, and still retain their pleasant splayed window-seats, and the transoms, and sometimes the whole 'croisée' of their windows. The fireplace in the third room is the most perfect, showing remains of sculpture on the columns of the chimney-piece; a fourth room closes the series; beyond this is a tower-stair and a yawning depth between the dwelling-house, or palace, and an external tower. A large wild-rose-tree grows in a corner of this fourth room and a narrow staircase leads down to—one shudders to think where.

Yonder, from a cliff-like tower, the breeze is

'wafting wall-flower scents,
From out the crumbling ruins of fallen pride,
And chambers of transgression, now forlorn.'

Out in the garden, or yard, across a bridge over a moat in which grow lofty walnut-trees, elder, nettles, and ivy-masses, are two round towers, one perfect in its battlements and machicolations, with a vaulted roof, like a chapel; the other more ruinous, and grass-grown on the top. A garden of pink roses, with a grass-plot sprinkled with peonies and poppies, sheltered by an arbor-vitæ hedge, leads to a further tower and more remains of the castle wall. There is a lovely view from this more distant tower, the Tour du Moulin, the oldest part of the castle, built by the Normans. It has a lofty, hexagonal vaulted roof and three arched loopholes, besides the window and the door. Above this vaulted room are gutters for pouring down lead upon assailants. The well appears to be still in use.

Chinon is as finely situated as Amboise: both were French kings' favourite castles overlooking towns built on islands of a river; but how different their story—one is a ruined Windsor, overgrown with weeds, the other is now a small modern château with a paradise of a garden.

Another tower contains the chapel of St. Martin, where Jeanne d'Arc retired to pray on the evening of the 8th of March, 1429, after she had had audience of the king. So says a tablet. Another wooden tablet hanging at the door of the Tour du Coudrai marks that it was inhabited by Jeanne d'Arc from the time of her presentation to King Charles VII. on the 8th of March, 1429, until the 20th of April, the date of her departure for Tours and Orleans. A statement full of inaccuracies, as is the way of such inscriptions, but yet a far more likely story than that she was sent to Château Coudrai seven miles off. This is more consistent with the fact of audiences with her by Charles's suite. It was outside the royal residence, beyond the bridge and yet within the fortress, a lofty round tower above the inner moat. Acacias and other trees surround the Tower of Coudray on the garden side, and honeysuckle, beautiful but scentless, clings about it.

The oblong portcullis tower of entrance to the ruins has its machicolations perfect, each one hollow and headed by a trefoil. This gateway is of later date than the rest of the castle. Murray calls it the donjon: here they call it the Tour de l'Horloge. It was built by Charles VII., at that later date when, thanks to Jeanne d'Arc, he was enabled to build. It commands fine views of land and river. It is inhabited by the guardian of the ruins and his family. One can mount the steep winding stair to the top and walk round this lofty tower outside. The machicolation holes, barred over by iron, command the approaches; on every side stones, arrows, or melted lead could be rained upon assailants. Its top stones are firmly iron-clasped together. From this height the garden and weedy courtyards of the castle look almost like a forest. The donjon is in itself a highly picturesque object, with its gable roof and two pointed spires, one of them a slate spire, the other an umbrella roof with weather-cocks, and stone chimneys of quaint fashion built between them.

At length Jeanne was introduced to the castle by the Count of Vendôme, and brought before Charles, this reckless inheritor of a glorious past. She recognised the king at once; she saw through the simple trick of a frivolous disguise. No child's play could deceive the clear eyes of one who was so in earnest. She could read features, and had often heard the king described. What were trifling differences of dress, or ornament, or of position in the room to her, who knew nothing about such things? She was sent there to work, to save France; the God in whom she trusted could lead her straight to him to whom she was sent.

'God give you good life, fair dauphin,' or fair king, for it seems uncertain which title she used on this occasion, though otherwise she never addressed Charles as king until after his coronation. Indeed, although he had already been king for seven years, since 1422, he is called indiscriminately king or dauphin by all historians, notwithstanding that Louis, his son, was actually dauphin; such stress was laid by contemporaries on the sanctity of the coronation and anointing.

Jeanne at once entered upon the subject of her mission—the four charges, or burdens (*quatuor onera*) laid upon her: 1, to raise the siege of Orleans; 2, to cause the king to be crowned and anointed; 3, to drive out the English (from the whole of France?); 4, to deliver the Duke of Orleans from the hands of the English. This captive prince, taken at Agincourt, had become for Jeanne a personification of the nation, like Charles VII. himself. The poet Duke of Orleans, ungrateful as Charles himself, has not dedicated a single verse to the memory of Jeanne d'Arc. The king was convinced of the truth of her mission after some private talk with her—at least, he professed himself to be so. Jeanne was cheered. Her king was another St. Michael to her, a prosopopœia of her own enthusiastic love.

'Ah! fallacies of youth's first flower,
  When all seems bright and good.'

Among the nobles round was the young Duke of Alençon, who lived in the neighbourhood at St. Florent-les-Saumur. The king named him to Jeanne.

'Be welcome,' she said; 'more there are together of the royal blood of France, the better it will be.'

It was a bewildering sight to the humble Lorrainaise to see these gay and jewelled darlings of a court, so young, so reckless, and so frolicsome, presenting in the varied costume of their office much the aspect of a fancy ball—priests, and the chancellor in robes of peace; knights and youthful nobles with the colours of their ladies; courtiers with what Froissart calls 'hattes of biever and eustrydes fethers;' and the poet Alain Chartier, the king's secretary, author of 'La Belle Dame sans mercy,' with his sugar-loaf hat hung by ribbons at his back. Add to these the train of ladies in the suite of the queen-dowager of Sicily, mother of the queen, Mary of Anjou, ('a princess of great merit and prudence,' who does not appear to have been there,) and Jeanne might well be dazzled. Yet her head was not turned; she was self-possessed and outwardly calm, very simple and speaking little ('moult simple et peu parlant'); but when she spoke her words were worthy of record. She was more remarkable to these people than they to her.

Great personages came to see her in the Tower of Coudray, and she showed good countenance before them; but when she was alone she wept and prayed. She yielded to grief, being too simple to deny pain.

Emotional persons—those who have the sensitive fibre of genius—in youth have their tears very near their eyes. Jeanne had this sensitive temperament, and she was only seventeen. She was high-strung and set to brilliant music; the tension once relaxed, the tones resounded in a melancholy minor. She was alone, too, in the midst of a strange life, different in her dress, her origin, her habits from everyone about her; watched with jealousy and curiosity, like an actress or an object in a show; thronged by people who had no earnestness, no heroism in their hearts; headed by a prince who was at best but another Second Charles Stuart, king of England, willing to let anyone who would toil for him, while he would only enter into their labours. 'L'initiative appartient toujours à quelqu'un.' That one was never Charles the dauphin, the natural leader. One wonders how Jeanne endured him for a day; but the reverential nature does not willingly see blemishes in its idol. He represented every principle of right for her, and perhaps, too, the strong nature unconsciously pitied and yearned over the weaker one.

Jeanne was a true Frenchwoman, essentially a Frenchwoman in her brightness, sense, taste (this is implied from old writings), vivacity of speech, and, above all, in her affections. This natural affection is pre-eminent among the French; it is this most of all that makes them bad colonists: they leave their heart behind them.

The Germans weep, but they go; we, too, go out into the world, but we do not weep. The bravest of the French have not strength voluntarily to quit their own people and their father's house.

They are right, no prospective good compensates for the sundering of all natural ties. That fine and picturesque young man, Alphonse Poulard, fisherman and baker of Mont St. Michel, was right when he told me, 'Non, je ne voudrais pas quitter ma patrie pour devenir riche autre part.' He spoke the French mind. It is not the best of the French nation whom we find cruising about the world.

It was this loneliness that made Jeanne's heart to ache amid all her glory. Yet Jeanne had sources of happiness that none around her understood, the companionship of her Voices, and the joy of supremely loving God. Her manners were necessarily good, being free and simple; as Burton, the Eastern traveller, says, 'vulgarity and affectation, awkwardness and embarrassment, are weeds of civilized growth, unknown to the people of the desert,' so they were to this peasant maiden. Although a peasant, Jeanne was a being all poetry, the heroic poetry of action. For me I dare not write her history in prose, I can only rub in the background. A Homer might approach the theme in lofty verse. Poetry, in life, does not usually survive a certain amount of civilization nor wealth. Madame de Staël says truly, the lower orders are much nearer being poets than the people of good society, for, as she goes on to say still more philosophically, 'Conventionality and persiflage are only of use to serve as fences (bounds), they can inspire nothing. The tone of society is favourable to the poetry of grace and gaiety, but let a being of superior order step in and the poet at once feels a want of harmony in the two creations,' one feels as if the lighter things must be swept away before the coming of a ruler. So Alain Chartier seems to have felt towards Jeanne; he, the poet, could feel that here was another type from theirs. 'The large and clear conception, the breadth of view, the passion held in leash, the tremulously earnest tone, the utter forgetfulness of self' of a conquering reformer were imaged in this young girl of majestic stature, but with still childish features and delicate bloom. History describes her as having had eyes of that uncertain colour between brown and green which are always so expressive and so melting; brown, finely-drawn eyebrows, and plentiful chestnut hair, cut round in equal length to the top of the neck; a sweet smile, a well-formed nose, delicate vermilion lips, the hollow between the lower lip and chin deeply marked, and the chin rather pointed. She had a fine contour of face, and a fair, white neck; a candid expression of angelic purity, with a tinge of melancholy. She had long taper fingers and nervous hands, well-formed, but thin rather than rounded. Her countrywoman speaks of her as 'having only the strength that comes from on high: inspired by religion, a poet in her actions, a poet also in her words when the Divine spirit animates them;

showing sometimes in her speech an admirable genius, sometimes an absolute ignorance of all which heaven has not revealed to her.' Madame de Staël knew Jeanne chiefly through the unnaturally coloured medium of Schiller. The only histories she could have read were Lenglet du Fresnoy's, which L'Averdy justly declares is *très médiocre*, and L'Averdy's compilation of old MS. which Lenglet de Fresnoy as truly calls *très précieux*.

We, whose Christianity is so much an effort of the intellect or of custom, cannot conceive the fervour of the lower classes whose hope, love, and expansion it was in the middle-ages, before printing had rendered other forms of soul-growth possible. The Rev. C. J. Robertson speaks of this as 'religious emotion, in which thought and logic are all but consumed in love.'

The inspired one has more, not less, native sense than others. The faculties of more clearly perceiving, and obediently listening to, the highest voice; the world, which runs after all manner of thought-reading, spirit-rapping, or mere unbelief, chooses to call this reverent spirit—mania.

Charles's court, occupied with making the most of their youth-time, with the dalliance of love and what ill-fortune had left them of the joys of life, felt humbled by this stern young follower of duty, who, while filled with enthusiasm, retained the innocent purity and sweet thoughts of earliest youth. Before this pure young Christian they were as Pagans lapped in sensual delights. Her overpowering influence was felt from the moment of her arrival upon the scene, a weight to some, an uplifting to others.

It was a god-like power and mastery which they could not choose but feel. At once historical and marvellous, the character and deeds of Jeanne stand out like fragments of Homeric tale. As in Homer, there are words and touches in the old chronicles of her life which give us the heroine in her image as she stood with a vividness which none of our modern lens-painting can achieve; crystallized—finished as an anthem by Mozart; and there is a spiritual side to her history which makes us hardly able to realize that these things occurred so late in recorded circumstance, so near to our own day: the age of divine mysteries being —as most people think—over. Noble ideas still lived in France, and were respected, but they were not practised, at any rate not by those whose highest use in life is the wide example their high position enables them to show. The glamour of sweetness that rests like the wing of a pardoning angel on the memory of Agnes Sorel is as firelight unto sunlight near the pure fervour of Jeanne d'Arc. Most people think of them together. When we mentally run over the history of France in the fifteenth century, it is not the kings and statesmen whom the memory calls up; it is the women. It is Katherine the Fair, foolish and feeble, the common man's feminine ideal; Isabeau, the infamous; Agnes Sorel, the beautiful and high-spirited, beneficent and tender-hearted, and Jeanne, the servant of the Most High. Even

Dunois, oak of chivalry, comes after these, and Charles is well-nigh forgotten. He is only a stumbling-block.

This picturesque figure in her male attire now occupied for over two weeks, from the 6th to the 20th of March, the attention of the triflers and the hopes of the serious. Concerning her dress, the Archbishop of Embrun sensibly remarks, later, 'It is more decent to do these things in man's dress, since one is obliged to do them among men.' Truly Jeanne was a wonderful person, yet—now rose the terrible doubt whether she might be a sorceress.

BOOK II.
THE TRIUMPH.

CHAPTER VII.

THE TRIAL AT POITIERS.

'En nom Dieu,' répliqua Jeanne, 'je ne suis pas venue à Poitiers pour faire signes ; mais menez-moi à Orléans, et je vous montrerai les signes pour quoi je suis envoyée. Qu'on me donne si peu de gens qu'on voudra, j'irai à Orléans.' ('In God's name,' replied Jeanne, 'I have not come to Poitiers to make signs ; but take me to Orleans, and I will show you the signs for which I am sent. Let them give me as few men as they will, I will go to Orleans.')

From Chinon the maid was sent to Poitiers, at the end of March, for examination by the doctors of divinity and laws. She had been gaining ground all this time, practising herself in all the necessary warlike exercises in which she soon became skilful and graceful. 'Taught by the willing mind that what it well desires gains aptly.' She is said to have ridden at the quintain, and her skill on horseback caused the Duke of Alençon to give her a present of a fine horse. She also practised the use of the cross-bow and other weapons. These exercises braced her physical frame, and counteracted her excitable mental temperament and kept it balanced. Now she was thought worthy of a hearing.

Oh, the relief of escape from a court and constant watching, to canter over the plains once more. These green plains of Ste. Maure, fairer than when she saw them last, these waving battle-fields of Saracens, under the caroub-trees and the blue sky. No wonder the Moors thought the climate would suit them, with its rich green, waving crops and cool shade, 'the food of vision,' as the Arabs call it. The country grows more decidedly southern in its character directly one crosses the bridge over the Vienne. Water-melons and great gourds and maize cover the ground with their quick growth, the shade of the walnut-trees is inky black in the dazzling white sunshine, and long bean-pods dangling from very large leaved trees give a juxta-tropical character to the vegetation. Two crops of hay and every other harvest come off the ground, ploughed by the tawny oxen twice a year, and the leavings support a teeming life of black fowls, geese, and other small stock. The rich red-coloured gravel soil is watered by a cool green river, which the road follows on to the foot of the steep hill leading up to the town of Poitiers. Here one enters by the Porte de Paris, near the ruins of the ancient château.

It is fifty miles from Chinon to Poitiers; a two days' ride for the more easy-going people who now accompanied Jeanne d'Arc; though her faithful friend, Jean de Metz, still remain-ed with her. They stayed at Chatellerault for the night, only next day following on the Vienne until it joins the valley of the Clain, whose rocky ravines are full of scenic beauty, of the kind that moderns admire, rather than did Jeanne d'Arc's contemporaries; to them 'the profit of our land must pass the beauty,' as old Chapman words Homer's meaning and his own feeling.

I know no town which so much reminds me of Jerusalem as Poitiers. The intense blue, burning sky, with a white heat round the sun; the arid rocky nature of most of the surrounding landscape, relieved by groves of verdure in the vales, and the keen air felt on the summit of the hill where the white stony town lies so closely packed. The sumptuous and peculiarly romanesque façade of Notre Dame much resembles the church of the Holy Sepulchre; and in both cities one soon gets the habit of examining every stone with interest; unlike the inhabitants of both, who have 'inherited a long past without thinking of it.' For all these reasons it also resembles Toledo. Poitiers is eminently what George Eliot calls 'one of those old, old towns which impress one as a continuation and outgrowth of Nature.' A town familiar with forgotten years, 'which carries the traces of its long growth and history like a millennial tree.'

Jeanne may not have been to the École de Droit, where our Bacon studied law, most of that building is of later date; but she must, during her stay, have seen the ancient curiosities of the place, for Poitiers is even now a museum of archæological history, dating from pre-Christian Rome to Napoleon

III., and the plain courtyard of the Law School holds an epitome of all this history.

Even now there are old capitals and sarcophagi strewn about the courtyard, in curious contrast with its trim central garden, full of asters. One of these stone coffins is shaped and hollowed for the head and shoulders of the corpse; one is a very curious double tomb, the bodies lying fan-wise, in wedge-shaped coffins, side by side. The Musée lapidaire, of which these things are the unplaced *débris,* contains many Roman and Gallic remains; one, an archaic female figure, holding an infant, inscribed 'Lepidava Lentise Reginiuxor lepidare gini fil pietati.'

One cannot find much remaining of the Roman amphitheatre. 'Ah, madame! il n'y a plus des arènes; on a tout démoli; les locataires ne voulaient pas que ça tombassent sur leurs têtes: c'est un quartier neuf.' And so it is; the inhabitants, true to their habits of burrowing, have burrowed it down over their heads; and the new stone, shaped by nature for building purposes, is as white as whitewash.

One gets a peep of Roman work—a crumbling arch; it is what remains of the arena. A petrified diorama, on which are traced the shadows of the Roman, Moor, and Gaul. 'Hélas tout!' they tell me, or nearly all, for by poking about, as only antiquarians care to do, one can discover more. There are four or five remaining arches of the Roman aqueduct still standing near the road to Angoulême. But the Christian antiquities are perhaps more abundant and more interesting than in any other French town. They dated from many centuries, even in Jeanne's time. St. Pierre, the ancient cathedral, built probably on an earlier foundation by our Henry II., whose rich façade shows a good deal of sixteenth century restoration (the date also of a fine brasswork canopy over the high altar), but where you descend eight steps, marking eight centuries; and Montiersneuf (in whose alleyed grove are ancient capitals for seats), where a Latin inscription tells us that, in 1086, Geoffroy, Duke of Aquitaine, this church's founder, died, and Pope Urban consecrated the high altar in 1096, long after its foundation.

Older still is St. Hilaire, dated 1049; and most ancient of all is the baptistery of St. John, one of the earliest Christian monuments in France, dating at latest from the sixth or seventh century. Some place it even in the fifth century, and Joanne calls it of the fourth century; and it looks as early. The wall-paintings of the interior are in the Byzantine style. It is about fifteen feet or so below the surface: the semi-domed stone roofs of the transepts just rise above the soil. These roofs are almost on a level with the eye, as one leans over the parapet of the surrounding area, and looks down upon the half-buried church. It is not that all worship was performed in caves in the olden time, but that the buildings have sunk. The antefixae of the stone slabs of these roofs have heads upon them and curved rays or scrolls, bearing the impress of a very early period, remounting to the antique. Its style, a bastard Roman, has little of the regenerated excellence of the romanesque.

These things would have interested Jeanne, the unlettered Christian, more than the Celtic antiquity, the Pierre levée, at a short distance out of the town, on the Limoges road, by way of the Pont Neuf. This, as a dolmen, is overrated; but Rabelais (who was to be born at Chinon later) says Pantagruel reared it, 'pour le divertissement des escholiers de l'université,' who came here to carouse.

Out in this suburb one sees the men working the inexhaustible white stone, and women, with high combs, or with caps high-crowned at the back, and stuffed with pads shaped like a chair-back, sweeping their houses and the road in front —a dusty job—and wine-shops, with bushes hanging out for a sign, and tubs full of the must of new wine staining the road with purple. Recrossing the clear but sedgy river Clain, shaded by poplars, one gains a pyramidal view of the town: Notre Dame and St. Radegonde spiring the hill above an old Gothic gateway in the Rue Barbate, near the rich and beautiful St. Pierre; and deep in the valley St. Jean de Montiersneuf, where you descend eleven steps, very much worn, into an early romanesque interior, very fine, with baseless columns, round but clustered. In one transept is a grottoed chapel, with tall fir-trees growing and fountains trickling. It is quite dark by the inner altar. Fir-trees stand also behind the high altar, reminding one of the antique worship in groves. One can read this church's history in its adornments. The chevet is very good old romanesque, the clerestory windows of the apse are decorated Gothic. The capitals are restored and ugly (egg and dart), but there are some old reticulated and other ancient capitals high in the deeply-recessed windows. Fergusson dates this church 1066. Near the entrance-door is the tomb of Count Guillaume VII., the pious founder. His effigy wears a strawberry-leaved coronet. Burton, speaking of the Mosque of the Genii, says, 'like all ancient localities at Meccah, it is as much below as above ground.' So are the old buildings at Poitiers.

Deeply interesting to Jeanne was the site of the battle of Poitiers, fought by the Black Prince. The site is fixed by Froissart at Maupertuis, five miles north-west of the town. There was also a great battle fought near Poitiers many centuries before this, in 507, when Clovis defeated Alaric, king of the Visigoths.

The place so teems with history under discovery's plough that one is too hard-worked at first. It is like the sight of a vast art-collection that gives one a fever of unrest which must be calmed before one can begin to enjoy.

As one goes down to the water's edge, the place reminds the oriental traveller more and more of Jerusalem (until one comes to the water, where it again vividly recalls Toledo), the arid rocks, parched ground, and the peculiarly blue hue of the few

K

sharp shadows are all so southern. An old tower and a further bridge form picturesque objects as seen from the bridge one stands on.

The churches in the town were Jeanne's favourite resort, and chiefest of all, the crowning glory of the place, Notre Dame. A labyrinthine monument of romanesque pell-mell, one calls it in one's first bewilderment. Even description must be confused. An enchanting church outside, but, on descending the steps (for of course one enters by steps downwards at Poitiers), and looking within, how coloured and patterny! It is said to be restored to its primitive appearance. It is enough to put one's eyes out: an æsthetic person would fall sick. There is a fine carved-wood pulpit, which at first I took for bronze, one is so blinded by the colours.

See that poor soul, with a long tale of sadness on her withered features, crouching down, telling her beads before the brocaded Madonna. What a picturesque figure! bringing her sorrows and her patience there among those real flowers placed by the altar. The church is always a consoler. She is soothed by the rapidly-recited prayers of the venerable priest, assisted by a deacon. The incongruity of his very thick shoes with his crimson damask cope does not occur to her; such hypercriticisms are part of our overstrained delicacy and heedfulness of outward apparel, and the spirit of levity, which only discovers trifles to mock at them—grains of sand or dust, to edge one's wit upon. Better have no culture than the habitual critical scoffing that savours of the comic papers, which kills even the hope that is in us. Not for the scoffer is the substance of that symbol of the sculptured figure of a man (the Root of Jesse), lying asleep or dead, and a tendrilled vine springing up behind him, with the legend, 'Aperiatur terra et germinet salvatorem,' there under the altar of St. Anne.

The choir is Byzantine romanesque, in colour and all. The round columns are baseless, but solid and lofty. Fergusson says : 'The façade of Notre Dame de Poitiers is strictly Angiovine, local in all its parts. Originally the one (!) window it possessed was circular, but in the fifteenth century, as may be seen from the mouldings then introduced, it was cut down to its present form, doubtless to make room for painted glass, which at that age had superseded all other modes of decoration ; whereas in the twelfth century, to which the church belongs, external sculpture and internal mural paintings were the prevailing modes of architectural expression. Sculpture is used in a profusion of which no example belonging to a later date exists. There is a richness and graphic power in the exuberant sculpture of the early façades which we miss in after ages, and of which no mere masonic excellence can ever supply the place.'

This wealth of sculpture was like a rich library to Jeanne, who knew no other reading than what the churches supplied, and whose soul was continually lifted up among the symbols of the Revelation, typified in these things.

Notre Dame is especially curious and striking to a modern, and it is peculiar in its perfectness, for, as Fergusson further says : 'No churches of the province have the characteristic corner towers, nor do they retain their pedimented gable so perfect as at Notre Dame de Poitiers.' It was founded in 1161.

We must not linger too long even at Notre Dame; there are so many other churches to be seen at Poitiers, and at these we must only glance, naming the most remarkable with the succinctness of an official catalogue.

St. Radegonde presents a remarkable admixture of age and restoration, reminding one unwittingly of an aged face under a youthful wig. It is curiously old in parts, though one enters by a florid and comparatively modern doorway, beneath a Byzantine tower. The nave of the church is sunken below the surface, though not deep, but beneath the romanesque choir is a very ancient round-columned crypt, hewn in the rock; containing the empty tomb of the saint. There are votive inscriptions all around, some of them quaint enough, as, 'Reconnaissance à Ste. Radegonde pour la conversion de mon père.'

St. Porchaire strikes one as elegantly strange, with its round columns inside the entrance, whence arches spring as from five tall palm-trees into the rounded vaults. The windows are ogival, but the portal is romanesque, and there is an old Roman-looking arch beneath the whitewashed plaster.

The Palais de Justice is the ancient palace of the Counts of Poitou. The Salle des Pas Perdus is a vast hall, with a timber forest in its roof, and rich fire-places of the twelfth and fifteenth centuries. The building is highly picturesque within and without. Besides the Palais de Justice, which is, next to the churches, most intimately connected with Jeanne d'Arc, there are many buildings of a later date which add to the interest of this most captivating town. Here is 21, Rue du Marché, which I take for the house where Francis Bacon occupied rooms as a law-student. It is covered with renaissance ornaments, ox-heads, &c. J. Masteau, ironmonger, has his shop on the ground-floor. Two plaques are inscribed, one | IN DÑO CONFIDO 1517. | the other { HOC EST REFUGION MEUM 1517 } There is another very quaint old house in the Rue Lebascle, behind the Musée, with a winding staircase tower outside. A curious old gateway below this house bears a legend on a scutcheon 𝕽𝖆𝖎𝖘𝖔𝖓 𝖕𝖆𝖗 𝖙𝖔𝖚𝖙, and on its little pointed battlements, in the style of the Veronese renaissance, 𝖙𝖔𝖚𝖙 𝖕𝖆𝖗 𝖗𝖆𝖎𝖘𝖔𝖓, 𝖆𝖉., 1581 : a letter on each crenellation.

But renaissance buildings have no connection with Jeanne d'Arc, nor have private houses, for we cannot identify the house of Maître Rabateau, with whose honourable wife she sojourned; so reluctantly, where each street has an attraction, I leave off sight-seeing. No, here is a street leading to a Gothic spire, and the nearest wall has a round

archway built in it, each stone carved with a
winged animal, and a gateway below it, all of
which might have sheltered or known Jeanne
d'Arc; and there are the old houses in the Rue de
la Poire Cuite; and another old house, which
truly for its age might have been her abode, and
another beyond again which has equal claims,
none of which can be proved in the absence of
written documents. One tradition—of some
weight—seems to show that she did not stay with
Maître Rabateau during the whole of the time she
was at Poitiers. We read in the 'Annals of
Aquitaine,' by Jean Bouchet, 'I have heard tell
in my youth, by the late Christofle du Peirat,
who then, in 1495, dwelt in Poitiers and near
my house, and who was nearly a hundred years
old, that in my said house there was once an
hostelry with the sign of the Rose, where Jeanne
d'Arc was lodged, and that he saw her mount on
horseback, all in white armour, to go to Orleans.
He showed me a small stone at the corner of the
Rue St. Étienne, of which she took advantage to
mount her horse.' This stone is preserved in the
museum at Poitiers.

The École Chrétienne, too, is a most interesting
specimen of domestic architecture in the decorated
Gothic style well worthy of an architect's study:
this alone would repay him for a visit. It is impossible to tear one's self away; not in Nuremberg nor
Augsburg is there so much to see as here in Poitiers.

Refreshing after this exhausting mental pleasure
is it to ramble through the surroundings of the

town, the woods and ravines of the river Clain; to alter our own poet's words—

> 'From where sweet Clanis wanders
> Through corn and vines and flowers;
> Below where *Poitiers* lifts to heaven
> Her diadem of towers.'

These environs are more pleasant than even the Blossac they are so proud of, a clipped avenue of limes, gritty and dusty, where the keen wind of Poitiers blows piercing cold at times. Yet this is full of charm, on calmer days, when one can sit looking over the old trefoil-arched parapet of this rampart promenade and enjoy the view over the clear green Clain, and see the cavalry winding up the opposite hill. It might be Jeanne's escort convoying her to see the site of the Black Prince's famous victory.

Vexed at the hindrance to her mission, Jeanne did her best; she took up the work that lay nearest to her hand while waiting for the doctors of the law to deliver judgment on the character of her message. She wrote to the English leaders now encamped before Orleans, or, rather, she dictated the letter, according to the commandment of her Voices, that it might be ready to send at the moment she should be authorized to send it. This letter bears date the 22nd of March. She also continued her military exercises.

She had been confided to the guardianship of one of the most honourable families in Poitiers, and here, instead of calling her at first to them, the council of the doctors came to examine her.

When she saw them enter the room, she sat down on the end of a bench and asked them what they wanted. They said they came to seek her, because she had told the king that God had sent her to him, and they showed her 'par belles et douces raisons' that she was not to be believed. They remained over two hours, each speaking in turn, and she answered them 'so that they were greatly astonished that a simple shepherdess, a young girl, could thus reply.' Her intellect illumined everything it touched, while her innocent childlike faith always believed in the nobility and good faith of others.

'Jeanne,' said Guillaume Aymeri, 'you ask for men-at-arms, and say it is God's pleasure that the English should quit France and return to their country. If that is so, no men-at-arms are needed, for the will of God can alone discomfit them and send them home.'

'In God's name,' returned Jeanne, 'the men-at-arms will fight, and God will give the victory.'

Master Guillaume admitted it was well replied.

This was the key-note of her message, that human means must be used, and God would enlarge and bless them. I need give no more of the examination, which lasted three weeks, and was marked throughout on her side by a practical good sense and piety which convinced even the Dr. Séguin, said to have been 'a very sour man,' who at first declared he could not, for his part, advise the king to confide men-at-arms to her leading, and to place them in peril on her word alone. He required a sign of her mission. Then came her reply which heads this chapter. It is brother Séguin who has preserved the minutes of the first day's examination, and 'sour man' as he was, and wounded at the girlish vivacity of some of her answers, he has honestly recorded even those which were made at his expense by the youthful Bœotian.

'Fine spectacle,' writes Alain Chartier, under an impression still lively, ' to see her dispute, a woman against men ; ignorant against the learned; alone against so many adversaries !' The beauty of the woman counted, perhaps, for something in his enthusiasm. So did Rienzi before the doctors of the law maintain his mission to restore a people to liberty ; but Rienzi was a learned man, Jeanne was an illiterate girl. God's power lay in her weakness.

' I know neither A nor B ; but I am sent by the King of Heaven to raise the siege of Orleans, and to lead the king to Rheims, to be crowned and anointed.'

They asked her of her visions, whether they were constant. ' My council is there. One voice stays with me always, another comes and goes, and visits me often, and with the third both deliberate.' Is this the natural fusion and confusion of ideas in a luminous but uncultivated intellect trying to burst the prison of ignorance ? or is it, as our best English writer* on Jeanne d'Arc has faintly suggested, a symbolical explanation of conscience and prayer ?

* Miss Parr.

George Eliot says: 'I don't think any of the strongest effects our natures are susceptible of can ever be explained. We can neither detect the process by which they are arrived at, nor the mode in which they act upon us.'

The highest knowledge, though it may bring to light the prophetic gift, does not confer it: it oftener smothers it. Jeanne had a gift, and it ennobled her.

> 'Nothing she does or seems
> But smacks of something greater than herself.'

Jeanne came victoriously through these trials of her mental attitude.

'There is more in the Lord's book than there is in yours,' said she, with her natural vivacity; and still the doctors admired her, and admitted that she had answered throughout with as much prudence as if she had been a fine scholar. Everyone agreed in the fact of her goodness, humility, virginity, devotion, uprightness, and simplicity. The matrons attested all this of her in their turn. These things are better than book-learning.

Without going so far as the distinguished journalist who says, 'Few things are worth knowing, and they can mostly be learnt in conversation,' many of us are beginning to feel that most books are only substitutes for thought, which is a better thing; or for conversation, our liveliest pleasure. The founder of our religion is only recorded once as having written; He lived, and we are expressly told that we should follow in His steps.

As the *Times* said lately of diplomatic intercourse, 'What we want is less clerical toil, and more personal insight.' In the household it is the same. Written orders are appealed to as having been given, they remain to witness of the fact; but, if they are not carried out, where are we? Politics—a different thing from policy—still prevailed over patriotism at the court.

The best evidence that could be obtained concurring in her favour, there was no hindrance to her being used as a moral support to the king's forces. More than this they did not expect of her; nor, indeed, did some of them wish for more. Preparations were now being made to push the war with vigour, and all was getting ready for the time when the cash should be collected.

Though the church and law had nothing to say against the Maid, the money question was, as usual, the motor of war, or else its impediment.

Jeanne had permission to go and stay awhile with her friends, the Duke and Duchess of Alençon, at their château at St. Florent, near Saumur. They took the liveliest interest in her, and here for about ten days she saw the best side of court life, while her army was equipped and her standard embroidered and emblazoned from her directions. This was of white linen, worked with silken fleurs-de-lis. The blazon was the Lord seated on the clouds of heaven, bearing the world in his hand, and blessing a fleur-de-lis presented on each side by an angel, with the inscription, 'Jhesus Maria.' On the reverse was the shield of France borne by two angels. She had also a pennon, or small banner, on which was painted the Annunciation. This she mostly carried in her own hand during battle. 'Never,' she said, 'had she killed any person,' and she loved her banner forty times better than her sword, even the sword that she sent to fetch from behind the altar at Ste. Katherine de Fierbois.

They formed her retinue, among whom were her guides, Jean de Metz and Bertrand de Poulengy, and, according to Wallon, her two young brothers, Jean and Pierre, who had just joined her. The Abbé Bourgaut says they joined her later at Tours, which is more likely. A brave and tried knight, Jean, Sire d'Aulon, 'le plus probe des chevaliers à la cour,' was appointed her esquire. Her page, Louis de Contes, was also brother-in-law of Jean Beauharnais, burgess of Orleans, a witness for Jeanne's rehabilitation. Prince Eugène was descended from this family.

It must have been a gay and pleasant journey to Jeanne, with growing reputation, and all thus preparing for her great enterprise, to ride in the midst of a bright company of friends, from Chinon, where she had now returned in triumph, to the charming residence of the Duke d'Alençon, who, by his parole to the English, had been hitherto debarred from battle. This young couple were of special interest to Jeanne from their relationship to the captive Duke of Orleans. Charles, Duc d'Orléans, married in 1406 Elisabeth, or Isabelle de France, young widow of Richard II. of England. She died in 1409, leaving a daughter married in 1421 (jubente patre, says Astezan) to Jean, Duke of Alençon. The Alençons had no children.

Down the narrow, paved way, since named Rue Jeanne d'Arc, the joyous cavalcade swept on; across the bridges, and through the suburb where the old women even now wear old-fashioned caps with broad strings pinned coronet-wise round the head—tall caps shaped like the head-dresses on old sculptured tombs; past the wine-shops with their bushes; perhaps these were mere booths in those days, but there must always have been wine-shops of some sort, as there must have been much gaiety surrounding a pleasure-loving court, though it was so nearly bankrupt. The third bridge crosses a swamp merely, and the road to the Loire lies through marshy meadows among walnut-trees shading blue and red corn-flowers. Chinon Castle from here looks low-seated, which is a curious optical illusion.

At five kilometres from Chinon a road turns off to Château Coudrai, which is six kilometres further yet. The château is ancient, yet it is impossible that Jeanne d'Arc should have been sent so far off at the time when it was required to cross-question her at every moment, and scrutinise her actions severely.

The landscape hereabout resembles Devonshire, only with walnuts instead of apple-trees. There are some orchards, however, as well as apple-trees in the standing corn, or in the abundant grass for hay. In some places there are moss-grown vines beneath the apple-trees, the produce of all of which speaks for the sun's power under the sky of Touraine. The spreading limbs of the trees are clothed with green velvety moss on the upper side. In the meadows are willows and poplars, for it is a well-watered country and spacious, easy for the poor to live in. All seems fainéant and easy-going like Charles VII. himself; though perhaps the rapid growth makes double work for somebody; for besides the two crops a year, which have to be tilled and harvested, the weeds also grow so quickly that it is hard to keep them under. A brimstone butterfly looks like the departing spirit of the primroses, as it flies along above the potato ridges.

Hale men in blouses and women with clear, agate-coloured eyes and pretty, regular features set in stiff, deep-frilled country caps, salute the passing traveller, and very dark-skinned gipsies eye him curiously as he follows the Vienne, where there are broad-sailed barges going up stream, and a ferry hard at work with pleasure-folk at the point where the Indre falls into the Vienne. At Candes the united river joins the Loire, which now becomes wonderfully islanded in its widened course, forming quite a plexus of rivers, so entwined are they, or braided together.

What a beautiful church this is at Candes, all white like a bride: an exquisite surprise. A slender column stands in the lofty, vaulted porch of the north doorway, which faces the road, sup-

porting deeply-groined vaulting in the early
pointed style. The church is castellated in a
peculiar manner, giving the idea of a warrior in
robes of peace; or conversely of Jeanne d'Arc, the
virgin, in her martial array. The battlements have
trefoiled cusps like those on Charles's clock-tower
at Chinon. Many churches of this date were
actually fortified. Bands of niched saints surround two storeys of the north front. The lower
frieze has sculptures of angels, crowned heads,
foliage, and animals in a richly-woven intricacy
of design. The church is niched in the slope
of a steep hill—the quarry, in fact, whence its
material is extracted. The rounded aisle within
the niche and the zigzagged windows betoken a
much earlier date than do the richer decorations
of the front towards the road. The interior is
elegant, but chiefly remarkable for containing
the tomb of St. Martin, who died at Candes.
The apsidal choir is of the twelfth, and the nave
of the thirteenth century. Candes is on the
border line between Touraine and Anjou.

There are many traces of castles, half-hidden
among honeysuckles and wreaths of roses, here by
the Loire. The principal of these, the château
of Montsoreau, is of large extent, and bristling
with machicolations. At a round-ended market-
cross, a road turns off to Fontevrault. The Duke
of Alençon's cavalcade would probably not have
turned aside to visit the abbey, with its tombs
of foreign kings, though doubtless he talked of

it to Jeanne. Although Fontevrault stands on a hill, it is not visible from their road.*

They rode on, following the tufa cliffs, by the caves of Souzé near the brimming Loire. Cave dwellings are hollowed all along here in the building stone. Doubtless the poor people dwelt in these quarries then much as they do now. The houses look comfortable and shapely, the fine stone being so easily hewn. They are set in banks of iris and roses, with delicate wistaria trailing along their eaves, and coloured vine-shoots glowing translucent above the walls. Their only ventilation or draught is by their chimneys, which sometimes crop up in the fields above: these chimneys also serve as speaking tubes, to communicate with the vine-dresser or labourer up there. All this was new and curious to Jeanne, being so unlike her own country.

Here the women's caps again alter in shape: they are plain on the top, with the borders goffred at the ears. These caps are survivals of the middle-ages. When we see them carved in solid stone on the tombs we marvel; in lace and linen, we understand them better. Another English royal tomb is here. Queen Margaret of Anjou died and was buried in the château of Dampierre here close by the Loire. Poor Margaret! a baby

---

* N.B.—Let all intending visitors to Fontevrault be warned that the abbey is now used as a prison, one of the largest in France. It is very difficult to obtain an order to visit the English royal tombs, and no ladies are permitted to enter the precincts on any consideration. A high wall prevents anyone seeing much of the abbey building. The village or town is uninteresting.

of a month old when Jeanne d'Arc passed by
Dampierre.

Ruskin thus describes this part of the Loire:

'The district through which it here flows is for
the most part a low place, yet not altogether at
the level of the stream, but cut into steep banks
of chalk or gravel, thirty or forty feet high, running for miles at about an equal height above the
water. These banks are excavated by the peasantry, partly for houses, partly for cellars, so
economizing vineyard space above; and thus a
kind of continuous village runs along the river-
side, composed half of caves, half of rude buildings, backed by the cliffs, propped against it,
therefore always leaning away from the river;
mingled with overlappings of vineyard and trellis
from above, and little towers or summer-houses
for outlook, when the grapes are ripe, or for
gossip over the garden-wall.'

Here are the windmills of Saumur, and here is
Saumur itself, with its strong, square, high-seated
castle, resembling in shape the White Tower of London, but with four rounded towers at the corners,
below which lies the town, with its churches
and picturesque Hotel de Ville. The Alençon
party do not stop, but, in the sunshine dappled
with the western clouds, they ride on through
Saumur, by the Loire bank, and across the meadows, then abounding in quail, by the meandering river Thouet, (a good part of these meadows
are now drained for the cavalry school,) and up the
slope to the convent on the left, with its church

and dwelling-house, now all restored, or new, and the parish church on the right. This is St. Florent-les-Saumur, and it is far more reasonable that we should find the site of the Duke of Alençon's house here than that we should follow down the Loire to the Abbey of St. Florent at Ingrande, beyond Angers, as some writers would have us do. (Berriat St. Prix only marks St. Florent-le-Vieil in his map.) It is three days' ride further off; less certainly by boat going down stream, but one would be indefinitely slow in returning. Jeanne d'Arc would hardly have consented to go so far for pleasure. Here, at St. Florent-les-Saumur, she was as near the scene of action as at Chinon, or nearer. St. Florent-le-Vieil would not have been called near Saumur, which all old chroniclers expressly state. Writers fall into these mistakes by trusting maps—which ignore ruins and sites of former places—instead of studying the ground, as Macaulay did for all the chief points in his history.

These convent buildings have all the appearance of standing on the site of an earlier house, the former abbey of St. Florent, which dated from the eleventh to the thirteenth century, and which was destroyed in the Revolution or, as Wallon asserts, between 1803 and 1833. The duke's house was a hunting-seat, not a castle. Much of the former interior is in good preservation, and the fine staircase still remains. It was a dependence of the ancient abbey, which had several extensive secular buildings belonging to it. Of the abbey church, which was called the 'Belle of Anjou,' only the narthex and the crypt remain.

The parish church, on the right-hand side of the road, has two aisles. An ancient, great, round stoup for holy water, bigger than a baptismal font, is noticeable on entering. The architecture is romanesque, and good early decorated Gothic. The exterior is castellated in the fashion prevalent about here. It has been carefully restored. There is every reason to suppose that Jeanne d'Arc worshipped in this church during her stay with the Alençons.

The present convent, presumably on the site of their house, lies high across the bridge beyond the rope-walk. There is even now a ferry over the Thouet, in the meadows below the bridge. The country here and further up the hill is well-peopled, and fertile with gardens and vineyards.

This was perhaps the happiest fortnight in Jeanne's life. This season, too, of April is so perfect in Touraine. There are masses of bluebells now, and foxgloves ready to come on. Truly we 'tourists, heaven preserve us,' flit like butterflies from joy to joy. We lounge here on these mossy stone couches in the sunshine and enjoy ourselves. What wealth there is for the people in these apple-blossoms; what joy is in their faces and thankfulness in their hearts for this countless bloom and the glad promise of the vines; the pear-trees all one foam, casting off their spray in a white shower of petals all around, the lambs nipping the lower shoots of the young quick-set hedges, the barley in the ear, the sounds of good feeding in the world of pigs and fowls, and geese and hens. How busy the sunshine is bringing things to life everywhere, and how the people smile and are glad! They have the true wealth of happiness, of usefulness, and interest in and enjoyment of their possessions, and do not need the money-wealth caused by sub-division of labour, which cramps life and destroys its healthiness.

Jeanne too saw all this, and sympathized with the joy of her fellow-peasants.

We may afford to linger on this glimpse of pleasure and of cultivated enjoyment in the society of persons of high rank in the laborious life of our heroine, foreign as it may seem to the tenor of her great purpose. One's surroundings are part of oneself, so, in considering the life of the Maid of Orleans, the ground she travelled over became part of herself and of her education. Though a strong character like Jeanne's developes itself and cannot be cast in a mould, yet the poetical, imaginative nature has a soft surface very apt to receive impressions.

In education there are two planes which meet each other, the nature of the being (within) and the educing power (without). The fineness of the nature is the most important factor of the result, and Jeanne's was of excellent quality. When it is of this fineness, it constitutes that genius 'which heaven and earth conspire to educate,' therefore the educing power we can apply does not matter so much as in the ordinary cases. Jeanne was a choice instrument in the hand of the Lord of the whole earth.

Percival de Cagny, who belonged to the Duke of Alençon's household, was the first historian of the Maid. He has given us many glimpses of the pleasant social life of the time, showing us that the warriors were not always sheathed in steel. The duke promised the Maid, that so soon as he should be liberated from his parole as prisoner of the English, he would join her standard in the army. The duchess, alarmed for his safety, would have withheld him from making this promise.

'Fear nothing, madame,' said Jeanne d'Arc; 'I will restore him to you safe and sound, in as good case as he is, or even better.'

CHAPTER VIII.

THE LOIRE.

> ' Le temps a laissié son manteau,
> De vent, de froidure, et de pluye,
> Et s'est vestu de broderie
> De soleil raiant cler et beau,
> Il n'y a beste ne oiseau,
> Qui en son jargon ne chante ou crye,
> Le temps a laissié son manteau.
>
> ' Rivière, fontaine, et ruisseau,
> Portent en liurée jolye,
> Gouttes d'argent d'orfévrerie,
> Chascun s'abille de nouveau,
> Le temps a laissié son manteau.'
> CHARLES, Duke of Orleans (father of Louis XII).

THE holiday was over. Jeanne must repair to Blois, or, according to Wallon, to Tours. He says the king delayed no longer, but sent her to Tours about the 20th of April, where they formed a complete military retinue for her, with two heralds and an almoner. The force had not been able to move earlier, as before the 21st of April they could not give the soldiers 'les arrhes de l'entrée en campagne.' Charles had only four écus left, says Marguerite de la Thouroude, wife of the receiver-general, who was with the queen of France at Bourges. The queen of Sicily, the soul of the national party, had undertaken to gather its strength at Blois, under distinguished leaders, and Jeanne was to join them there. It does not appear that she returned to Chinon from St. Florent.

Another ride, at a more energetic pace this time, through Saumur and across the double bridge, which gives such a good view of the castle. In the Quartier des Ponts, in the island, at Saumur, there is a house built by King René, called 'La Maison de la reine Cicile' (de Sicile). It was highly ornamented then, for René was a king of taste. It is now much defaced.

They rode across the fertile plain, watered by many streamlets, on the opposite side of the Loire; past Langeais, with its turreted castle, where, later on, the monarchy of France was strengthened and firmly established by the marriage of Charles VIII. with Anne of Brittany; through the fertile district of Chouzé-sur-Loire, just opposite Souzé—here, what a feast of roses! Who has not contemplated the awakening of Nature in Touraine on the fair banks of Loire, has never known 'the time of roses?' Palaces of foliage, temples of verdure rise as by enchantment from the ground. So writes an exuberant Frenchman, revelling in his country. How the sun smiled on the Maid, and wreathed her path with flowers, as she swept on, joyous with her bannered army! Her energetic nature, too, was effervescent with delight. Hope was gladdening into fruition.

They rode past the remarkable Pile of Cinq Mars, that extraordinary monument, which has perplexed all antiquarians by its seeming uselessness. It has been supposed to be Roman, Celtic, cinerary, astronomical, monumental, a beacon, or only built for the purpose of puzzling posterity. It is a square brick tower, ninety-five feet high, looking like a pinnacled chimney; it is sixteen feet wide in each face. On the south side the pattern of the bricks forms twelve compartments. It had formerly five pinnacles, each ten feet high; one of them has been thrown down. The pile is perfectly solid, and has no openings of any kind. M. Joanneau computes its age at two thousand four hundred years, but then eternity itself is a trifle in the hands of a thorough-going antiquarian or geologist. Near this is the castle of Cinq Mars, with two round towers and a fine rampart; then comes Luynes, with its cave dwellings and limestone cliffs, whence one can look across the broad valley of the Loire and Cher, which run parallel with each other for leagues, and the Roman aqueduct which led from Luynes to Tours.

Yonder is Tours cathedral, a landmark in the grey distance above those glowing fields where ordinarily nothing is busy but the butterflies. Tours was then humming with warlike preparations; all were looking forward to excitement as a change. The languor of the monarch had infected all classes; the martial energy of the Maid revived them.

She stayed about a week at Tours, happier with

the bourgeois people, who were nearer her own rank, than with the courtiers and nobles among whom she had won her place, always excepting her kind friends the Alençons. Lonely in her high-wrought ascetic self-devotion, a very vestal of purity, she was maidenly in all her ways. She ever associated, spoke with, and was beloved by women. There is no shadow, or rather no brightness, of love-tale in her tragic story. She loved children, and was often asked to be sponsor to them, and she loved young girls. Her friendship at Tours with the daughter of the painter, Hennes Poluoir, who emblazoned her banner, is a pleasant feature in her outwardly stern career. When this young girl married, Jeanne asked, in a letter addressed to the town-council of Tours, for a hundred crowns to be given her for her trousseau, as an act of friendship towards herself. This, and her request that her native place might be exempt from taxation, were the only favours Jeanne ever asked in return for her services to the king. She desired nothing for herself, 'fors bonnes armes et bons chevaux.'

During her stay in Tours, the king caused a complete suit of armour to be made for her, and he gave her horses for herself and her people; but in place of the sword he offered her she wrote from Tours to Fierbois to the priests, asking if they would allow her to have the sword marked with five crosses in the church of St. Katherine; an armourer of Tours was sent to fetch it. It was sent to her with two magnificent scabbards, one of red velvet, the other of cloth of gold. She caused a sheath to be made for it in strong leather for every-day use.

At once she set to work to purify the camp and reform the manners of the soldiers. It is a fine example of the influence of womanhood that La Hire, the reckless, who heeded no claims on his veneration, and cared only for military glory, who was accustomed to swear and take God's name in vain all day, even he dared no longer swear 'but by his baton' before Jeanne d'Arc, the village maiden.

Schiller puts her feeling into beautiful words when he makes her say, 'Heaven is for France; angels whom thou seest not fight for our king; they are all decked with lilies. The standard of our noble cause is white as is the lily; the pure Virgin is its chaste symbol.' Tours was not then the common-place capital of a flat surrounding that it now is—the 'nicest place on the Continent' to the common-place Britannic mind, though a sleepy residence for persons requiring intellectual stimulus. The Revolution did what most revolutions do, it ground everything down to a dead level, devoid of all the picturesque of memory; only the dust of history remains, and there is plenty of historical dust in Tours. But Tours has its beauties of climate, of which no revolutions can deprive it. There is a great timber-stemmed magnolia-tree in the courtyard of the Hôtel de l'Univers telling of more rapid wood-ripening than they make with us. One can sit in the Square de l'Archevéché looking towards the cathedral, whose doors are wide open, comparing its tall renaissance towers with the young straight palm-trees as they tower above the sub-tropical plants, and the crowned heads of all the trees. There is no inner door to the cathedral, so that the nave of the church is completely exposed to view, giving a grand effect that we miss in our northern churches; and the altars are loaded with real flowers; no cambric artificialities, rag flowers.

But there are some churches in modernized Tours of Jeanne d'Arc's time and older, ever so much older. St. Julian's, built in 1224 upon the remains of an earlier church, whose nave is eight steps lower than the street; another of those churches which has half-buried itself with age. Darwin tells us that this is the work of worms, who industriously raise the ground outside with their worm-casts. If Darwin's theory be true, then churches also are a prey to the worms. Though the heavier buildings being deepest buried, makes it seem that worms have but little to do with the matter. There is a pretty garden behind the high altar. This church has a straight east end and no chevet, only a passage under the large east window. This is unusual in France, especially in this part of France. There is a very lightly traceried triforium gallery. This church has a fine romanesque tower and vestibule.

The neighbourhood of the Rue St. Martin naturally contains the most precious relics of ancient Tours. In front of the church of St.

Saturnin are many old, overhanging houses, cross-barred and abounding in beams of carved wood, and hard by one sees the fine old tower called after Charlemagne, and another, its companion, equally conspicuous; the spring of former arches with zigzag mouldings show that these once belonged to the same magnificent building, the vast basilica of Tours originating in the fourth century. All the ground hereabout was once covered by this world-famous cathedral of St. Martin, whose gorgeous shrine, though not his actual tomb, is in an adjoining subterranean chapel.

In about a week the army was ordered off to Blois to form a junction with the main body of the force and the convoy of provisions for the revictualling of Orleans. The money had come in at last; if sparingly, it had come, and all was activity and haste to be at Orleans before the need of the besieged became too pressing.

Jeanne rode to Blois in company with the Archbishop of Rheims and several nobles in command of the army, which she reckoned at not less than ten or twelve thousand men, when united to the force which the Queen of Sicily had collected with the convoy at Blois. She was cheered by the arrival of her two young brothers, who had lately joined her standard.

Out again into the fields striped with golden buttercups in bands of green and yellow. The hill-slopes are thickly studded with villages and dwellings cut in the chalky tufa, set among sweet buds and shivering poplar branches and young sunny leaves of acacia, all soft, filmy, and tender like French landscape-painting. The vale lies deep in rushes and water, and white water-flowers, and tender shadows, mysterious and soft as love, bounded by glaucous-blue wheatfields and hazy distances all tremulous in the warm, moist atmosphere of latest April before it blushes into May, their hues melting into each other with no harshness, scarcely an outline, aerially soft as the pale, pink, feathery-flowered tamarisk, falling like a fountain, which veils the shimmering sunshine on the Loire, leaving only lesser suns in the yellow flowers de luce in the pools, gleaming like patines of bright gold. There is nothing out of harmony in this sweet country; even now in this age of sin and sensuality I see a man with a rose in his mouth—instead of a cigar.

We seldom see the tamarisk in flower in England. In October of 1884, after a hot summer, it was admired and marvelled at in Cornwall, where no one remembered having seen it flower before. I had seen it flowering profusely in Touraine and Berri in early May of the same year. The orientals call the dove the 'Bird of the Tamarisk,' perhaps because both are so soft to touch and so tender in hue; one can hardly call it colour, or only dove-colour. An Arabian poet speaks of a maiden's form 'waving like the tamarisk when the soft wind blows from the hills of Nejd.'

And all this fair land was to be saved! Jeanne d'Arc must have admired it, even if, like Jeanie Deans, she only thought it was 'braw feeding for the cows.' To Jeanne it was more than a rich picture, it was a grand reality, filling her heart with praise and thanksgiving, for she was appointed to win back this land for her own people and make it smile again. She too had the peasant's habitual faith and trust in the outpouring hand of the Creator that He will give the blessing which follows faith. This is not our cold idea of self-help, which only trusts our own right hand; so that we remain shorn of joy because we look to create for ourselves a hard and bare subsistence, with no overflowing, including only what we make, not what God gives besides. Bread perhaps, for we have earned it, but little wine and—no roses.

How beautiful is life when young, yet perfect in its strength! How beautiful too is Nature, clad in the intense young green of a spring morning! Nature never grows old. She blooms now in our late century as fair as ever; as we can see in the countless blossom of these nurseries of young trees, kept here to make avenues for the high-roads. The French have always liked to trim their straight roads with green fringe and flowers.

The land was not devastated by the army's passage, this garden of France in its glad time of rosy promise. The armies of those days spared the peasants' toil, not for the peasant's sake truly, but for their own subsistence, and also because the soldiers themselves became peasants again when the battle was over. Jeanne was hailed by the common people as a deliverer. Everything was hopeful, everyone was young, in feeling at least, and Jeanne's heart was unchilled, unblighted. That 'fulness and luxuriance of life which has in it something of divine' was in her followers, but in herself this was intensified by a spiritual conviction of having her powers especially called forth by the Creator for His own use.

The army crossed the bridge at Tours, and kept to the left bank of the Loire, the southern side; as in the season of floods there was only a scrambling path across the hills between Tours and Frillière, and the southern road was well defended by the castle of Amboise, which commands it both ways from Tours to Blois. The Loire was then more of a torrent flood than now, because of the vast and numerous forests that gathered the rain. The north side is especially liable to inundations of the river, which often devastate the land for miles. There has existed from Carlovingian times the great embankment of the Loire on the right bank, from Blois to Angers, one hundred miles; but this was not always available as a road. The most important works of these dykes were made under Henry II., King of England and Count of Anjou. But in times of poverty and disturbance, public works of utility are left to loss, and the embankment was out of repair. Vernon is built up on the hill, and so are many of the villages, which now look like one bright, continuous suburb of Tours, in order to escape the floods. A break of a few inches in the soft dyke of light gravel is enough to make the river effect an entrance; a molehill giving way when the river is swollen, in rushes the flood, melting the land before it; and on the first rush of the torrent both men and cattle make swiftly for the hills, where many people keep a dwelling on purpose to take refuge in.

But it is a quickly recuperating country, the sun soon sets to rights the mischief of the floods, which retiring, leave a fresh deposit of rich soil upon the fields, and the vineyards are seldom much damaged by their bath; the acacias and glorious judas-trees, now a mass of pink flowers, are firmly rooted, the land is soon as glowing and beautiful as ever. The women, clad now-a-days in blue cotton and worked Touraine caps with narrow frills, knit while they lead down their cows and tether them to within an inch, it seems, of the standing corn, and the black and white cattle stand breast-deep in the crimson clover. Men quaff the sparkling wine of Vouvray, which, as it will not travel, the inhabitants keep for themselves, and they are gladdened with Nature's bounties even through her chastisements.

The people here are gay and happy, though their country is less neat and trim than Normandy and the northern provinces, which are an agricultural pleasure-ground. Up the country in many parts, in La Brie for instance, people are stern like their hard climate, here they are gay and sparkling, like their wine. Perhaps vif too, like their Loire, whose devastating fury cannot be calculated on nor controlled.

Fifteen miles from Tours is Amboise, another of the islanded Loire towns, with double bridge, whose castle is its high-seated citadel. Amboise, where nearly a century later Leonardo da Vinci was to live and die: 1452—1519 are the dates graven on his monument in the castle garden. A risky-looking place is this low-lying island, barely secure from floods; a charming place this lofty castle, with its towers of many different heights all intermingled with foliage of remarkable variety, and valerian and pinks tufting the outer walls; its gardens an ordered labyrinth of beauty and delight, its varied views each one lovelier than the last, culminating in a rapturous scene which includes the length of the winding Loire, with its bridges and wooded islands, and a nearer scene of arches, gardens, gurgoyles, and the delicate white miniature chapel of St. Hubert, florid to profusion with its minutely fondled sculptures, wrought like silversmiths' work, and its panel in high relief, above the chapel door, of St. Hubert discovering the miraculous stag with the cross between its antlers.

The modern château itself is insignificant; but the old round towers seem part of the natural rock they rest upon, and some of these date from Roman times. Amboise is one of the choicest scenes in Europe as a mingling of all the beauties of mediæval romance. In its ancient castle, its scenery and gardens, Art has perfected Nature. No pen or pencil save Turner's could do justice to this delicious place. He has given us the scene, yet even he cannot revive for us the forms that haunt this place, nor give back to the world their spirit. The armoured figures on their tapestries and canvas mock us with their 'scorn of our dull, uninspired, snail-paced lives,' that we think so energetic, but which are only so fatiguing.

Leaving Touraine and entering Le Blésois, the cavalcade rode on through the still exquisite valley between the densely-wooded slopes on both sides of the Loire, crossing the bridge and arriving at Blois in time to hear the nightingale's song before taking refuge within its solid old walls. After their day's ride of thirty-five miles, they were just half-way to Orleans, their goal.

Blois had not then its present gardened appearance, nor was its castle then bristling with porcupines and carved with the badges of Anne of Brittany and the salamanders of Francis I., for the present castle on the western hill was not then built. But the town's situation was always fine as any on the Loire, with its cloven hill and amphitheatral distribution of the ground, which is made available by terraces and streets of stairs.

The cathedral, which now occupies the eastern height above the river, is neither old nor grand. The bishop's palace is splendidly situated, with its kitchen gardens among the ancient walls and terraces of the former castle, which received Jeanne and her companions. The prospect from the dense chestnut promenade is delightful, embracing wide sweeps of the Loire and its beautiful rich vale. It is delightful, too, to sit in the more open lime-tree avenue listening to the evensong of birds.

The western hill holds the chief attractions for the traveller. Here is the piled castle of Louis XII. and Francis I. This solid fortress of roughly herring-boned masonry is softened to the eye by the oleanders growing near the huge walls, cliffs of masonry one might call them, and so one might the walls of the inner dwelling of the castle, a tremendous building with its rounded bastions. It is a relief to get inside the courtyard, where the castle looks less threatening and more habitable. This inner front is highly decorative, with its statue all gilt and coloured of the king on horseback, and its carvings of the porcupine of Louis the Well-beloved and the ermines of Anne of Brittany.

The bridge of Blois is one of those high-raised structures of uneven arches built to suit the erratic current of the shifting Loire, meeting at an obtuse angle in the centre like that of Gien. This bridge, which was built in the time of Louis XV., is surmounted by an obelisk in the centre. The view of Blois is fine seen from the willowed waters of the Loire.

The grand old church of St. Nicolas, half-way down the western hill beneath the castle, is far more interesting than the renaissance cathedral. It has a small cupola and fine romanesque columns. This church, however, has little to do with Jeanne d'Arc, on her first visit to

Blois, because she would not have been allowed time to wander across to this western hill, for there was a council to be held and much to set in order. She had, besides, to write to the English, summoning them to surrender, marking thus the peaceful character of her mission, which, as her own words tell us, was 'one of peace to men of goodwill.' Heralds were the great ordnance of those days, so Bacon says, and the Maid especially wished to employ them thus, even though this wish might be misinterpreted by friend and foe. So she sent her letter, written at Poitiers on the 22nd of March, summoning the English leader to surrender Orleans to the Maid, who had been sent by God. It commenced thus:—
'Duke of Bethfort, the Maid prays and requires of you that you should not destroy yourself.' If he agrees to surrender the place, she suggests that together they might do great deeds for Christendom, which is interpreted to mean a crusade against the Turks. Quicherat gives this and others of Jeanne's letters in full in his work. Perhaps the army thought it was her failing courage which caused her to insist on sending heralds to the enemy to beg them peacefully to cede their conquests. Her message was received with insult and derision.

The time has come; the blow has to be struck. The Maid has to witness for the God who sent her. Away with woman's natural fears.

The work and council over, she goes to pray in the church and nerve herself for battle, for to-morrow is to begin the great adventure of her life, for which she has been preparing for years; yet a new experience and trial of her faith.

We may presume there was a fine cathedral here on the present site close by the former castle, for at Blois, Astezan, the Duke of Orleans' secretary, a contemporary of Jeanne's, admired an organ, the largest he had ever seen, having, so they said, fourteen hundred metal pipes (d'étain), of which some were so large that a man could pass through them. Such an organ could never have been built for the church of St. Nicolas. Another huger pipe and more ancient marvel is still to be found in Blois; this is a subterranean aqueduct, called the Arou, and by the common people the Pont de César, which traverses the town from end to end. It is so wide and so lofty that several persons can walk in it abreast. It is supposed to have been pierced through the solid rock by the Romans.

CHAPTER IX.

THE MAID OF ORLEANS.

'En nom Dieu, le conseil de Messire est plus sûr et plus sage que le vôtre. Vous m'avez cuidé décevoir, et vous êtes déçus vous-mêmes, car je vous amène le meilleur secours que eut oncques chevalier, ville ou cité.' ('In God's name, the counsel of our Lord is more sure and more wise than your own. You have intended to deceive me, and you are deceived yourselves, for I bring you the best succour that any knight, town or city, ever had.')
Jeanne d'Arc to the Bastard of Orleans.

THE Maid wished to march directly upon Orleans by the right bank of the Loire, on which the town is built; but her chiefs, fearing the English strongholds, insisted upon taking the left bank, the side of La Sologne, leaving the river between their march and the principal strength of the enemy. Jeanne affirmed that the English would allow them to pass without attacking the convoy; a statement which the leaders could hardly be expected to act upon. They corresponded with Dunois, who commanded in Orleans itself, about the most prudent line of march, and, considering the south side of the river the least hazardous, they resolved upon this, and also upon concealing their resolution from Jeanne till the last moment.

They deceived her, accordingly, as to the true position of Orleans.

This was not easy, for of course she had inquired its situation before this at Gien and elsewhere, and had thought about it. She was not a person to decline informing herself of facts advisable for her to know. Facts of this kind never clash with one's duty to God. But they did deceive her. A truthful nature does not readily suspect others of untruth, and to her ignorance the word of a knight or noble was sufficient to make her believe she had apprehended the fact wrongly. It was one of the many lessons they gave her in unfaith; they did not corrupt her, but she learned contempt of their ways.

The convoy crossed the bridge at Blois on Thursday, the 28th April. The army followed the convoy for its defence. Jean Chartier speaks of the 'grant force de buefz, moutons, vaches, pourcheaulx,' &c., that were being driven on to victual Orleans. Jeanne led the march, the priests followed with the troops singing 'Veni Creator Spiritus.'

The road by the river skirts the forest-land on the right for miles, part of what is now the beautiful oak forest of Boulogne, which breaks insensibly into the Parc de Chambord, passing the fine Château de Chambord, the Versailles of Touraine, which at a distance looks like an ornamental forest of chimneys, roofs, and dormer gables, with a tall stone lily rising proudly in the centre.

The convoy marched safely along the level

road, defended by the river on one side and by detachments of the army in front and rear, while strong bodies of troops scoured the forest roads to guard the slow-moving caravan from ambush and marauders, the Cosson river being too small for a defence of the convoy on this side.

The forest now-a-days is one of those radiated labyrinths that all woodland pleasure-grounds become in France, focussed here and there by sign-posts, with dozens of names sticking out from them like wheel-spokes, not one of which names does a stranger know, and rays of straight road run from these round-points like the gathering of avenues at the Arc de l'Étoile in Paris. 'Il n'y a pas à s'y tromper,' as everybody says, provided one knows the way, that is all that is necessary, for the names one is in search of, such as Chambord or St. Dié, are not posted up, being too well known to the natives to need it. The cuckoo calls the echo repeatedly, women drive their tinkling herds through the forest glades, the song of birds is continuous, the paths are agreeably shaded, yet enlivened by numerous butterflies, the scent of pine-trees is delicious, the breeze refreshing, so that a walk here seems the most delightful of travelling when one hears it is only six kilometres to Chambord.

One prolongs the pleasure by seeking parts of the forest bearing the wild aspect they had in 1428. It is so heaven-bright above, yet the forest is so dim in 'embalmed darkness,' that one goes on gleefully until one comes to a second sign-post with seven rays, and names unknown outside the forest. The verbal direction had been, 'Take the road to the left, il n'y a pas à s'y tromper.' But was this left at the first or second sign-post? It was the second to us coming from Mont, but was it so to the speakers coming from 'Marie Leczinska,' the other way? The roads are like a wheel, and there are three to the left; now which, if any, is most to the left? As in French politics, here we have *gauche, centre gauche,* and *extrême gauche*. The problem serves as a reason for sitting down to rest and enjoying the sense of bliss that a snatched pleasure in fine weather gives. A man with a game-bag passes. One might have waited for him the whole day. It was a chance if anyone might pass. We are to go straight on, and at the next sign-post turn 'à votre gauche.' The man did not remember the name on the label, but it would be à gauche, and he explained the particular angle. It was marked six kilometres to Chambord! Had the beauty of the glades really beguiled us so far out of our way?

Here goes for another sign-post. Still six kilometres to Chambord! On again. 'Yes, madame, it is the right road—il n'y a pas à s'y tromper. It is six kilometres to Chambord.' This was certainly an enchanted forest; another sign-post marked Chambord, six kilometres! Such reiterations may become monotonous at the close of a day, but a true walker never grows tired before four or five o'clock, and now only one was sounding from the distant castle clock. There would be plenty of time to admire the views from the roofs and the central lantern with the great Bourbon lily, to go up and down the great double staircase of carved white stone, whose involved and interlacing spiral is such a puzzle to visitors, and to be dragged through the labyrinth of upholstery, the four hundred and forty rooms that have weighed upon one's spirit since first hearing of them. In one of these rooms a great picture in needlework represents the vow of Louis Treize. On the right of the king is Jeanne d'Arc bearing her standard, on the left St. Michael presenting the banner of the Sacred Heart. This was worked in 1878 in cross-stitch by ladies, like the rest of the hangings of the room on which the deeds and faiths of the Bourbons are depicted on a ground of royal blue sprinkled with golden lilies.

One re-emerges on the high-road by the Loire near the tall church of St. Dié, a fishing village whence there is a delightful double ferry, between the broad detritus banks, across to Suêvres. The tepid, sunshot Loire here teems with fish, small fish in shoals, and some big ones; they cannot hide themselves, the water runs so clear. It is hot crossing the low cornlands by the Loire.

Was it here that Jeanne first suspected that she had been deceived as to the side of the river on which Orleans was placed? The deception vexed her greatly, because the leaders of the force were acting contrary to the counsel which she believed came to her from heaven. It was too late now to re-cross by the bridge at Blois, and ferries such as this at St. Dié were unavailable for an army. Beaugency was a stronghold of the English, and, until they should reach Orleans, there was no other bridge save the strongly-fortified one at Meung, which was also in the hands of the English. Perhaps she herself tried the passage at this spot, to retrieve the unfortunate step that had been taken. This is very likely, as there has always been a fishing village here, which implies many boats. They have now quite a fleet of them, with tall narrow sails, and the men of St. Dié are all more or less fishermen and sailors.

The river looks so shallow here, besides, that it seems as if almost all the passage might have been made by wading. Did she as leader, and the most venturesome of the army, reconnoitre the passage and the road by Suêvres beyond? Being on horseback, she rode in advance of the convoy with its mules and drovers on foot, and waggons which moved still more slowly, and so she had ample time to look about her. It is always the slowest animals which determine the pace of a caravan. I ponder over Jeanne and her difficulties with the stubborn team she had now to drive, more violent in their temper than her cattle of former time, while sitting on a bridge over the mill-stream that lies between the Loire and Suêvres. A herd of cows have come down to drink and wade; the dog that guards them is enjoying himself in the stream where it is shaded by the alders. Here waddles down a convoy of ducklings. The stream is swarming in fish, perch and some good sizeable trout. Yes, thick with fish like gold-fish in a crowded globe. Here comes another fleet of bigger ducks, all dipping and gobbling. What a happy life it looks! Jeanne, does it remind you of your own loved native rivers? What are these large black flies, or moths, fluttering over the water, with blueish bodies?—or are they lustrous blue wings that glance so in the sunlight? I cannot tell. There are myriads of these flies. These three poor little squeaking ducks have not yet found their brethren; here they come squeaking back again. One might idle away time for ever toying with these country objects. Up and away again, unless we can get into the little romanesque church hereby.

There is another larger church at Suêvres, but this one interests me most. Jeanne d'Arc may have found here the sustaining power she needed. It was, unconsciously, a lesson to the army that Jeanne had not the miraculous power they credited her with, founded on some coincidences of her words with after occurrences at Chinon and elsewhere. Had she immediate revelation she would have known which side of the river Orleans was on, and they could not have deceived her. Human sense and knowledge were sufficient for this purpose; these are never stultified by unnecessary revelation. Jeanne was not a very gullible person. She had the keen wit and business capacity of her nation, and their clear expression in words; as Voltaire says, 'Ce qui n'est pas clair n'est pas Français,' but she had also the boundless capacity for belief in the highest, which is characteristic of great souls and warm hearts. It was only by repeated experience that she learned to suspect treachery in the rulers of her people.

Yet why did the river flow this way, and why were they marching against the sun, if they were really on the side of La Beauce, as her leaders had told her? It must have been difficult to choke back conviction.

The convoy has had time to come up. Let us all move forward upon Orleans.

They could not make the thirty-five and a half miles in one day encumbered by their convoy. Jollois says Jeanne's army arrived the third day before Orleans; but this includes a détour, and they arrived early on the third morning. Wallon and others say she arrived on the 29th of April, the day after leaving Blois. The truth lies midway, perhaps; the later portion of the convoy arriving after the vanguard. They hastened past Beaugency, with its spire and tall massive tower of Julius Cæsar, all splendid with the setting sun. This huge, square tower is one hundred and fifteen feet high, and very broad. It is really of the tenth or eleventh century. Look at Turner's view of it in the 'Rivers of France,' and see what a covetable place Beaugency was; for it is not materially altered, and Jeanne saw the town across the river from about the point where Turner drew it.

A road diverges near St. Laurent des Faux from the main road to Orleans towards the bridge of Beaugency, an old-fashioned structure of thirty-nine arches, and rejoins the main road near Lailly, about four miles further on. Doubtless Jeanne would have taken this détour to guard her convoy against the probability of a sortie from the English garrison at Beaugency. See how its tall donjon dominates the fruit and corn land of La Beauce. Jeanne knew within herself that this strong place would soon be in her hands, for this was part of the promise; but so far none else fully believed in her. She had given no sign, or none that could be universally recognised as such, though there were many floating rumours of her marvellous gift of prophecy. Yet some steps were gained, for she was nominally leader of an army: it is even said that Baudricourt, castellan of Vaucouleurs, also marched to Orleans with Jeanne.

At a safe distance from the garrison of Beaugency and the red castle of Meung, the army encamped in the open field, and were again early afoot. Jeanne was the first to be up, though tired and ill with having rested 'for the first time,' so Martin says, 'in all her armour upon the hard ground' (sur la dure). Others say she slept fully armed upon the ground during her journey from Vaucouleurs. [Axiom: When in doubt, follow Quicherat.] Again the truth lies midway, in an average of both statements. He says that in riding from Vaucouleurs, she wore and slept in the plain military dress of the time, now she was equipped in a suit of armour.

On again with morning light, leaving the bridge of Meung well to the left, they passed close by the little town of Cléry, not yet boasting its square and massive church of Notre Dame, so famous in the succeeding reign; then again forgotten till revived by Walter Scott. The church of Cléry had been destroyed by Salisbury last year, 1428. In the upper part of a modern-painted window in the present church of Notre Dame de Cléry Jeanne d'Arc is represented leading the attack on the bridge of Meung.

Orleans is nine miles further yet. The way is pleasant and easy by the borders of the small river that flows parallel with the Loire for miles, as so many named and unnamed rivers do. The scenery is monotonous, which few people cared for at that time, any more than American settlers do now. They looked at the foreground, not at the distance. The Loire is invisible here until you come close upon its borders, but the western towers and slender central spire of Orleans, how near they look from this plain!

Now the decorations of the cathedral can be traced, and another tall church behind it, and other towers beyond the bridge; and now one makes out the flying buttresses of the cathedral, soaring over a large city of roofs and chimneys, a heart led up to by arteries of road. This plain is now a populous suburb.

The army did not follow the present high-road all the way to Orleans bridge, but branched off to the right about two miles beyond Cléry, and gained Olivet (now famous for its cream cheeses), on the Roman road from Vierzon, not far from the source of the Loiret. This was just behind the English bastilles of the left bank. Then Jeanne knew for certain that her leaders had played upon her ignorance, and treated her as a child. She was indeed before Orleans, but divided from it by the Loire. At this moment of excitement the deception used towards her was too much. She was deeply angered; she felt but too keenly how the belief which possessed her seemed like madness to others. It was impossible to force the bridge, though Jeanne would willingly have prepared the way by attacking the most westerly and isolated tower of St. Jean le Blanc; but this project was overruled, and the convoy moved five miles further eastward towards L'Ile aux Bourdons, beyond Chécy, where they found it safer to embark the provisions and send them down again in boats to the eastern and least strongly defended side of Orleans. Boats could only be procured from Orleans itself, and it was a matter of great difficulty to send them up stream with a contrary wind and under the enemy's fire.

'Are you the Bastard of Orleans?' said Jeanne, when Dunois himself arrived from Orleans to consult with the rest upon the means of introducing the provisions into the town.

'Yes, and I am rejoiced at your arrival.'

'Was it you who gave counsel that I should come by this side of the river, and not directly where lie Talbot and the English?'

Dunois admitted that he and the most experienced leaders had advised this as safest and wisest.

'En nom Dieu!' cried Jeanne. 'The council of Messire' (God) 'is safer and wiser than yours. You thought to deceive me, and are yourselves deceived, for I bring you the best succour that ever knight, town, or city had: the help of the King of heaven, Who, at the prayer of St. Louis and Charlemagne, has had pity on the town of Orleans, and would not suffer His enemies to hold the body of the Duke of Orleans and his town.'

As she spoke, the wind changed suddenly, and the boats were enabled to leave Orleans. They placed the corn and other provisions on board, and the 'beeves,' for Lent at Orleans had been perforce prolonged till now, and the flotilla re-descended the river and unloaded at the eastern gate. But they had not means sufficient to bring the army itself into the city, for the Loire was now too high and rapid to construct a bridge of boats here in the very face of the English. There was no other passage than the bridge of Blois, and accordingly the army had no choice but to return to Blois and come back again by the road Jeanne originally recommended.

Dunois besought Jeanne herself to enter Orleans that night with him to cheer the townspeople, who so longed for her presence; but she was fearful that the captains might again betray her, and possibly not re-appear with the army, and she had promised to deliver Orleans, and not only to revictual it. The captains gave her their solemn promise to return, and she lent them her banner, under which they had been encouraged to enter on the campaign, with Pasquerel, her almoner, to carry it, and the priests who led their devotions. Then Jeanne, with Dunois, La Hire, and two hundred lances, descended the river by the right bank, having previously crossed over in the provision boats, and defended the convoy in the boats from an attack on that side.

Saint Loup is situated on the right bank of the Loire, above Orleans. To understand what follows, I must explain that the convoy having stopped on the left bank, opposite St. Loup, at a point called Port St. Loup, they went to fetch boats from Orleans to cross the river, going round a large island that divides it at this place, and entering the town by the road leading to the Porte de Bourgogne.

On this eastern side the English had only the bastille of St. Loup, and, in order that they might not fall upon the provisions, the townspeople assailed this fort with the courage and success of desperation; the boats, thanks to this timely diversion, were safely unloaded, and Jeanne and her companions stayed near at hand in the fields by

Chécy till this was accomplished. She selected this point, Chécy, in order to guard the Roman road, which was the only way a sortie could have been made by the English to attack the convoy; after which she rested some hours in the house of Gui de Cailly, a gentleman of Rully, at some distance to the north-east of Chécy, before entering Orleans.

At eight o'clock in the evening of the same day, Friday, 29th of April, she entered Orleans, having put on the Duke of Orleans' colours, whose city she had come to deliver: the huque, a sort of blouse of dark-green cloth, and the lévite, a long flowing-sleeved mantle of fine crimson Brussels cloth, lined with white satin, which she wore over her armour. Mounted on a milk-white horse, preceded by her own banner, and having on her left Dunois, richly accoutred, she headed a procession of the nobles and notables, and made by torchlight a triumphal entry into the town, accompanied by her brothers and her two guides from Lorraine. She was like moonlight to imprisoned eyes. Her prestige was worth her whole army to Dunois.

We are well acquainted with this illustrious man. It suffices here to remember that he was only created Count of Dunois on the 29th of July of this same year, 1429. Until then he had no other name than that of Bastard of Orleans— Bastardus Aurelianensis. 'Birth is the boast of the fainéant.' Jeanne and Dunois had to make their own name, and where shall we find a name more nobly won than that of the Maid of Orleans —more valiantly than that of the elder Dunois? He was now twenty-seven, having been born in 1402, the same year as Charles VII.

The people welcomed Jeanne d'Arc as an angel of God, and followed her into the cathedral of St. Croix, there to return thanks to Almighty God, and thence to the house of Jacques Bouchier, the Duke of Orleans' treasurer, where she would be under the protection of his excellent wife. This was close to the Porte Renard, which no longer exists, though a remaining portion of the house is still cherished in Jeanne's name. Here she was sheltered on that first night of her arrival from a violent storm of thunder and lightning, which would have been terrific had it assailed her on the previous night in the open fields. There is little in the appearance of the house, No. 32, Rue du Tabourg, to remind the visitor of Jeanne d'Arc, nor does the present cathedral resemble the one wherein Jeanne worshipped Him who had brought her so far.

Fergusson says, 'Orleans is the only first-class Gothic cathedral erected in Europe since the middle ages,' the original church having been destroyed by the Calvinists. The present cathedral was commenced in 1601 by Henri IV.

The cathedral is handsome and purely flamboyant, but it looks modern and unpoetical. It is plain inside, and, though like Chartres in plan, it appears low and too neat to be sublime. It has double aisles, certainly, but no mysterious entanglement of shadows, no colour, or none that is entrancing. [My first sight of Orleans cathedral was just after seeing Chartres; it is but fair to say this. On my third visit to Orleans I liked it better.] There is, however, a fine effect on looking westwards, from the series of coloured chapels round the chevet, between the very tall lancet openings behind the high altar, through the nave to the western wheel window: a really grand arrangement of lines and masses. The church is clean, well-cushioned, and curtained and fitted up throughout for comfortable piety, and—I do not enjoy upholstery in churches. The carving is mechanical and shoppy, as befits a cathedral made to order and furnished by—Gillow. No one would exhaust himself in rapture here, nor roll the eye in frenzy. The west front is fine, with its central door and lofty archways on either side, and three wheel windows placed evenly above, all alike, with columns uniform as a regiment, and a pair of steeples each of three storeys, and a gallery of arches; fine, yes, but little inventive, perhaps.

Orleans has been greatly altered even within the last ten years. The restorers, those housemaids of our towns, have been at work; they found it picturesque, and they left it tidy and respectable, after the example of the cathedral. On my first visit, among other relics in what were the slums near Diana of Poitiers' house, I came upon an old wooden-fronted house in crossbarred work, which was in the act of being destroyed, and near it one tall, slender column of an ancient building. It looked spiritually light hovering above its own ruins. I seized both in a sketch before the fairy column fell. To-morrow had forgotten them. The society for the conservation of historical monuments dusts and takes care of the best of these relics, and leaves the rest as lumber to be swept away. The guide-books catalogue these remaining chattels. Let us see Orleans by the light that still burns; though not even Agnes Sorel may be thought of in the Maid's own city. One historical possession of Orleans can never be forgotten—that is, its deliverance.

Thus runs De Commines' monumental tribute to Henry V. of England and Agincourt: 'When God was weary of doing them (the English) good this wise king died at the wood of Vincennes, and his unwise (insensé) son was crowned king of France and England.' He calls Harry of Agincourt 'le Roy Henry le Bel et tresuaillant.'

We all know the story of Orleans and Patay, so it will not destroy the interest if we hear the English view of the reason for their defeat in Bedford's letter to Henry VI.

'And alle thing then prospered for you, till the tyme of the Siege of Orleans, taken in hand, God knoweth by what advis. At the whiche tyme, after the adventure fallen to the persone of my cousin of Salysbury, whom God assoille, there felle, by the hand of God as it seemeth, a great strooke upon your peuple that was assembled there in grete nombre, caused in grete partie, as y trowe, of lakke of sadde beleve, and of unlevefulle doubte, that they hadde of a disciple and lyme of the feende, called the Pucelle, that used fals enchantements and sorcerie. The which strooke and discomfiture not only lessed in grete partie the nombre of your peuple there, but as well withdrowe the courage of the remenant in merveillous wyse, and couraged your adverse partie and enemys to assemble them forthwith in nombre,' etc.

So great was now the French enthusiasm that while formerly, as Dunois says, two hundred English could have put to flight more than eight hundred French, now four or five hundred soldiers dared to brave the whole English force. But they could not act successfully without Jeanne among them, for on the next day after her arrival, the 30th of April, the most impatient, under Florent d'Illiers, who had arrived on the 28th with four hundred men, charged the English and drove them to their bastille on the Paris road, but the French could not support their attack, and had to retire.

Jeanne did not wish to fight until she had again summoned the English to retreat peaceably, so she wrote a second letter, demanding also her previous herald, whom they retained prisoner. Again they replied with insults. They thought her an agent of Satan, and it was not the custom of the English to tremble before the fiend, but rather to defy him. It never occurred to the minds of that day to disbelieve in the agency of spiritual powers, and the remarkable coincidence of event with her predictions confirmed their belief in her ungodly power.

Now she wished at once to fight and drive the enemy from Orleans, but Dunois would not attack them until the arrival of their own troops which were coming round from Blois; and, to hasten their arrival, he rode off on Sunday morning, the 1st of May, to hurry them up. He passed proudly under the English forts, the Maid having established herself for his defence between the forts and the town: the English did not stir. Then she rode through the streets of Orleans to give her people confidence, saying, 'The Lord has sent me to succour the good town of Orleans.' She came near the Morin Cross, again inviting the garrison of the neighbouring fort to surrender it and return with their lives safe to England. They derided the idea of surrendering to a woman. The next day, Monday, she rode out and carefully inspected all the positions, followed by the people in great crowds, who showed no fear while under her protection. She returned to attend vespers in the cathedral. On Tuesday, the day of Holy Cross, assisting at the cathedral fête, she joined the grand procession with her captains, and when the aged men told her, 'My daughter, the English are strong and well-fortified; it will be hard to drive them off,' she replied, 'Nothing is impossible to the power of God.'

On this day contingents from Gien, Château Regnard, and Montargis all arrived, but from Blois, no one as yet. Dunois had good reason to go to meet the army, distrusting their movement if he were not there. Their departure was already in question on his arrival, for they were deliberating with the chancellor of France! Dunois showed them that if the little army, gathered with so much difficulty and already reduced by two-thirds of its number—for it was melting away—were entirely dispersed, the town and the cause must fall. He carried the day, and they resolved to march to Orleans with fresh munitions, moving thither by the right bank as Jeanne had at first advised. On Wednesday, the 4th of May, hearing of their approach, the Maid went forward about a league from Orleans with standards displayed, to meet her own sacred banner. The whole army passed under the strongest bastilles of the English in the manner of a procession, the priests chanting psalms, and leading their war-song, the Veni Creator Spiritus, the enemy seeming impotent before the Maid whom they had insulted.

After dinner, Dunois came to tell the Maid that Fastolf was bringing up reinforcements of men and provisions for the English. She desired him to let her know when he arrived, and not to attack without her knowledge. Nevertheless the attack was rashly begun while she was resting. Awakening D'Aulon, her squire, to arm her in readiness for a call, they suddenly heard a great noise and a cry in the town that the French were being beaten. Hurriedly she sent her page for her horse, while she armed herself with the help of Madame Bouchier and her hostess's little daughter, Karlotte, and receiving her standard through the window, not waiting for it to be brought round to her, she rode rapidly by the main street towards the Burgundy gate, her horse's swift feet striking fire from the pavement. Here by her personal efforts she supported the attack so rashly begun, and they carried St. Loup, the strongest fort of the English, before nightfall.

This success was celebrated in Orleans as the first act of deliverance. Jeanne, who had led the men to victory, reminded them Who was the author of it, and told her companions of the true conditions of the promised conquest. It was Ascension Day (May 5th), one of the most solemn festivals in France: Jeanne, who had never ceased to battle against vice and disorderly conduct as their greatest enemies, and the obstacles to their triumph, commanded that no one should go out to fight to-morrow without confession, and she wrote a final letter to the foe desiring them to quit their forts and return home: 'otherwise,' she writes, 'I will make you such a *hahu* as shall be held in perpetual memory.' She sent no herald this time, as hers were retained by the enemy, but she took an arrow and tied her letter to it, and had it fired at the English with the cry, 'Read it, there are news.' We know the rest of the great victory of the Maid, of how her captains disputed her advice, where, had they followed her plan, Orleans might have been delivered with little or no more bloodshed. Her ascendancy had not yet had time to work upon Dunois. We know how she at length prevailed, and how valiantly she fought at the old bridge, which was a double one in those days, after the fashion of Loire bridges, and built a good deal higher up the river than the present bridge, with its centre planted upon an island. How she waved her banner and led her countrymen to glory, crying, 'Ne vous doubtez pas, la place est votre,' and was wounded in the fight, as she had predicted, but still they were not to fear, though her womanly tears flowed at the anguish of the wound in her neck.

Her wound dressed with olive oil, she came to Dunois, who had fought like a paladin of old, as Froissart declares that a knight hath double courage at need, when animated by the looks and words of a beautiful and virtuous woman. She told him and his men to rest awhile, to eat and drink, although it was Friday, to gather strength. They did so, for they were subdued by her words and manner.

'Now,' she said, 'return in the name of God to the assault, for the English will no longer have strength to defend themselves, but will be taken in their outworks and their towers.'

She called for her horse and returned to the charge, after a private prayer, and, taking her banner from her squire, she told a gentleman to observe when the end of her pennon touched the rampart.

'Jeanne, it touches the rampart!' he soon cried.

'All is yours now. Enter therein,' she said; and they scaled the walls at her word. Her sense of pain was lost; filled with strength inspired by overwhelming emotion, she swept on with the rest, her banner still their vanguard.

It was nightfall when the Tourelles were taken, and, after waiting to see all safe, the Maid re-entered Orleans by the quickly-repaired bridge, as she had threatened to do, while all the bells of Orleans saluted this fresh victory.

'God knows with what joy she and her people were received,' says Perceval de Cagny. It was here that the brave Salisbury, whom De Commines calls the Comte de Salberi, was killed. [But why does De Commines here date the siege of Orleans 3rd November, 1428 ?]

There are various accounts of the incidents of Friday and Saturday, according to which attack the witnesses were engaged in. Wallon follows the 'Chronique de la Pucelle.' Lebrun des Charmettes relates the account which I epitomise. On the day after Ascension, Jeanne arrived early before the tower of St. Jean le Blanc. The English, having erected another very strong tower at the foot of the city bridge, the French made a bridge of boats across another arm of the Loire from an island. They passed over only to find the tower dismantled and abandoned by the enemy, who had retreated to a much larger and stronger tower, called Les Augustins, too strong for the French to attack. The French were retreating in good order when the enemy sallied out on their rear. La Hire and the Maid, whose horses had been conveyed to them in boats, mounted and turned on the assailants so furiously as to drive them back to their citadel, into which two men, one a Frenchman (d'Aulon), the other a Spaniard, Alphonso de Partada, animated by a recent dispute respecting their valour, gained a passage, closely followed by their comrades, and the garrison was taken.

How true it is what Captain Richard Burton says: 'In the days of European chivalry, battles were a system of well-fought duels.' It is interesting to follow up this short account with d'Aulon's own version of it, given in evidence at Jeanne's trial. Being her squire, and always about her person, his word as relating to Jeanne is of great value. I have met with this account in no history of the siege. Quicherat gives it in full among the testimony in the trials. I have abridged it.

D'Aulon says, a Basque came forward, when they had sounded the retreat, and the Lord de Villars, being fatigued with carrying Jeanne's standard (at Orleans), gave it to the Basque to carry, for that he knew the Basque to be a valiant man, and the beloved standard would be followed by the soldiery. He asked the Basque, if he entered on foot into the boulevart, whether he would follow, which the Basque promised to do. Then he entered the ditch, and went to the foot of the boulevart, covering himself with his target for fear of stones, and left his companion on the other side, expecting to be followed closely. But when the Maid saw her banner in the hands of the

Basque, she feared to lose it, seeing that he who carried it was entered into the said ditch. Came the Pucelle and grasped the banner by the end, so that he could not have it, crying, 'Ha! mon estandart, mon estandart!' and brandished the standard so the 'ymaginacion' of this witness was that it seemed like a sign to the others; and then the speaker (d'Aulon) cried, 'Ha, Basque, is this thy promise?' Then the Basque tore the standard from the Maid's hands, went to the speaker carrying the standard; then all those behind the Maid gathered up and rallied, and by si grant aspresse assailed the boulevart that in a short time the boulevart and bastille were taken (par eulx prins), and the French entered Orleans by the bridge.

The Basque is the Alphonso de Partada of Lebrun's account, and d'Aulon, the deponent, he who led the attack. He, or De Villars, for the story is here somewhat confused, weary, gave the standard to the Basque, and fearing that evil should follow from the retreat, and the bastille, &c., remain in the enemy's hands, he imagined, if the banner were led before them, the men-at-arms would follow it from affection, and they could thus gain the boulevart.

D'Aulon seems always to have been fired by the Maid's enthusiasm. He says she was a very good Christian, and 'qu'elle devoit être inspirée.'

You may make an impostor, you cannot make a heroine; she must be born as a poet must.

It is hard before such deeds to keep strictly

within topographical lines, to leave to other historians the pomp and circumstance and glow of battle, the excitement of war and enthusiasm, every word of whose language is poetry. It is hard to leave to others these adornments. My tale is stripped of these as it is of the flowers of love. I am not a battle-painter, and the siege of Orleans has been described by those who are able to depict such scenes.

Near the end of the former bridge stands the Cross of the Pucelle, which marks the spot where the fight took place. A dirty, damp cellar is all that remains of the famous fort called Les Tourelles, the taking of which was the principal feat of arms in the saving of Orleans, and this was achieved by Jeanne d'Arc herself. The ancient prediction was fulfilled, 'Quand les hommes auront tout perdu, une femme viendra tout sauver.' ('When men shall have lost all, a woman will come and save everything.')

On Sunday morning, the 8th of May, the English retreated in good order from before Orleans and fell back upon Meung, and, their backs turned, the French, guided by Jeanne d'Arc, visited all the churches to return thanks to the Giver of Victory, improvising, as Wallon says, in the joy of triumph that procession which the Bishop of Orleans instituted soon afterwards, and which has been perpetuated from age to age in memory of the Maid of Orleans, the pious girl who, in the day of peril, saved her country. The Maid had shown her sign.

To this day the statues of Jeanne d'Arc, from the semi-classical standing figure in bronze, by Gois, on the bridge, to the fine and feeling statue by the Princess Marie of Orleans in front of the Hotel de la Mairie near the cathedral, are all wreathed and illuminated during almost the whole of May in her honour. The Société Agricole holds its fête and Orleans is gay with bunting by day and coloured lamps by night. Jeanne's equestrian statue, by Foyatier, is garlanded with laurel and arbor-vitæ, the illuminations round the pedestal light up the story of her life, written there in bronze bas-reliefs. Flags wave in all the main streets, and arches and Venetian masts line the way to the railway station, which is surrounded by theatrical decorations of painted scenery. The shop-windows are full of souvenirs of the Maid, while of the newspapers describing the festival of the 8th of May soon not a single copy remains.

There is at Orleans a museum of works of art executed in honour of the Maid, and objects connected with her history; among them is a portrait of Jeanne painted from the best authorities in the year 1581, but her best effigy was the Maid of Orleans' monument on the bridge struck down by the cannon of the Calvinists in 1567. It was restored, and destroyed, this time entirely, in the great Revolution.

The raising of the siege of Orleans was begun and finished within a week, and out of this three days, Sunday the 1st of May, Tuesday the 3rd, Holy Cross, and Thursday the 5th, the Feast of the Ascension, were consecrated to prayer. On Sunday the 8th the siege was raised. Jeanne left Orleans on the 9th of May, returning to Blois and Tours, whence she went to Loches to seek the king, to tell him the good news, and persuade him to go with her to Rheims to receive his crown. How was she to know that the laziness of man, the vis inertia, is a power indeed, and one of the greatest? It was not so often felt in those active days as we feel it now.

Out in the fields again, a joyous, sparkling cavalcade, beaming with success with banners floating among the flowering hawthorn and guelderoses which shelter the barley and young wheat, their steel reflected in the pools whitened with arrowhead and frogbit. The larks, fluttering up, joined their song of triumph.

The bridges are now free across the Cher, no scouts need watch their road nor patrol their night camp; they are among friends now. The trees are white with blossom, whose crops will not be wrenched from them by the stranger; the warm yellow earth will be moistened by those heavy clouds for themselves and for their children. Now they mount the higher ground at Montbazon studded with fir-plantations and genista.

How among these genista-covered commons one goes back into history's morning, and one's own school-days too, riding in fancy with Plantagenet. A railway now runs through these landscapes, but though one can see the outlines of the country and of history from the train, one fills it in best on horseback or on foot.

They cross the Indre and follow its course in the shade of poplars filled with mistletoe. In the valley stands the old romanesque, two-storeyed tower and stone spire of Cormèry; the distance is purple-shadowed by the lowering clouds that enhance the emblazoned fields of crimson trefoil and blue vetch, the pink lucerne, and yellow enclosures full of sheep, all belted in by the purple zone of the horizon. To-day their land seems of a richer colour than ever. Their hearts have not been so light for many a long day.

Past Reignac, and Chambourg with its high-tiled roofs, and then come the rock dwellings, and now the towers of Loches. It is the first time Jeanne has entered Loches; at any rate, the first time she has been welcomed there as an honoured guest. All hearts are open to her now, though it is less her victory at Orleans than her 'strong faith and pure life which stamp her as the messenger of God.'

Here Charles was staying. He received the victorious Maid with honours, and made her good cheer. Indeed, when she met Charles, he looked so glad the people thought he would have kissed her. But he did not follow her advice, which was made with her usual straightforwardness. This would have been to disarrange himself and put himself to inconvenience with his idle court; who placed obstacles in the way of pushing the victory—who tried how not to do it. It was easier to argue than to act. They needed their little money for pleasanter purposes than to pay armies. They did not care to buy a kingdom: it seemed like a white elephant to some of them.

How could they go to Rheims, they pleaded, leaving the enemy entrenched behind them in strongholds on the Loire at Jargeau, Meung, and Beaugency? Driven from Orleans, the English had strengthened themselves within these towns, and when the French captains, under the leadership of Dunois, taking advantage of the impression produced by the name of Joan of Arc, sought to take Jargeau, they had to give up the enterprise.

Then to assemble a sufficient following to accompany the king to Rheims needed time, and how could this be better employed than in dislodging the English from their strong positions on the Loire? Jeanne adopted the project, and the Duke of Alençon was to join her in the campaign.

This might take a long time; at least, it was postponing indefinitely the evil day in which their own courtly persons would be called upon to pay. They had gained time, and could be comfortable under a distant prospect of restored royalty, which included its cares. Jeanne had taken the work in hand, let her finish it, and get the kingdom ready warmed and aired for them to enter upon, while they relished their good Vouvray wine and gigot de Berri, to the sound of viols and rebecks, and roundels by Alain Chartier. They were not a romantic, nor a chivalrous set of people, but amiable butterflies merely, who only asked to flutter merrily through life. Harold Skimpole the First was Charles the airy dauphin.

Loches Castle is too serious a residence for such a feather-headed monarch. It is a far more picturesque place than Chinon, though not yet grim with the terrors Louis XI. caused its strong castle and tall donjon to gape with, which give a shudder even now to the careless casual visitor to Loches. It was brighter, gayer in Charles the Dauphin's time, when the court occupied the more domestic palace that has since been converted into the Sous-préfecture: a home-like place, softened further by imprints of the gentle Agnes Sorel, the patriot, La plus belle des belles, on whom for her kindness and charity even the sternest moralist must look charitably.

The castle of Loches sets the seal on the horrors of the middle-ages. It is well-known as one of the finest fortified castles in France. Its cliff-like height and prodigious strength make one quake while standing in the courtyard by the provision-well, all moss grown, that goes down deep into the subterraneans, and has or had an outlet in the town below. One enters twilighted dungeons, at whose loopholes weeds and blanched ivy-leaves, winding on long white stems, straggle in with a weary grace, wan with lost light. The finest summer can only foster round these gleams of outer day some thread-like sprays of attenuated pale green foliage and half-developed flowers, still in their weakness a solace to the prisoner; though his hand could not reach them, nor his lips kiss them, they told of Nature's sympathy. Here is Ludovic Sforza's strange, weirdly-pictured prison, a room with vaulted roof all painted over by himself with patterns and inscriptions, and his remembrance, in colossal outline, of his own head as seen mirrored by daylight long ago. He did not willingly let himself die. This is his sundial! to measure such sun as could reach him through an embrasure of wall seven mètres thick, so the guide says; though the castle walls generally are only eight feet thick; this embrasure is deeper through the splay and copings outside and in, one cannot get at it to measure it through the seven ranges of gratings. To unused eyes it is a mockery of daylight, only a dim, ghastly twilight that the sundial measures. Poor wretch; he existed here for ten years, and died of joy at hearing he was free.

Here are Cardinal Baluc's dungeon, his cage door, and other grisly sights, and '* 𝔥𝔢𝔩𝔭𝔥 𝔤𝔬𝔡 𝔞𝔫𝔡 ✝ 𝔪𝔞𝔫,' an inscription traced by some unknown English prisoner at Loches. Did Jeanne d'Arc ever shudder in these castles with predictive sympathy? Her friend, the Duke of Alençon, was imprisoned here in 1456.

Loches is a clean, pretty town, rising on a conical hill. It is highly picturesque, with its tall, romanesque belfry-tower, and its numerous portcullised gates, from which its streets, lively with shops and attractive 'bits' for the artist, slope upward to the donjon and the many-steepled church of St. Ours, an early romanesque building of marked peculiarities. It has a Roman altar in its porch, hollowed with a leaden basin for holy water. There are fine sculptures, formerly coloured, round the portal. The octagonal stone spires are hollow within, forming pointed cupolas supported on pendentives. Two tiny low arches, just wide enough to squeeze oneself through, divide the aisles from the nave. The church has an apsular end, beneath which is a crypt, part of which is known as the prayer chapel of Louis XI.

Fergusson says of this church, with reference to the construction of domed roofs, 'At Loches, we find the pointed arch introduced evidently for this purpose, forming a class of roofs more like those of mosques in Cairo than any other buildings in Europe. The variety of form and perspective they afford internally, and the character and truthfulness they give to the roof, as seen from without, are such advantages that we cannot but regret that these two expedients of stone external roofs and domes were not adopted in Gothic.' It was commenced by Geoffrey Grise Gonelle, Count of Anjou, in 962, and continued by his son, Foulques Nerra.

The king soon left Loches for St. Aignan, in Berri, accompanied by the Maid, who was again joyous so soon as they were in movement. Here, on the higher ground, there is fine air and windy blue sky, the ground is also blue with milkwort. Apple-trees line the road with rosy blossoms, fairer than the flags at Orleans, and these vine-trails are richer than those festoons. Here, too, Charles sees what all France might be, if it were only free and strongly defended; for the country is well-farmed hereabout, and the corn (now in May) is in three stages of its growth, from the autumn and spring sowing; the barley is in full ear, and the latest wheat just sprouting.

The Maid, having the king's interest at heart, rode again to Selles, four leagues from St. Aignan, where the troops were to be reviewed for the campaign. It does not appear that Charles inspected the army, though he rode with Gui de Laval to see the Maid on the 6th of June, just as she was setting off for Romorantin with a portion of the troops. The Maid was always the first to move.

Gui de Laval, writing pleasantly to his mother and grandmother about the great fight of Orleans, beginning, 'Mes très redoutées dames et mères,' says of Jeanne's appearance and manner at court, 'Et semble chose toute divine de son faict et de la voir et de l'ouïr.'* Gui was the first Count de Laval of his family, and was by turn admiral and marshal of France. The ladies, driven from Laval by the English, lived at Vitré Castle, in Brittany. Anne de Laval, the grandmother, had been in her youth married to the famous Constable du Guesclin. Gui de Laval wrote from Ste. Katherine de Fierbois previously to this letter, written on the 8th of June, 1429, 'et fit laditte

---

* And there seems something quite divine in her deeds, and in seeing and hearing her.

Pucelle tres bonne chère à mon frère et à moy.' The Maid sends the aïeule a ring, 'un bien petit anneau d'or;' a trifle, she would willingly have sent more 'considéré votre recommendation.'

The famous, or rather infamous, Gilles de Laval, Lord of Retz, Ingrande, and Chantocé (the original of the story of 'Bluebeard,' that same year Marshal of France, executed in 1440 for sorcery, aggravated by detestable crimes), also joined the Maid's army, on Wednesday, 8th of June, with the Duke of Alençon, Dunois, and Gaucourt. They said the king himself meant to follow on the morrow, but he seems to have been hindered in some way. Perhaps the courtiers were afraid of Jeanne's personal ascendancy leading the king to battle, or perhaps even to Rheims. The person who exercised most importunity always gained him over to his side, and it was chiefly La Trémouille who stood near him. The king dared not trust his own sense of right: perhaps he was deficient in this sense.

In thinking of Charles, one has to make a good deal of allowance for his unfortunate bringing-up, by an evil mother and a mad father. It was lucky for him that they also neglected him.

The Maid wished the queen to go to Rheims. It was discussed, and the queen wished it also. It hinged on a question of money probably. However, the favourite, La Trémouille, wished her away, and the queen returned to Bourges.

CHAPTER X.

A WONDERFUL WEEK—JARGEAU AND PATAY.

> PUCELLE. Of all base passions, fear is most accursed.
> Command the conquest, Charles; it shall be thine.
> Let Henry fret and all the world repine.
> CHARLES. Then on, my lords; and France be fortunate.
> SHAKESPEARE.

A WONDERFUL week's work then began. On the 9th of June, the little army had returned to Orleans, where the Maid was enthusiastically welcomed, and on Saturday, the 11th, she advanced with her force towards Jargeau, some twelve miles from Orleans.

Another joyous, hopeful march, for the victorious Maid was with the army, and in chief command. She had as her principal aide-de-camp her friend, the Duke of Alençon, now free to fight for France. Taken prisoner at Verneuil, he obtained his liberty in 1427, leaving hostages for part of his ransom. He redeemed them by the sale of lands —and a loan from Charles VII. (?) some say a gift (!) The Duke of Bedford declared him quit, even from his faith and promise, on the 21st of May, 1429: so that he could return to the king's service. There were no schemes of deception now towards Jeanne d'Arc, among her army at least, whatever wiles court intrigue might mesh around her.

'Then was a time of colour, when the sunlight fell on glancing steel and floating banners.' All the picturesque of war; as Joshua Barnes says of Poitiers, 'then you might have beheld a most beautiful sight of fair harness, of shining steel, feathered crests of glittering helmets, and the rich embroidery of silken surcoats of arms, together with golden standards, banners, and pennons gloriously moving in the air.' Leighton's fresco of the Industries of War pales before this picture. 'Their gorgeous heraldry and silken surcoats glittering to the midday sun,' as Southey hath it. The Maid with the mercurial temperament of the Frenchwoman, or the artist, revelled in all this lustre on her glory, rejoicing yet more in the glowing warmth of her soldiery as in these battles a roused love of country sharpened their swords. Jeanne was too young and innocent, too womanly to conceal her satisfaction at all this pomp and brilliancy. Her transparent character reveals these natural instincts of vanity, and love of toys and trinkets, of finery and spangles, that is only subdued when custom has staled them to us. These touches of child-like nature seen through the hardness of her heroism are like the charming fibrous ramifications of moss in agate or in rock crystal, not blemishes but beauties. She could at once sacrifice these pleasures at duty's call, as she gave up her friends and animals, her home itself, at the call of the spiritual voice commanding her to go forth.

Their route was by the left bank of the Loire, across the level country where a continuous village now lines the road to Jargeau. At Sandillon, twelve kilometres from Orleans, they were greeted by the villagers, who even now flock out to see who comes in the diligence, or any chance passing carriage, and nod a friendly welcome. A simple, happy peasantry who live their life and enjoy it, who understand, without learning it from lecturers on political economy, that a woodstack is real property, a hedge of white roses a real luxury. Grass is to be had for the cutting by the old woman for her cow, sticks for her picking to make her cooking-charcoal. No one destroys, all use and enjoy, and by the cross where the roads fork they think of Whose children they are. For social gathering they have the all-sorts shop, a miniature Army and Navy co-operative store, a country club giving opportunity for the good-natured local gossip that is the mortar of society. In all, we know and hear and see, we feel how vastly different Paris is from France.

At Darvoy stands the tall May-pole for the vine-dressers' festival. How happy life is here, with no machinery to hurry it on, making one civilized, rich, luxurious, troubled, in one's own despite.

Objector. Yet the Bible seems to prophesy of machinery and exalt it, and symbolise the power of mind over matter in the vision of wheels within wheels. The spirit of the living creatures was in the wheels.

Rejoinder. Bah, by your own reading, machinery is a type merely of the sublimer meaning of this heavenly mechanism; a symbol of a movement, as the clock face images the mere time-beat of the solemn dance of the universe to the music of the spheres. Do not attempt flights; let us not be as shuttlecocks which fly upwards only to drop down again. Look at what lies before us. In the trenched ground with vines planted at each side of the ridge, as the way is here—for vine-culture holds its local traditions as well as other arts—see the old woman among the vines, seemingly amusing herself: the toil is not hard even for her age. It is true Nature here does much for the people; they need not trouble themselves to do much more than hope, gather in, and enjoy. See, too, a man stirring mortar; the fine white stone lies so temptingly to his hand that it is a pleasure to build with it. It is work, while it lasts, but not slavery, like the ten-hours daily grind in towns. They all have a smile and a word for the traveller as he passes (much more had their forefathers for Jeanne d'Arc, their saint and their deliverer). So far are they from the whirr of iron life, the traveller is at once their newspaper and their book of travel. Flowers grow by their doorsteps, where dust lies in towns in lieu of flowers. A month since they were great scented stocks, each plant as big as a flower-bed, which bloomed here; I saw it so, a perfumer's shop was nothing to it: now in June the air is spicy with pinks and roses. Money is such a poor form of wealth: pleasantness is real property. Emptiness of joy is itself a great sorrow. As for the world, 'they lose it that do buy it with much care.'

Objector. Are you inditing a new copy-book?

Rejoinder. A sardonic smile is no answer. Look around you. Are we better off than these people, or better in any way, though we read everything new as it comes out?

Objector. True; but are they better or longer lived than we?

Rejoinder. They are healthier while they live, and less anxious. Our life is a battle with Nature; theirs is peace and co-operation with her. Their wealth, like truth, springs out of the earth, and drops down like righteousness from heaven. Each year brings its increase, that best of interest, which God gives to the labourer——

Objector. And man takes from him for the capitalist.

Rejoinder. In each year they can pay a cheerful tithe to the Wealth-giver (no earthly capitalist grasping his per centage), Whose benign influence they see; helping their belief. Faith is harder for us, for we cannot see—some, alas! cannot believe. They are content to live happily upon their labour; they do not, like the greedy gentleman farmer, expect to live luxuriously and lay by a fortune as well.

Objector. The roads are good, and good roads are the foundation and proof of civilization.

Rejoinder. Yet the swallows skim all the same

and children leap and run. Still good roads are good things, and there you meet me.

Objector. Yet railways are the pulses, as rivers are the nerves of a country.

Rejoinder. Similes are poor stuff. These roads are an inheritance from their forefathers; they hand them down righteously to their children, with vineyards, windmills, wells, and other conveniences. Anyway, it is a well-peopled country; the people do not care to leave it.

Objector. If you like it so much, why don't you come and live here? It would cost you nothing; you would turn a profit.

Rejoinder. I have my reasons.

Objector. Good ones, doubtless.

Rejoinder. There is no end to wrangling raised on questions such as these.

Objector. So let us agree to differ and travel on with Jeanne d'Arc.

On she must go. Her king commands it, and she has put herself at his service. Albeit not to-day supported by direct commandment from above; yet if she fail now all is lost: the patient past, the glory of Orleans, the promise of the future. She must not fail; the strength of a host lies in her single will. Onward with the banner.

Jargeau was then a small compact town, altogether a fortress, very strong, and resolutely held by the Earl of Suffolk with six or seven hundred picked men, provided with cannon. The Maid's force was seven thousand men; yet, so used were they to tremble before the English, that on the road many of Jeanne's soldiers wished to turn back on the report that Fastolf was coming to the help of Jargeau with a numerous troop. Many fled, and Jeanne only retained the waverers by affirming that God certainly led the enterprise. She meant the large general enterprise of freeing France from the invader, of which this formed an episode.

Jeanne meant to lodge her army in the suburbs for that night, but the common people, not the army, filled with the might of her presence, threw themselves into the moats and at once began the attack, without waiting for her to direct them. They were repulsed by the English, when the Maid, taking her standard and coming among the army, restored their courage, and they were located in the suburbs, as she had intended.

Jeanne, according to her custom, sent a herald to the besieged to bid them depart with their lives and their horses safe. 'En leur petite cotte,' that is to say, with nothing but the clothing worn beneath the armour. They demanded a fortnight's truce. By this time succours would have come. Jeanne said they must depart immediately, or the onset would begin; and on the following morning, Sunday the 12th of June, at nine o'clock, the trumpets sounded, and she called to Alençon, 'Forward to the assault, fair duke.' He thought it was too early to begin, but she replied, 'Doubt nothing; it is the hour when God pleases—we must work when God wills. Work, and God will work,' and she added, 'Ah! fair duke, dost thou fear? Thou knowest I have promised thy wife that thou shouldest return safe and sound.'

In this very assault she was the means of saving his life. A catapult was pointed towards the spot where he stood. 'Retire,' she said, 'for here is an engine that will kill you.' He retired, and a minute afterwards the Lord of Lude was slain by it on the spot where the duke had stood. The English held firm for four hours (or till four p.m.) Jeanne and the Duke of Alençon themselves descended into the ditch, and the Maid holding her banner, mounted a scaling ladder. The banner was captured, and Jeanne was struck and stunned by a stone which broke upon her helmet. She fell, but soon rose again, crying, 'Up, friends, the English are condemned; they are ours now. Be of good courage.' The French, emboldened, took the town, and Suffolk was made prisoner. What remains at Jargeau besides the history of that day?

The walls are levelled in many places, and the moat is filled up and planted in gardens, the town having spread beyond its former limits. It has now 2,358 inhabitants. I was being taken for a scamper round the place by a man of sixty-four, who well remembered the levelling of the old fortifications, when he was eight years old. We made the circuit of the old town, that is, of what was formerly within the fortifications. The rest he called 'the fields.'

'At the corner of the boulevard was a tower. The present street where the yard of the "Hotel de la Boule d'Or" now is, was once within the fort: the wall was carried round where the opposite houses now are; their gardens are in the ditch.' The moat is filled up. 'Here are the last remaining battlements. The wall was one mètre thirty centimêtres thick. This is the Porte de Berri.' Its square pillars remain. A chestnut promenade follows the line of the former ditch at this part. My friend in the blouse saw it filled up. 'Je l'ai vu bouché, moi. There are subterranean passages under the avenue. Les couloirs existent.'

'This is the church'—this at least I could see for myself. It has a square tower, with three small, round-headed windows at the top of each side—'near the hospice and the ancient chapterhouse of St. Vrin, demolished. A house here was the Tourelle des Vieilles prisons'—now Rue des Vieilles prisons. 'This is the Rue de l'ancien Pont.' It was written up. 'The present suspension bridge was built in 1834.' It is a long, lofty bridge, connecting the town with the railway. At Jargeau was formerly one of the many fortified (towered) bridges on the Loire. 'In Jeanne d'Arc's time' (so the man in blue says) 'there was a bridge of seventeen arches in stone, one of the most ancient on the Loire, a stone's throw above the present bridge. It was destroyed in 1794.' His grandfather remembered it. 'You see the ditch is all planted. This is the Porte Neuve. The ancient passage under it exists. The place

P

where Jeanne d'Arc was wounded' (? struck down) 'was here at the angle of the boulevard Porte Madeleine. Ah, oui, madame, c'était une bien brave femme. Elle se donnait pour la France: elle se dévouait. The strongest and oldest gate is ninety mètres' (one hundred yards) ' or so further on. Les couloirs existent. There is the tourelle, there was another tower formerly on the other side.' He saw it all at twelve years old, the year of his first communion; he remembers it well. He used to play in the moat.

The Inn of the Boule d'Or (a nice young couple keep it) is built over the ditch. The front gardens of the houses facing it are in what the man in blue called ' the fields.' The greater part of the present town of Jargeau was formerly faubourg. Flowers grow on the ancient wall, and tame rabbits are kept in the thickness of the arches. The quiet, gloomy, thick-walled streets give the idea of the interior of a fortress. The faubourg is more modern and cheerful. The women about here have wonderfully fine, rather fair hair. They look like a Gothic rather than a Gallic race. The girls have a naturally fresh-coloured complexion. The church is romanesque, with a small dog-tooth moulding round the south door, where I entered. It has round arches inside, small, deep-set clerestory windows, and slabs of flat stone on the round columns supporting the round-arched vaulting. This, at least, has been unaltered since the siege of Jargeau. I dipped my fingers in the ancient holy-water stoup used by the Maid of Orleans, the heroine of Jargeau.

The taking of Jargeau was a great day for Jeanne, for she was the leader of the enterprise, and it was reckoned an especially strong place. Much of the success was due to her own personal courage and military skill. She rode back in triumph to Orleans, with the prisoners and trophies, on Monday, 13th of June, where she rallied her troops. On Wednesday, the 15th, she rode to Meung, and took the fortified bridge, leaving alone the capture of the town for the present. This bridge opened up the road to her army, and she pushed on to Beaugency on the 16th. This town capitulated on Friday, the 17th. The English at Meung, knowing Beaugency had been given up, retired at once, with their garrison.

A dispute between Alençon and the Constable de Richemont, who wished to assist in the liberation of the realm, threatened to divide Jeanne's compact little army, and had nearly compromised their success at Beaugency. Jeanne mediated between them, and offered to reconcile Richemont with the king, who hated him, perhaps chiefly because he was the personal enemy of La Trémouille, his chancellor and favourite. English reinforcements coming up, under Sir John Fastolf, gave greater weight to Jeanne's intercession, and Richemont and Alençon fought side by side before Beaugency. Fastolf reached the spot too late to save Beaugency, whose garrison, conquered by the Maid at Orleans, retreated in good order upon Paris, under the command of Talbot, the Achilles of England.

Jeanne followed the foe across the Beauce to Yanville, and the battle of Patay was fought on Saturday, the 18th of June, very near the site of the 'Battle of Herrings' fought near Artenay and Rouvray in the early spring. How different were the fortunes of France at this time! The numbers engaged in this battle are differently given by different writers; only this much is certain, Fastolf won himself eternal obloquy for his over-great prudence in this battle. Shakespeare's Talbot says, when tearing the garter from Fastolf's knee,

> 'This dastard, at the battle of Patay,
> When but in all I was six thousand strong,
> And that the French were almost ten to one
> Before we met or that a stroke was given,
> Like to a trusty squire did run away;
> In which assault we lost twelve hundred men,
> Myself and divers gentlemen beside
> Were there surprised and taken prisoners.
> Then judge, great lords, if I have done amiss,
> Or whether that such cowards ought to wear
> This ornament of knighthood, yea or no.'
>
> GLOUCESTER.—'To say the truth, this fact was infamous
> And ill-beseeming any common man,
> Much more a knight, and a captain and a leader.'

Talbot believed Jeanne's power was from beneath; his patriotism seemed to clash with hers, and he thought he defended himself better in fighting her than in hearkening to her. Like an awful reverberation, or earthquake roll, grimly sounded the ghastly charge of sorcery, that capital crime, the one unpardonable sin of the middle-ages.

In the battle of Patay Monstrelet says, 'Les François moult de près mirent pied à terre et descendirent la plus grande partie de leurs chevaulx.' Hear, too, De Commines' reason for the practice. 'Divers lords fought on foot, for at that time among the Burgundians it was most honourable to fight in that manner among the archers, and there was always a large number of these volunteers among them, to encourage the infantry and make them fight the better. They had learnt this custom from the English, when Duke Philip made war upon France, during his youth, for thirty-two years together without truce.' He adds this remark, 'But the greatest part of the burden of the war lay upon the English, who were powerful and rich, and governed at that time by Henry V.' In these thirty-two years the English lessons of warfare had not been lost upon the French. We had trained them to fight us too well, and Jeanne and Dunois were persons well calculated to apply those lessons.

Talbot was taken prisoner. 'It is the fortune of war,' said he, gravely, to the young Duke of Alençon. 'After Patay,' says Lenglet de Fresnoy, 'Jeanne presented to the king a captive hero, in himself a host, the renowned and formidable Talbot.' Saintrailles, the captor of Talbot, had the generosity to send him back without ransom, which Talbot some time afterwards returned by a similar service, so says Martin. Shakespeare, however, makes Talbot say,

> 'The Duke of Bedford had a prisoner
> Call'd the brave Lord Ponton de Saintrailles;
> For him I was exchanged and ransomed.'

On this or some other occasion after Patay Talbot was afterwards ransomed and created Earl of Shrewsbury. In 1443 he was killed when nearly eighty years of age, with his son, Lord Lisle, at the battle of Chatillon.

The Maid returned on Sunday morning from Patay to Orleans. A week only had elapsed, the campaign which the king had ordered upon the Loire was over, and the fortresses were in the king's hands. In this life-sized game of chess the king was in check no longer; the castles were taken, and Jeanne was the all-powerful queen.

She attacked Jargeau on the 11th of June, took it on the 12th, and on the 13th was again at Orleans; the bridge of Meung was taken on the 15th, on the 16th she was before Beaugency, it capitulated on the 17th. On the 18th was the battle of Patay. What a wonderful week! Two sieges and a pitched battle, and the strong bridge of Meung taken, which caused the evacuation of the town. The mere journeys over the country traversed is work enough to fill a week of great interest. Between Orleans and Patay one crosses part of La Beauce, teeming with fertility, a monotony of wealth; a country widely differing from Jeanne's green Lorraine, that being pastoral, this entirely agricultural land. A broad level dominated by the vast height of Chartres cathedral. Truly it may be said of all this northern part of France that the mountains are entirely of man's making, and they give the feeling of the sublime in the same way as do the natural mountains of other lands, by their intrinsic splendour and the far-reaching views to be obtained from the summits of both.

What was once the forest of Orleans, haunted in geological ages by animals whose fossil remains in the fresh-water limestone tell us that they were gigantic quadrupeds (Deinotherium), is now a great cornland, intermingled with residue of forests, sloping upwards from the vineyards by the Loire. A vast expanse of corn, hay, clover, and lucerne, so wide that, standing at any point, one feels as on a variegated island in a lake of blue, the distance melting off everywhere into width like that of the ocean. A wide, exposed plain, almost treeless, dotted with hamlets and peasants' villages, each headed up by its little church of no particular style; the teeming fields, the banks embroidered with spikes of dark-blue flowers, the fields of pink lucerne patterned over with hawkweed and white stars, the hawthorn hedges still white with bloom, and at intervals, dark upon the verge of the distance, a short line of wriggling elm-trees, writhing skywards against the pressure of winds.

In all this campaign Jeanne had shown a steadiness marvellous in one so lately risen to power. The rapid rise had not dizzied her brain, nor had the transition made her reel, which even heroes have not always been capable of bearing calmly. Charles XII. was possessed by mad chimeras of ambition, Napoleon rushed to Moscow from his newmade empire; Jeanne kept steadily to her purpose, and did not enlarge her horizon with her higher standpoint. Her enthusiasm was a gift laid on her from without; it was no selfish ambition surging up from within, exciting her to extravagance. Her pure life proved her a child of God, and to children of God all things are possible. To make France brave again, this was what was needed, the current of enthusiasm from the heart of Jeanne d'Arc. 'To Rheims!' cried the crowd, 'électrisée.'

Who could now doubt that Jeanne would lead her king to be crowned at Rheims? None but those whom long, sad experience has convinced that lazy indifference is the greatest force on earth. An empty money-bag, besides, is a greater weight than a full one. 'Il n'y a point de soulde,' writes Gui de Laval, that charming letter-writer and gossip. Yet the king had a good bargain in Jeanne. If Charles had recovered his realm by the help of James I., King of Scotland, a treaty which had been drawn up at Chinon, November 10th, 1428, would have obliged him to give James the duchy of Berri or the county of Evreux. Jeanne did it cheaper. A few pleasant words and a war-horse or so sufficed to pay her. His friends relieved him for the most part even of her equipment. There exists an order given by Charles, Duke of Orleans, for paraphernalia for Jeanne d'Arc, about June, 1429, at the time when she rested at Orleans after Jargeau and Patay, to the value of thirteen golden crowns, of the weight of sixty-four to the mark. This costume was likewise made in the Duke of Orleans' colours.

CHAPTER XI.

THE CORONATION AT RHEIMS.

'Gentil Dauphin, ne tenez plus tant et de si longs conseils, mais venez au plustôt à Reims pour recevoir votre digne couronne.'
('Gentle Dauphin, do not hold so many and such long councils, but come at soonest to Rheims to receive your just crown.')
Jeanne d'Arc to Charles VII.

THE prestige of the English was broken: the French no longer dreaded the irresistible archers of Cressy and Agincourt. But the secret of the English weakness was that their councils were divided, and the king too young to fight for himself. There was lack of will on France's side also. There was nothing now to hinder the coronation at Rheims but the vacillating weakness of Charles himself and the selfish policy of his court.

Jeanne was at Orleans; the king was at La Trémouille's castle at Sully-sur-Loire, kept carefully out of the way of her personal influence. Nevertheless, Jeanne was bound to appear before him there to perform her engagement made with regard to Richemont. The king pardoned him at her intercession, but he refused to allow him to join the court in their journey to Rheims on account of La Trémouille, which displeased the

Maid. La Trémouille was none the better satisfied that people flocked to the camp, desiring to serve under the Maid at their own charges. He wished to be all-in-all to the king, and could not bear that gratitude should be due to others besides himself.

Charles himself seemed to prefer being King of Bourges with La Trémouille than King of France by means of the Maid. It must have been discouraging to any ardent spirit to work with or fight for such a fainéant king; but Jeanne acted under the orders of the King of Kings, and hers was no self-asserting, common mind that took offence readily. Loyalty first, then patriotism, was the creed she had been brought up in, and she could not allow herself to believe that her king could be her country's enemy. To her he was Pater Patriæ. Even the wise and learned Sismondi admits of her that she was 'impelled (rather than excited) by a thoughtful patriotism,' of which loyalty was the first principle.

What most wearied the Maid was the hesitation of the king and his delays. She wept before him, and begged him not to doubt but that he would recover his kingdom. She followed him consecutively to St. Bénoit-sur-Loire, where there was at that time a monastery, whose church is even now one of the oldest and finest in the department; its portal is an assemblage of round arches and round columns, with sculptured romanesque capitals, forming a triple colonnade of great magnificence. Then on to Château-Neuf, also on the right bank of the Loire, where there was then a fine château, whose remains are still to be seen; and to Sully, an old castle overhanging the river on the left bank. The English, when they invaded the Orléanais, in 1428, spared Sully, the lordship of La Trémouille, a fact which gave colour to the rumour that La Trémouille was bribed to keep the king in a state of inaction. But this condition coincided too well with the natural disposition of Charles 'the Victorious' to have required much fostering.

The contagious fervour of the army and the devotion of the Maid at first fired even Charles. It was decided that the troops should come from Orleans to Gien, where the king would join them from Sully, which is about ten miles from Gien. Jeanne, who never spared her labour, and who made light of exertion, returned to Orleans, to prepare everything for the march to Rheims. On Friday, the 24th June, she left Orleans, and arrived at Gien the same day (thirty-eight and a half miles), so eager were the troops, so devoted the Maid. But the wranglings at court were by no means at an end; and, at length exasperated, Jeanne left the town on the 27th, and went out to dwell in the camp with the troops.

This decisive measure made the sluggards move, and on the 29th of June (St. Peter's Day), the cavalcade set out for Rheims. All now was joy, the clang and stir of progress. They were moving towards achievement, as they rode forward in the brisk air of the common-land, odorous with thyme and the genista, trampling the flame-crest of the Plantagenets, glimpsing among the openings of the pine and birch-forests, the broad, blue distance of their own reviving country, girt by the silver ribbon of the Loire: the evening ride lighted by innumerable sparkle of fireflies and all the 'argent luxuries' of night, the moon soaring 'passionately bright' above.

Even to-day there is not, across the wild country of Puisaye, any direct communication between Gien and Auxerre; the difficult bridle-paths by which Jeanne had made her way in coming to the court, would have been impracticable for a cavalcade. 'The king and Jeanne would probably,' says Wallon, 'have taken the only high-road known to have existed in the middle-ages, the Orleans and Auxerre road passing by Perrigny, Fleury, Laduz, Senan, Sépaux, Villefranche, gaining Montargis by Château Renard.' Therefore he adds Montargis to Quicherat's itinerary. Possibly the army may have divided itself, and the main body may have taken the main road; but, as it seems proved by the old chronicles that Jeanne herself took the path by Briare, the royal party may be held certainly to have followed the line of march sketched by Quicherat, who says distinctly that they made a feint of taking at first the road to Montargis, so that it might be thought they were marching upon Sens; but they turned off towards Auxerre. Jeanne halted at Briare on their road to Auxerre towards Rheims. The king followed her next day.

Jean Chartier says it was near Auxerre that Jeanne d'Arc broke the sword of Fierbois on the back of a 'fille perdue,' elsewhere he places the breaking of the sword some time after Patay. Lebrun says it was at Château Thierry; Alençon, an ocular witness, puts it at St. Denis. I follow Alençon. There is wide variation among the different historians in matters of detail, but all the old chroniclers agree right well as to the principal facts. The chain of evidence is splendid.

They were not admitted at Auxerre, although the time-serving towspeople did not absolutely declare against Charles. Jeanne wished to take the town, an act of vigour which would doubtless have been successful, and saved much subsequent trouble. But La Trémouille, who, it is supposed, was bribed by the town, caused a truce to be granted, the burgesses promising ultimately to follow the example set them by Troyes, Chalons, and Rheims. They also provisioned the army—upon payment.

We are not told if Jeanne entered Auxerre on this occasion; perhaps she only looked up at France's peculiar architectural pride, the great wheel windows, from the camp at the distance, whence the city looks its best. But the fine neighbouring abbey of Pontigny may easily lay claim to a visit from her, even if she did not stay there during great part of the three days that the king wasted before Auxerre. This abbey is especially interesting to the English, from its possessing the relics of St. Edmund of Canterbury, and having been the retreat of Thomas à Becket, as well as from its great architectural beauty. It is externally plain, which is a characteristic of churches built by the Cistercian order, and it is said to be the only perfect church of that order remaining; but its chevet of seven small bays, lighted by tall, lancet windows, is exquisitely beautiful. It is an unaltered building of the middle of the twelfth century, in the severe Burgundian Gothic style.

On leaving Auxerre, the king went to St. Florentin, which was given up peaceably. From Pontigny it is only six miles to St. Florentin, which lies on the direct route from Auxerre to Troyes. It stands at the junction of the Armance and Armançon.

How fertile is this Burgundy, a glorious country! This is about the highest north latitude where maize can be grown to any advantage. There is great richness in all the crops, besides the famous vineyards, which of course are the chief wealth of the province. The numbers of magpies hereabout is a sore exercise to those who know an adage or a superstition connected with any and every unit of them. The country even in winter-time here looks green, fresh, and pleasingly varied; especially delightful was it to an army that had just marched through the darkness of the then vast Forest of Morvan, which even now supplies Paris with fuel, which is transported down the Yonne and Seine in rafts of faggots. Brinon-l'Archevêque and St. Phal stand also in the chronicle of their route as halting-places for refreshments.

This leisurely travelling was different to Jeanne's former rapid ride. She had plenty of time to look about her, for not till the 5th of July did the royal army arrive before Troyes, then a larger city than now, if one may judge by the decrease in the population, now not quite twenty-six thousand. In Henri IV.'s reign it numbered sixty thousand. Here they likewise found the gates shut against the king.

Jeanne had written to the municipal authorities the evening before, inviting them to submit on pain of compulsion. They used insulting expressions concerning the Maid. The resolutions of the town were controlled by a garrison of five or six hundred English and Burgundians; but really the nobles of Troyes, as well as the town, had too much to fear from Charles. 'Their town had given the name to the famous treaty of exhereditation, and was the first subscribed to it.' This town did not even supply provisions to the army in the business-like manner of Auxerre, and the soldiers were thankful to find great beanfields outside Troyes, providing them wherewith to thicken their soup. The price of provisions was high as in famine times, and Charles's purse was short. Fortunately there was abundance of green wheat and young beans.

Friar Richard, an Augustine monk, famous for his preaching, was anxious to see this inspired Maid of Orleans, of whom he had heard so much, but he only dared approach her under shield of crossings and holy water. 'Approach boldly,' said the Maid. 'I shall not fly away.' Five days they waited more or less impatiently for the town to capitulate, and the leaders were for giving up the hope and retiring, when Jeanne, who had asked leave to capture the town in her own way, prepared for an assault, and took the place by the mere appearance of being in earnest. 'Let them (the soldiers) only follow me and set hands to the work, for God wills that we help ourselves,' said Jeanne before Troyes.

The 'Edinburgh Review' says that the small English garrison was overwhelmed at Troyes. Morally overwhelmed, I presume, as there was no bloodshed whatever on this occasion.

On the 10th of July the king entered Troyes with great pomp. Nine years before he had been here deprived of his birthright, now he was a king marching to his coronation. The garrison wished to carry off their prisoners as they marched out, as by treaty they were to carry away their property; but Jeanne would by no means permit this form of traffic in human flesh, and the prisoners were set free.

The Seine, dividing here into numerous branches, adds much to the beauty of the situation of Troyes; though seated in a plain, one's eyes are not pained by the usual monotonous reach of a level country. Above the brushwood clumps and alder thickets the tall poplars and lofty cathedral carry the eye upwards like the lines of a well-composed picture; the flying buttresses giving diagonals like mountain slopes.

The description of a French town necessarily begins with the cathedral, and, if I have seemed to sow my book with churches, it is that there are so many of these in France, all interesting to the historian, if not delightful to the artist. Cathedrals are to French scenery much what trees are in an English landscape, what the sky is to Italy, or the temples to Greece. The French have always been great builders. A general view of France must necessarily comprise a series of architectural pictures. And if I dwell sometimes longer than seems consistent with my purpose, or in a way that seems irrelevant, on the condition of the peasantry, it is because they were especially Jeanne's brothers. The churches and the peasantry are the survivals of the middle-ages that she knew and fought for.

Troyes cathedral was begun in 1206, and continued steadily in building for more than three centuries; hence it is a fine study for the architectural historian and for him who compares a nation's glory with its art. Fine art is seldom the outcome of a nation's happiness, it symbolises rather its aspirations and its hopes. Three centuries of growing beauty were a fine school of architectural criticism for the people of Troyes, while the lesser churches would make the celebrity of a lesser town. Troyes cathedral is more than usual the history of the finest art of those three centuries, which, if not dark, we have been until lately accustomed to consider as twilighted ages. The interior is full of forest-like perspectives; the roof, branched with liernes, clustering into stars in its vaulting, with a delightful variety of grouping, such as cannot be looked for in a one-idead cathedral, although the one idea may be noblest and carried highest. The tracery of the outside gives the deepest impression of a succession of kings, and counts, and municipalities, each wishing to offer of their finest an oblation to the Almighty. It is of all cathedrals the most French and most loyal in its emblems, this expression culminating in the crown of fleur-de-lys at the coping of the roofs; the tracery is flamboyant to that pitch of luxuriance whence the next step is towards decay. It is like a handsome woman who has just attained the zenith of her prime: people will now begin to talk of how beautiful she has been.

Troyes is full of 'bits' of architectural interest of a Prout-like character, timbered houses and carvings, iron-work and unrestored mediævalism; so that it bears the unprosperous aspect of an old-fashioned town a good deal out of repair. To many tastes, this makes it the more interesting, and it is much the more instructive. It is one of the few cities in France which did not lose its ancient character in the Revolution; it is therefore worth the while of those who study comparative history to visit it. Troyes was built before the craze set in for well-drilled streets, and before everybody was educated in precisely the same way: built in ages of self-reliance, one of the lost virtues which we are always talking about but never see.

From Troyes the army moved on to Chalons by way of Arcis-sur-Aube and Bussy Littré, where we know Jeanne to have stopped on the 14th of July. Vitry-le-François is also said to have been on their route; if so, this town must have come before Bussy Littré. Vitry-la-Ville would have been less of a circuit, and they might have taken this small town en zigzag between Bussy Littré and Chalons.

They now came in sight of the spires of Chalons and the prettily-wooded borders of the Marne.

At Chalons the army was submissively met by the notables, who had heard of the surrender of Troyes, and saw how the tide was setting. Here Jeanne had the joy of meeting folks from Domremy, her own kith, Jean Morel and Gérardin d'Epinal, formerly a Burgundian in politics. Here all were friends, for a home-friend is loved, whatever his persuasion. Affection prevailed over astonishment at her celebrity, and greatness had not made her proud. They had long, familiar talk of people and of places, rekindling the embers of old associations, and to Gérardin (whose child she had held at the font) she confided that she feared but one thing—treachery. This glimpse shows us Jeanne's really lonely condition amidst all her triumph, how the heart ached for sympathy under the rich velvet robe; for she now went splendidly arrayed: this was part of the king's pomp, and also it was politic, or held so, to enhance her consideration with the soldiery, who judge so much by outward appearance. Her own woman's nature, too, rejoiced in beautiful and becoming garments.

Chalons-sur-Marne contains few objects of interest beyond the slender and many-pointed spires of Notre Dame, and the less elegant, but more ancient cathedral, which is of the heavier-columned romanesque type: one descends three steps to enter it.

The king and his army were lodged for the night in the town, and next day they continued their march, passing at six miles on the road the elegant little church of St. Mary of the Thorn, a miniature cathedral, commenced about 1329. It boasts one of the very few open-work spires in France. There are one or two of them in Normandy. Having so few, the French rather overrate them. Hazebrouck, near the Belgian frontier, has another of these much-cried-up spires; well enough, certainly, but without novelty for us. I once walked eleven miles to look at it; I would not do it again.

St. Mary of the Thorn was built by an Englishman named Patrick. He worked here about 1419, so that the church was exquisitely new when Jeanne passed by. It was begun a century earlier, and not finished till a century later; many lives were thrown into its building, but Patrick was the principal architect. Jeanne's friends from Domremy rode with her, doubtless, as we meet them again at Rheims.

An old MS. chronicle of the reign of Charles VII., from 1422 to 1429, describes this part of Charles' journey. The spelling is modernised somewhat. 'Charles left Troyes, and took the road to Chalons, in Champagne. La Pucelle tousiours devant armée de toutes pièces' (I wonder Charles was not ashamed to be behind a woman) 'et chevaucha tant qu'il vint devant Chalons. De Chalons il reprit le chemin pour aller à Rheims, et vint en Chastel nommé Sepesaulx, à quatre licues de Rheims. Après diner sur le soir entra le Roy, lui et ses gens dans la ville, où Jeanne la Pucelle était fort régardée, et là vinrent les Ducs de Bar et Lorraine' (was it not all one duke?) 'et le Seigneur de Commercy bien accompagnez de gens de guerre, eux offrans son service. Le lendemain, qui fut le Dimanche, on ordonna que le Roy prendrait ou recevrait son digne Sacre, et toute la nuit fit-on diligence que tout fut prest au matin, et fut un cas bien merveilleux; car on trouva dans la Cité toutes choses nécessaires—le 17 Juillet, 1429, par les mains de l'archevêque Renaud de Chartres.' ('The Maid, always in front in complete armour, rode before him to Chalons. From Chalons he regained the road to go to Rheims, and came to a castle called Sepesaulx, four leagues from Rheims. After dinner in the evening, the king and his people entered the town, where Jeanne the Maid was much gazed at, and there came the Dukes of Bar and Lorraine and the Lord of Commercy, well accompanied by men-at-arms, offering their service. The next day, which was Sunday, they ordered that the king should take or receive his worthy anointing, and they were diligent all night to have everything ready by the morning, this being a very extraordinary case; they found in the city everything that was necessary—the 17th July, 1429, by the hands of the Archbishop Renaud de Chartres.')

The sun was setting behind the full-leafed trees and purple hills of the vale of Saulx, the young Marne glancing under the crescent moonlight from among her sedgy marshes, alder tufts, and aspens; the same Marne that Jeanne knew so well as flowing through her own Vosges hills. Jeanne's heart, softened at the sight of her friends at Chalons, was touched anew by the sight of this familiar object. Nothing in Nature speaks to one so feelingly as does a river; especially one's own beloved river. While Charles received the deputies of Rheims at Septsaulx, a castle belonging to the Archbishop of Rheims, Jeanne rode out seeking a place for the cavalcade to ford the river. She may have ridden to Wez-Thuisy to pioneer the path. Any way, we are told that she followed straight up the Vesle from Septsaulx to Sillery. The landscape by these villages must have reminded her of home. It was no longer the superb Loire breaking its way among the detritus like an army through the country which it ravages, but a clear green river peeping among leaves and woods, tenderly nurturing the juicy ground. The evening grew softer and lovelier at each minute, until the mist, rising from the marshes (beyond the present canal-bridge), veiled the foreground, making more deeply purple the vineyards on the hill slopes. Some of the sweetest views paint themselves on the memory in colour, and this is one of them; one can conjure up the purples and the russet brown. Some scenes are remembered best in light and shade.

The villages hereabout are built of sun-dried bricks, and there are fields of wheat and clover. At Sillery itself, the land of sparkling wines, there are no near vineyards; they all lie on the slopes beyond the plain. From here there is a near cut into Rheims, pleasanter than the highroad or the rail, through the long straggling village of Taissy. This road by the Vesle is pretty, and gracefully embowered in its hedgerows, a delightful path to travel on. It joins the high-road near the caves of Goulet, the wine manufacturer, and one enters Rheims by way of the fine abbey-church of St. Remi.

'St. Remi is the exception to the assertion that nothing remains of the round Gothic style within the limits of central France, of which Metz, Paris, Soissons, and Orleans are the capitals. It has been much altered; it nevertheless retains the outlines of a vast and noble basilica of the early part of the eleventh century.'

Even in archiepiscopal Rheims St. Remi's abbey commands especial attention; it is a fine link of the chain which connects Roman antiquity with our day. Clovis and Clotilda founded this church.

It has the romanesque, or rather Norman, character in its towers and elsewhere. In the chancel stand the fine elaborate Flemish-Italian tomb of St. Remi, and a rich silver chasse of relics.

Although Chatillon, the governor of Rheims, was an obstinate Burgundian, yet Jeanne declared they would enter without drawing the sword. Indeed, at the news of the approach of the French, the Rémois showed such disposition that Chatillon quitted the place.

Jeanne had fulfilled her word, and brought her king in triumph to this city, where the kings of France are always crowned. This was the 16th of July. Five months ago she had left Domremy an obscure peasant; now civilized Europe rang with her fame, and here, close by the crowning scene of triumph, at the inn of L'Ane Rayé, now La Maison Rouge, Jeanne was folded in the arms of her father. What a moment for both! L'Ane Rayé (Zebra) has been altered, though it is still an old-fashioned inn. It must then have resembled those numerous wooden-fronted, overhanging houses which still exist near the markets at Rheims, carved with Crusaders, foliage, and quaint animals (one a dog, or a lion, having its mouth wrenched open). L'Ane Rayé, where Jacques d'Arc lodged, was kept by a widow, Alix Morian. The bill, amounting to twenty-four livres Parisis, was paid by the king. This inn was within a bow-shot of the archiepiscopal palace where Charles stayed, and where Jeanne herself was lodged. This is now a plain renaissance building, but it contains some internal arrangements of early date, a fine hall of the twelfth century, used for the banquet, and an elegant chapel with a Gothic crypt. Noël! Noël! resounded on all sides, and the hammering and noise of workmen. People were too busy or excited to sleep much on that Saturday night. The cathedral must have reminded Jeanne of Toul, her first cathedral, and she had seen so many since then. But this was a glorified Toul.

This city, where trams now run, and which reminds one of Brussels in its brilliant gas and electric lighting, has revived again after its melancholy appearance when occupied by Prussian troops after the Franco-Prussian war. It is gay as its own flower-market, which is an ever-shifting scene of bright blossoming begonias, pink dracænas, and things most sweet and pretty—gay now as in Jeanne's time, when Rheims was bent on welcoming her king. The busy market-place was bright with colours, even as it is at this day, when we still see eager faces bending over the heaps of various fruits or stuffs and housekeeper's gear of every kind, shaded with blue or striped umbrellas, selecting just such artichokes and vegetables as I saw to-day at the Saturday's market, each busy purchaser a picture, with her gathering of comestibles for to-morrow and to-day. One lady struggling with a dozen lithe live black crawfish, others choosing among the great barnacled lobsters with their feelers all moving; women with frilled caps carrying live poultry, and fashionably-dressed young ladies carrying fancy baskets garnished with parsley and carrots, pretty as a beau-pot.

It was more solemn in the cathedral square, in 1429, for all the workmen, with their scaffold-poles and the striped baudekin cloth for the procession; the church dwarfs such objects to insignificance. There it stood, as now, the mighty cathedral warm with the golden light of evening, the sun smiting with starry blaze the outside of the great rose-window above the door, with its inscription, DEO OPTIMO MAXIMO. The workmen were busy draping the entrance with crimson cloth, the pigeons, wheeling about the lofty, slender-shafted towers, sought their nests in the shrine-work canopies of the kings above the higher great wheel-window.

The clouds rolled back behind the building, the dangers were past, the sunshine was in front, the work was achieved; now came the crown of glory, deathless fame. The cathedral flushed into the rose light of peace, and repose for France for four hundred years was gained at the price of martyrdom for Jeanne the Maid. The rich calm evening light rested on the warm, golden-toned sculptures of Notre Dame of Rheims.

The grey deepened, the rose-hue became fainter and more lurid as the cathedral stood out cold, with but a faint flush on the grey masonry: shadows from the opposite houses stretching up and up dimmed it from the ground, until an unearthly sublimity of dying daylight rested on the great niched archway of the western portal, now whitened into a ghastly, corpse-like pallor, like fading faith, upon the towers above. Death seemed to set its seal upon the work.

The workmen were all trooping home to sup and talk and rest awhile. There came an afterglow. The rays of the sun's last reflections flashed blood-crimson on the rose-window above the central door, as in memory of those who fell in fight. The bloodshed was not wasted, the end was gained. France was delivered. The bells rang out a last joyous peal, the cooing of the doves 'died away in ardent mutterings,' and the city was wrapped in peace and thanksgiving.

It was lovely to Jeanne d'Arc to think of sleeping under the shadow of this saintly thing, the scene of so much royal splendour and worship. It was the culmination of her life's hope. But could she sleep? I doubt it.

The young moon shines with Dian's own crescent of pure light, the Pleiades shed their sweet influence over the archiepiscopal palace where Jeanne dwells—Jeanne, the church's vassal. She owed obedience to the chancellor, Archbishop of Rheims, being a daughter of Domremy, Dompnus Remigius. Charles Martel's Wain, that we call the Great Bear, beams on the further side of the cathedral. Sleep, Jeanne, if it be possible, sleep on; but—your work is not yet finished. You have led your king to his earthly crown, your crown awaits you in glory.

That evening and busy night were spent in preparation for the anointing which was to take place on the morrow, Sunday, July 17th, and the city was early astir. Besides the nine heavy strokes of the bells, which toll at intervals for the offices, there was all night the noise and bustle of relays of workmen. The sun rose crimson over the archiepiscopal palace, pouring its blessing on the head of the sovereign. Too fair a sunrise for the Maid, so ominous as morning red. The bell tolls loud again for early service, a troop of military, horse and foot, winds its way by the north side of the cathedral with fanfarons and drums. The pigeons are whirling about looking after their morning meal. The cortége of priests and high lay functionaries is gone in procession to the Abbey of St. Remi to fetch the Sainte Ampoule.

Under their escort, the abbot, in full pontificals, carried it in solemn procession as far as the church of St. Denis, where the Archbishop of Rheims, at the head of the chapter, took it from his hands to place it on the high altar of the cathedral, under oath to return it safely to the abbey. At the foot of the altar stood the king, now knighted by the Duke of Alençon, surrounded by the proxies or representatives of the twelve peers of the realm, six lay and six ecclesiastic, and supported by his vassals and foreign nobles, headed by Réné, Duke of Bar and Lorraine, brother of the Queen of France.

All was fulfilled according to ancient prescription, but there was one in attendance at the high altar concerning whose office there was no tradition, standing like an angelic presence at the king's side: the Maid of Orleans holding her banner, which she said had shared the dangers, and now justly shared the glory. She was full of emotion. Perhaps in all that assembly no heart was so thankful as hers. Hear the old chronicler.

'Et y estoit Jeanne la Pucelle tenant son estendard en sa main, laquelle en effet estoit cause dudit Sacre et Couronnement et de toute l'Assemblée. Si fut rapportée et conduite ladite Saincte Ampoulle par les dessus dits jusques en ladite Abbaye; et que eust veu ladite Pucelle accoler le Roy à genoulx par les jambes, et baiser le pied pleurant à chaudes larmes, en eust en pitié, et elle prouoquoit plusieurs à pleurer, en disant, "Gentil Roy, ores est executé le plaisir de Dieu qui vouloit que vinssiez à Rheims recevoir vostre digne Sacre en monstrant que vous estes vray Roy, et celuy auquel le Royaulme doibt appartenir."' ('And there was Jeanne the Maid holding her standard in her hand, who in fact was the cause of the said Anointing and Crowning and of all the Assembly. And made to be brought and carried back the Holy Anointing Oil by the above-mentioned as far as the said Abbey; and the said Maid came and on her knees embraced the King by the legs, and kissed his feet, weeping hot tears, touching to behold, and she provoked many to tears by saying, "Fair King, now is executed the pleasure of God who willed that you should come to Rheims to receive your just Anointing, showing that you are true King, and he to whom the Kingdom ought to belong." ') She calls him king now and no longer dauphin.

The whole religion and bravery of France was for the moment personified in this young girl. The bells rang out proclaiming to the whole city and the country round the fact of the coronation and her great deed.

The bells chimed, those bells among which she heard her Voices clearest, loudest, best. In the choral anthem of oblation, grand sounding as the trumpet bursts of Spanish organs, her fervid emotional piety realised the passionate longing of her youth to serve her country and her God.

The service proceeds with quiring voices and organ peals, and solemn tones are drawn from the great bass-viols near the lectern. A priestly voice requires the coronation oath. The sun streams in from the jewelled clerestory windows on to the pavement, and the wondering people weeping for joy. The trumpets sounded 'à faire fendre les murs de la cathedrale.'

The dazzling gleam from the clerestory enhances the intense depth of shade, clear shade, not blackness, in the roofs and upper parts of the church, which is one of the first things that strikes the stranger on entering Rheims cathedral.

Tapestries line the aisles behind the tall cruciform piers, each formed of a central shaft and four slender columns clustered round it. These ancient tapestries are delightfully harmonious, draping the walls with a soft green and red sumptuousness of aged, but not faded, colour. They illustrate biblical scenes from the creation onwards. Two pieces representing the Annunciation are especially fine ; in one the Virgin is weaving a band of coloured tissue, richly patterned ; in the companion tapestry she is reading, while a company of angels descend and encompass her with their wings. Pheasants, partridges, flowers, hares, dogs, &c., are wrought in labyrinthine elaboration of design round the inscriptions on the lower borders of the tapestries. Two larger and more ancient tapestries at the western end of the church clothe the wall from the floor to the lofty triforium. These are more faded, and the design is almost too intricate to be decipherable, but they are evidently legends of the kings of France. In one that seems to be the legend of chasing the hind, there are the Frankish banners, emblazoned with three frogs. The other depicts St. Remi crowning Clovis. These dimmer hues of green and brown, and ancient grey, enhance the bright but delicate colours of the high-raised eastern window, which is divided from the still more aërial windows and light shafts of the vaulted Lady Chapel by the dark belt of the triforium gallery, in which the sculptures and columns stand out as a deep grey patterning on a ground of brown, so deepened as to be almost black. The sarcophagus of Jovinus, Roman prefect of Rheims, takes one back still earlier into the morning of French history. This monument memorialises the defeat of the Alemanni in the 4th century. The tomb is of white marble, sculptured in bas-relief.

Another exquisite effect of light and colour occurs at the west end, where the great wheel-window is all crimson, purple, and other jewelled colours; below this is a range of saints and kings pictured in glorious light, for the new-crowned king to follow, if he will, to an eternity of glory: the lighted western wall, niched all over with saints and ancestors of his, culminates in a focus of ideal beauty formed by the central ogival arch with its lesser wheel-window filled with softened blue and fainter pinks, paler, quainter, and more delicate, if less superb, than the coloured splendour above.

The north side columns are all in light, flooded with rays from the southern windows.

The spectators of Charles VII.'s coronation standing on the steps in the chevet behind the high altar rails, must have seen from here the rays falling from the south upon the beautiful enthusiastic face of the Maid of Orleans as she stood beside her king; the flood of illumination filling all the scene, the rays falling especially on these two: the centre of that sumptuous assemblage of all that was most dazzling in France. Below the range of tall candlesticks at the foot of the high altar, amid the heralds, nobles, and foreign magnates, the banners, trumpets, and insignia, was held in place of honour that sacred banner which 'shared the dangers' of the war. Above these glancing forms rose the shaded colour of the clerestory and triforium arches, the blue-grey gloom in the lofty roof and the dim unillumined window above the great organ.

The sacred pageant is acted out; at last reverberate the fugal 'Amen' intricacies, and echoing vocal music from more distant clergy, and a hearty cheer from the loyal crowd outside; the silver voice of the saintly youth of France, in white dalmatics, and the rough-voiced people hail their consecrated king; then nothing is left but the antiphonal chanting of the priests, for the procession has swept in lordly fashion down the aisle, and the flood of brilliancy streams out of the great west door, into the dazzling blaze of outer day, scattering largesse; the trumpets blare, the bells chime themselves to frenzy, and these things have passed into history, now perhaps never to be seen again.

Over all Time's changes the cathedral exists benign, serene, shedding a holy influence upon the city. Careless of the pomp of kings, the pigeons coo among the sculptures outside, building their nests in the very bodies of the monstrous gurgoyles, in the huge leaden bull's head and the Behemoth, its fellow, and all the other sculptures which constituted the free libraries of those earlier days before these things were writ in light and colour on the jewelled glass. And Jeanne had now read all these sermons in stones.

Fergusson says, 'The painted-glass style is a truer name' (for the finest period of Gothic architecture) 'than the pointed-arch style. Painted glass was the important formative principle of Gothic architecture.' And further he adds, 'Here is the whole history of the Bible written

R

in hues of the rainbow by the earnest hand of faith.'

What glass was internally, sculpture was without.

'In a perfect cathedral of the thirteenth century the buttresses, pinnacles, even the gurgoyles, every coign of vantage tells its tale by some image or representation of some living thing, giving meaning and animation to the whole. The cathedral thus became an immense collection of sculptures, containing not only the history of the world as then known and understood, but also of an immense number of objects representing the art and science of the middle-ages. Thus the great cathedrals of Chartres and Rheims even now contain some five thousand figures.' The history of the world, its creation and redemption, are told, so Fergusson says, ' with a distinctness and at the same time with an earnestness almost impossible to surpass. The statues of the kings of France and other potentates carry on the thread of profane history to the period of the erection of the cathedral itself. Interspersed with these, a whole system of moral philosophy as illustrated by the virtues and the vices, each represented by an appropriate symbol, and the reward or punishment its invariable accompaniment. In other parts are shown all the arts of peace, every process of husbandry in its appropriate season, and each manufacture or handicraft in all its principal forms. Over all these are seen the heavenly hosts, with saints, angels, and archangels. All this is so harmoniously contrived and so beautifully expressed that it becomes a question even now whether the sculpture of these cathedrals does not exceed the architecture.'

Thus ornament was not without its meaning, which the unlettered poor could read as clearly as the learned could read Dante or the Fathers. The flippant mind of our day cannot endure these things, it prefers pseudo-science, or, still more, the smart levity of the weekly press. We have given our people cheap newspapers and an unreadable art. 'In the middle-ages the sculpture, the painting, the music of the people were all found in the cathedrals, and there only.' With all our resources, we have hardly surpassed their arts, if indeed we have approached them.

The importance of these things is why the churches and cathedrals figure so abundantly throughout mediæval history. These were the crystallised facts of the time, the rest were the passing phantasmagoria bounded by each man's little life. The stones remain memorials of their soul-power to our day. Man's faith lifted him above himself, and he is immortalised in his work; not by name always, but collectively with the body of working saints.

The pageantry of kings and courts is soon forgotten like last year's flowers, but the memory of Jeanne d'Arc lives for ever. She had performed her promises to Charles, and for the reward he offered she asked that her birthplace should be for ever exempt from taxation. This would cheer her poor people, for Domremy and Greux were charged with many dues to the crown of France. The news of this would be taken back by her father after the coronation, sealing her forgiveness for having left her parents against their will, recognising a higher authority, loving God more than father or mother, as her Master did. She did not love her parents less than others do, but more, according to the deep capacity of her nature. Other daughters leave theirs for a husband, Jeanne only quitted hers at the call of her Redeemer. Her request was not much to grant, and Charles truly had not much to give; his successors, who shared the benefit, would share this payment with him.

It seems certain that Jeanne also made the request now to be permitted to return to her village home. Villaret, in his 'History of France,' says she implored to be let return home from Rheims. 'Mon fait,' said Jeanne, 'n'était qu'un ministère,' and this was over. All tradition agrees upon this point, though modern writers question it, and Martin, having a theory to support, denies it. The sight of her father caused a great longing to surge up in her breast to see all who were dear to her at home. Her kind uncle, Durand Laxart, too, was at Rheims, for we hear that Charles encouraged him to tell him over and again, in his homely way, the tale of his niece's journeys to Vaucouleurs. Doubtless Jeanne felt it would be sweet to return in all her fame to her people, to rest after her labours and live in peace with her honoured, though not yet ennobled family. That came later—in November. She had seen the vanity of courtly life, and could not reconcile herself to live at court. But Charles would not consent to part with his best weapon, he could not spare her who was worth an army to him. Besides, the coronation was far from being the term of the enterprise; it seemed now but the point of departure for the conquest. The crown was the earnest of the kingdom. So Jeanne remained obedient to her king.

Amidst all this splendour and the adulation she received, she retained her simplicity and purity of manners. In the letter of three gentlemen of Anjou to Queen Yolande, written on the day of the consecration, they say, 'It was a fine thing to see the beautiful manners of the king and also of the Maid.' She was no mystic, her disposition was full of spirit and vivacity. She arrogated to herself no exclusive powers. The thing most miraculous about her was her skill in war, where her disposition of her pieces of artillery was especially admired; but even this extraordinary quality was considerably due to keen sight, and a clear perception of what she meant to do pointed out the best way to do it; while she was cool and self-possessed in battle, feeling herself only an instrument in the hand of God. · Yet she was no blind instrument. It is a fatal mistake to suppose that the Lord wishes a blind obedience. St. Paul says, 'I will pray with the understanding also.' 'More light and fuller,' is our want.

The great lesson her story reads to women in modern times is the true influence of womanhood. To us her purifying of the camp, and her testimony to the excellence of virtue in a licentious age, speak of the noblest warfare of all. How good and upright must have been her own conduct when men dared not blaspheme in her presence, nor behave amiss; not even the envious could slander her; no man impeached her life. Yet she was only a poor village maiden, no high-born dame for chivalry to worship. Frank and open in speech, she was not presumptuous, though when she had won a certain rank and position she kept it without mock modesty.

> 'No longer on Saint Denis will we cry,
> But Joan la Pucelle shall be France's saint ;
> Come in, and let us banquet royally,
> After this golden day of victory.'

BOOK III.
THE TRAGEDY.

CHAPTER XII.

THE ABBEY OF ST. DENIS.

(On lui demanda ce qu'elle aimait le plus, de sa bannière ou de son épée. 'J'aime quarante fois plus la bannière que l'épée.' Elle ajouta qu'elle portait sa bannière quand elle chargeait l'ennemi, pour éviter de tuer personne. 'Et je n'ai jamais tué personne,' dit elle. (They asked her which she loved most, her banner or her sword. 'I love forty times more the banner than the sword.' She added that she carried her banner when she charged the enemy, to avoid killing anyone. 'And I have never killed anyone,' she said.)

THEY wrote the details of these events to the queen and to her mother, the queen-dowager of Sicily; and, the coronation accomplished, the Maid and all the king's well-wishers desired that he would at once advance to claim his capital. Jeanne's task was performed, the king's efforts should now begin; but the slothful sovereign, who dreaded the daily duties of government, forced the conquest into her hands to complete, while he sought only the pleasures of royalty. Who could expect God to help him who would not help himself? He might as well have held a distaff as a sceptre. Bedford fully expected him at once to enter Paris, where he might have 'walked over the course;' but he loitered in Champagne, seeking pleasure. Victor Hugo—in 'Notre Dame de

Paris'—speaks of a water-party whereat Guy Vertaut, boatman's minstrel at Rheims, played before King Charles VII. after his consecration, when he descended the Vesle river from Sillery to Muison, and Jeanne d'Arc was in the same boat.

Yet it seemed not impolitic to remain four days at Rheims, receiving the homage of the great province of Champagne and, avoiding all appearance of haste and dread, performing all the customs of a newly-anointed sovereign. He went, according to prescriptive usage, to the Abbey of St. Marcoul, at Corbeny, not far from Laon, to touch for the king's evil, leaving Rheims by the Porte de Mars, one of the four ancient Roman gates of which only this Porta Martis remains. It stands in a hollow, age having sunk it deeply in the ground, which has, however, been cleared away from its base. On this side of Rheims there are now well-planted boulevards and public-gardens, and, what would be a valuable institution in any town, a garden of instruction for horticulture and viticulture. The views by the canal and the Vesle river with its two bridges are very pleasing. It is highly probable that during the king's stay at St. Marcoul Jeanne d'Arc visited the high-seated and extremely beautiful cathedral at Laon, whose picturesque group of towers forms the chief feature of the surrounding landscape, but we have no record that she did so. The royal cortége next proceeded to the little fortified town of Vailly-sur-Aisne in the valley, where the notables of Soissons and Laon brought him the keys of their towns. Jean Chartier says the king and his 'ost' came from St. Marcoul to a town named Velli belonging to the Archbishop of Rheims, where he lodged one day and sent messengers to Laon. On the 23rd of July, he went four leagues onward to Soissons, where he received submissive deputations from Château Thierry, Crécy-en-Brie, Coulommiers, and Provins. Nobles and people flocked to his standard, or rather to the Maid's, for they saw that victory followed her. Their road to Soissons was defended by the friendly castle of Coucy, then held by Saintrailles for the captive Duke of Orleans, but they did not turn aside northward from Anisy to visit this famous feudal fortress.

Jeanne made everything ready for further conquests, for these easy submissions presented no solid basis of strength to the sovereignty. The English power had yet to be coped with, and that, driven to bay in its strongholds in the north, was a formidable obstacle to peace. The object was to divide their force, and to bring back the Burgundians to their allegiance. Jeanne took her measures for the completion of the conquest. On the very day of the coronation, she wrote to the Duke of Burgundy beseeching him to make peace with his own country. Shakespeare, who, against his will, cannot help putting eloquence into the mouth of the Pucelle, tells us how she pleaded with him.

'Brave Burgundy, undoubted hope of France!
Stay, let thy humble handmaid speak to thee.'

Bur.—' Speak on; but be not over-tedious.'
Pucelle.—' Look on thy country, look on fertile France,
And see the cities and the towns defaced
By wasting ruin of the cruel foe.
As looks the mother on her lowly babe
When death doth close his tender dying eyes,
See, see the pining malady of France;
Behold the wounds, the most unnatural wounds,
Which thou thyself hast given her woful breast.
Oh, turn thy edged sword another way;
Strike those that hurt, and hurt not those that help.
One drop of blood drawn from thy country's bosom
Should grieve thee more than streams of foreign gore;
Return thee, therefore, with a flood of tears,
And wash away thy country's stained spots.'
Bur.—' Either she hath bewitch'd me with her words,
Or Nature makes me suddenly relent.'

She then goes on diplomatically to show him how the English will use him as a tool and then cast him aside. This is poetry, not history, but tradition and a good deal of historical truth besides are embodied in Shakespeare.

Jeanne's clear business capacity was so marked that, besides all the letter-writing and negotiations being left to her to do, she had to manage much or most of the business work of the campaign: victualling the army, and such-like matters. The military chest was in her hands, or rather in that of her brothers, who held it in deposit for her. The treasure was not large, according to our ideas of the cost of warfare; but we are told later on that she held the sum of twelve thousand crowns for the purpose of providing for her troops. In these earlier and more prosperous times with Charles's army the sum would have been more considerable.

All, all was joy; they were at length moving

upon Paris. Leaving aside the temptation to dally with easy conquests, the royal army again swept to the southward, nearing Paris as if intending gradually to hem in the capital. But their progress was too slow for success. At first it excited wonder and suspicion, next it allowed the enemy a breathing space and time to recover courage. The king, who arrived at Soissons on the 23rd, made no further movement for nearly a week, and did not reach Château Thierry till the 29th, his people waiting, meanwhile, in battle array, hoping the Duke of Bedford would fight them. At vespers the place surrendered without a blow, and the king lodged there till Monday the 1st of August.

Chatillon, the Burgundian governor of Rheims, who had fled to Château Thierry, did not attempt to hold the place a day after the king had made up his mind to take it. Still the court seemed disposed to linger, and, had Jeanne had much historical knowledge, she must have drawn a parallel, as she wandered impatient by the Marne and looked up at the ancient castle, not then in such a fragmentary condition as it is now, between this inactive Charles and young Thierry, another of the fainéant kings of France, for whom Charles Martel built this castle. Jeanne, with the five-crossed sword of Charles Martel in her hand, must have longed to strike the blow which the sovereign dared not deal nor look upon. I do not pretend to write the political history of the time, I only sketch the leading events in outline as they bear upon Jeanne's journeys. When one has divested events of the policy and opinions that surround them, their clothes or draperies, there is little to be said but that a fact is a fact, and that a lazy man lives according to his nature.

It seems as if the court cared more to soothe Jeanne's impatience than to fulfil her wishes, for from Château Thierry, on the 31st of July, is dated the formal exemption from tax of Domremy and Greux. Anything to delay a decisive movement. This want of plan increased immensely the difficulty of feeding and providing for the wants of an army.

On the 1st of August the king went to Montmirail (en Brie). This, though south-eastward, did not appear a retrograde movement; although no nearer Paris, still they were moving in a circle marching parallel with Paris. On Tuesday the 2nd they recrossed the Marne and were well-received at Provins, famous for its roses; here they stayed till Friday. This moving off at a tangent betrayed the secret wish and intention to return towards the Loire and its luxurious castles. Most historians blame La Trémouille exclusively for these delays; but viewing Charles's dilatory character as a whole, and remembering the trouble Agnes Sorel took later on to make a man of him, we may well believe the fault lay mainly with the king himself: though La Trémouille readily acquiesced in what suited his convenience. Charles wanted to have the kingdom won, by war or by treaty, he was indifferent which; but his advisers were to conduct the negotiations, and he was not to be troubled to fight the battles.

These strategic movements gave Bedford time to look about him and assume the offensive. The Cardinal of Winchester's men, collected for a crusade, were eager to take the field against the 'sorceress.' On the 4th of August, Bedford, his own recruits reinforced by this impetuous band, advanced to Melun by way of Corbeil, and seemed likely to cut off the king's retreat towards the south. The royal army abruptly left Provins on Friday the 5th, and went westward as far as the château of La Motte-de-Nangis (en Brie) to meet them; but seeing no one, and hearing that Bedford had returned to Paris, the king again took the road towards the Loire. Bedford thought it more important to strengthen Paris than to pursue that unusual object, a flying conqueror.

The courtiers had already found the campaign long enough; but they had to return, nevertheless, for when Charles came to the bridge of Bray, where he intended crossing the Seine, he was again foiled by his own dilatoriness. The people of Bray appeared submissive, and the king put off crossing the river till the next day. The inhabitants of Bray had promised to surrender their town to the king, but they did not keep their word; they let a detachment of English enter during the night, who occupied the town, and intercepted the passage of the Seine, and the courtiers did not care to fight their way. This incident rejoiced the Maid and the leaders of the royal army, who were very bitter at seeing their hopes of victory so recklessly flung aside. So they had to return to the plan of the Maid, who dates her reassuring letter to Rheims, 'd'un logis sur champ, au chemin de Paris.' The king took the northward road by Provins, and on Sunday, 7th August, he dined, supped, and slept at Coulommiers en Brie. We hear a good deal in the old chronicles of where he did these important things; the diarists have so little else to tell. It reads like the 'Court Circular.' Narrowing his spiral round Paris, on the 10th the king was at Ferté-Milon; on the 11th at Crépy-en-Valois; on Friday, the 12th, he slept at Lagny-le-Sec; on Saturday the army encamped all day near Daumartin-en-Gonelle—easy journeys all, and the king was keeping an army week after week in the field, incurring all the expense of a campaign, and putting it to no profit.

While the king thus went from Rheims to Daumartin, the Maid made much diligence to reduce many places to obedience. 'Many places were by her made French' (faictes Françoises). She seems to have been everywhere, carrying victory in her hand.

An anecdote related by Dunois gives us a few pleasant lights on the attitude of the army and the people towards Jeanne. When riding from La Ferté to Crépy-en-Valois, as the people ran towards them, crying, 'Noël!' Jeanne, who was riding on horseback between the Archbishop of Rheims and Dunois himself, exclaimed

'What good people! I have never seen people so much rejoiced at the arrival of so noble a prince. Ah, might I be happy enough to end my days and be buried in this earth!'

'Oh, Jeanne,' said the archbishop, 'in what place do you believe you shall die?'

'Where it shall please God,' she replied, 'for I am not assured of the time and place more than yourself. And I would that it pleased God, my Maker, that I might return now, quitting my arms, and go back to serve my father and mother by keeping their herds with my brothers and sister, who would be rejoiced to see me.'

Crépy-en-Valois is set in a country of alternately plain and wooded undulations, with no great interest or beauty save that of calm. It is only famous besides for the peace of Crépy between Henry VIII. (of England) and Charles V., 1544. The vegetation, seen by eyes that have lately viewed the richer central France, has lost its southern character with the vines and acacias, the growth is fresh and sweet, but it seems a shade darker than in the regions by the Loire. Murray does not even mention Crépy. No tourist goes there, yet there are some things to be seen. Entering by a pair of handsome Renaissance entrance-gate pillars without gates, one passes through this old-world, old-fashioned town, which reminds one of the most retired and least visited of the Belgian towns. 'The very houses seem asleep.'

There are traces of long bygone days about

s

many of the buildings, and bits of old arches left in the walls of dwelling-houses, giving the idea of town-halls converted to domestic uses. There is the old bell-tower of St. Thomas, belonging to an interesting ruin. It is part of the west front of a former abbey-church, and what remains of an old pierced and crocketed spire, strongly buttressed. Viewed towards the west front, one sees a lancet light set in a large circle, with four rosettes forming angles or spandrils. There are eight quatrefoils below this circle, then two more lancet windows and a rather small doorway below between them. On walking round by the north side towards the ruined east end, one perceives that this tower was indeed one of two western towers. The second has lost its spire and upper storey, but it was formerly the richer of the two. The nave of the building has disappeared. At the other end of the town there are considerable remains, and nearly the whole of the surrounding walls of the castle, a portion of which is still inhabited. The walls are firmly buttressed, but do not look impregnable to men accustomed to Loches and Chinon, though a slanting bastion wall at the lowest part of the fortress, where the ground slopes off into the fields, is a fine, strong, smooth-surfaced fortification. The castle covers a wide extent of ground.

The poets Shakespeare and Schiller both create an imaginary scene at this time of the Duke of Burgundy falling repentant at his sovereign's feet; it is pretty, but less astonishing than the truth that he did nothing of the kind, but only coquetted with his sense of patriotism.

What made Charles so difficult to deal with was his indecision, a fault less common then than in our days, when the complexity of civilization renders decisiveness more difficult and more rare. It has been said of highly-educated persons, 'You cannot get them to come to a decision. They want always to inquire and to investigate, and they never come to a result.' They cannot see with 'half an eye ;' they know too much about the stereoscopic effect of binocular vision. Sir Arthur Helps says, 'There is a great reason for thinking that of all the qualities which are needful for the wise conduct of human life, decisiveness is the one which can least afford to lie dormant. It soon dies away by inanition, if not exercised. Moreover, it is very questionable whether it can be revived.' Indecision should be used as a weapon when all others have failed : when nothing can be done, wait; a chance may turn up and point out an opening—seize it swiftly.

The king's indecision lost him his chance of gaining his capital without a pitched battle. Though Bedford was alarmed at the northward movement, still he wrote in insulting terms to Charles offering him battle. The king refrained —of course—and Bedford returned to Paris for reinforcements. Bedford had too much to lose ; he could not afford to be rash. The party which held Paris was virtually the sovereign of France, and De Commines says Bedford resided at Paris as Regent of France, and had twenty thousand crowns a month, at least, to support the grandeur and dignity of his office. This income was drawn from France, and the English side possessing it, naturally made Charles so much the poorer. Bedford took up his position beyond Senlis on the evening of the 14th of August. After some skirmishing the French drew up at the village of Baron, near Montépilloy (Mont Espilloi or Mont Piloer, as the old writers spell it), about two leagues from Senlis, where the Maid and the captains, and six or seven thousand combatants, were lodged at vespers under a hedge in the fields. The church of Baron dates from the thirteenth to the sixteenth centuries. It has one of the rare pierced and crocketed spires. It is supposed that in this church Jeanne took the communion with the Dukes of Clermont and Alençon.

The next day, notwithstanding it was the great festival of the Assumption, the 15th of August, the armies joined in battle; but the English, numbering eight to ten thousand, remaining intrenched in their position, gave the action more the aspect of a siege. The Maid could only provoke them to several obstinate skirmishes. La Trémouille himself showed much personal courage in the fray, charging the enemy, lance in rest; but his horse fell and flung him among the English, from whence his friends extricated him with difficulty. The king, seeing the English were not to be driven from their intrenchments, returned that evening to Crépy. The Maid, the Duke of Alençon, Dunois, La Hire, and their army passed the night on the field of battle, a fact which generally argues victory, but this engagement decided nothing. Early next morning, to try if the enemy, seeing them less numerous, would venture to follow them, the French retired to Montépilloy. The English only profited by this movement to retreat at their ease. Towards one o'clock the Maid was informed that they had regained Senlis, and were marching towards Paris. It was too late to follow them, so she rejoined the king at Crépy.

If the numbers are correctly given by the old historians, this indecisive action shows more than anything else the terror the Maid's presence inspired in the enemy.

Compiègne and Beauvais received Charles's heralds gladly, and at Beauvais the people sang 'Te Deum laudamus' to the great displeasure of the Count-bishop Pierre Cauchon. The people proclaimed that all who would not submit to King Charles might go away and take their goods; but Cauchon could not carry off his county and bishopric. He preserved his hatred, as Wallon says. It was felt to the Maid's cost later. He henceforth follows Jeanne like an evil genius, sowing the tares of a cruel suspicion around her.

On the 17th, the king received the keys of Compiègne, an important stronghold, whither he went next day, and was received with effusion. Here he also heard of the submission of Senlis.

Loyalty was closely hemming in the capital. It seemed they had but to march thither. But this entailed personal fatigue, the weather was hot, and the courtiers felt they had a right to grumble. Had not the indefatigable Maid insisted, they would not even have ridden to Compiègne.

The fortified side of the town of Crépy slopes into a narrow valley with dells formed of deep quarries. Into this leafy vale the glittering cavalcade descended with their banners and bright armour; Jeanne in the centre of the troops, brilliant, alert, and in dazzling array. They rode through the sylvan country like a hunting-party, with all the brilliancy of war brought into festive relief. This was the side of war that Charles loved best to look upon, and it was necessary to coax him into good humour. The aspect of this district between the Aisne and the Oise is agreeably diversified, it looks like the broad sweeps of landscape of golden harvest melting off into blue distance that we see in Vicat Cole's pictures. Forests spread away deep into the blue, and the wooden crossbar-fronted dwelling-houses are set in a jewellery of flowers. They crossed the Aisne (by a ford?) and arrived at Compiègne on the Oise after an easy ride of about fifteen miles. Alas! they were still sixty miles away from Paris!

The bridge at Compiègne was then lower down the river than it is now, but this makes little difference to the aspect of the town, whose Hôtel de Ville, with the effigy of a king on horseback, like that at Blois Castle, and whose decorated

Gothic church of St. Jacques, stand almost unaltered since Charles's time, with the town gathered on the hill around them. The bourg of Compiègne was enriched (manured) by inundations.

The most changed object is the château, which, from having been a strong castle, is now a modern palace built in the time and style of Louis XV., altered by the Napoleons for a hunting palace, with a broad margin for state pageantry. These Louis XIV. and XV. palaces lend themselves well to pomp. With modern splendour of palatial frontage and wide pavement, it has the modern inconveniences of exposed, unbroken surface, biting bleak in winter, fiercely hot in summer, with heat of radiation from the flag-stones sufficient to cook a dinner. This enhances the charm of that modern revival of the most ancient luxury, a garden, with long glades of grass surrounded by woods fading off evanescent into the blue distance, wave upon wave of foliage, filled with an orchestra of birds: forests beloved of French monarchs from Clovis to Napoleon III.

Here at Compiègne they saw return their own ambassador to the Duke of Burgundy, soon followed by an envoy from the duke himself. The fifteen days' truce agreed upon before Burgundy should cause Paris to be delivered to the king was ending. Nobody had credited this promise, however, and they now spoke of a general peace, and prepared a truce to last till Christmas.

Meanwhile the Duke of Burgundy proposed to receive Compiègne itself from the king, a town which was justly regarded as the key of Picardy on the Burgundian (Flemish) side. The Romans called it Compendium, because they kept their military stores there. But there came no submission from Paris.

The king remained five days at Compiègne receiving the submission of all the neighbouring towns. All Picardy was ready to join him. Henry V. had been King of France, Henry VI. seemed king only of the Isle of France. Charles was flattered by the semblance of sovereignty, but the high-minded Maid regretted to see that in receiving the submission of these lesser towns he neglected the capital city, which was the symbol of possession of the entire kingdom. So long as Bedford held it, Henry was King of France. She took a step on her own responsibility to allure Charles from his false tranquillity. She said to Alençon, 'Fair duke, make ready your people and those of the other captains; I will see Paris from nearer than I have yet seen it.' So on Tuesday, the 23rd of August (Lebrun says the 22nd), the Maid and the Duke of Alençon left Compiègne with a numerous following of men-at-arms. As she was mounting her horse to set out, a messenger brought her a letter from Jean, Count of Armagnac, concerning the rival popes, whose claims were then distracting the spiritual world, and between whom he invited her to judge. She dictated an answer at once—that is, a letter was dictated; but Jeanne did not recognise it for hers at her trial. Most historians agree that she deferred making any definite answer till her return.

They gathered in passing part of the force which was billeted at Senlis, where they stayed two clear days, as we know from Albert d'Ourches, who testifies that he saw her confess herself to Friar Richard, the only man, it seems, who attempted any contact with her mind, under the walls of Senlis, those ancient pre-feudal walls whose sixteen watch-towers show traces of Roman construction. D'Ourches tells us she received the Holy Communion on two consecutive days with the Dukes of Clermont and Alençon. She who made such abundant claims on her spiritual life could not work without this constant refreshing, and of confession she says, 'One cannot too much cleanse one's conscience.' ('On ne peut trop nettoyer sa conscience.')

There is much of old-world interest in Senlis: including many picturesque and curious houses and the remains of the castle. Of the stately church of Notre Dame, which is mainly of the twelfth century, the most decorative portions are later than Jeanne d'Arc's time, having been restored by Louis XII. and Francis I. St. Frambourg, with its fine lofty walls, was not then desecrated as a building-shed, nor the rich, flamboyant church of St. Pierre as a cavalry stable. Senlis was then closely surrounded by a forest. Several writers mention the king giving Jeanne a second horse at Senlis in September, but I cannot find that they were at Senlis together at any time, and I cannot help suspecting that this horse of Senlis was the one that caused the dispute with the Bishop of Senlis, that was brought up against Jeanne at her trial: she sent the full payment to the bishop for his hackney, which he declared he never received.

On Friday, the 26th of August, the Maid with her forces settled at St. Denis. The famous abbey is not well seen from the road. The country alternates in plain and wooded undulations, with no great interest, except what the mind derives from knowledge of its situation and history; or beauty, except where one comes upon peeps of the Seine winding in deep bends among the woodland slopes. The burgesses of St. Denis delivered the town to Jeanne. 'She restored to the royalty, in despite of the king, the town of royal tombs as well as the town of the anointing.' Charles was obliged to join the army much against his will, for fear of being left alone at Compiègne. He came as far as Senlis, for at first he dared not approach Paris nearer. But it was not to attack Paris that he changed his quarters, but to abandon Compiègne: he pawned it, or tried to do so.

Bedford left Paris to secure Normandy, which he feared might catch the infection of loyalty to united France. Two thousand English were left in Paris under a knight called Radley, and the Burgundians under the command of L'Isle Adam. They fortified Paris morally and mechanically. The Duke of Alençon's invitations to them to welcome the king were ill-received, and the French army prepared to fight its entrance. The Maid assisted at the skirmishes, and attentively examined the situation of Paris to see where to make the assault, which was perforce deferred so long as the king did not arrive with the remainder of the troops. Their messages to the king receiving no answer, the duke went himself to Senlis on the 2nd of September; and again, as his journey was fruitless, on the 5th: this time he so far prevailed that the king put himself in marching order and arrived on Wednesday, the 7th, in time to dine at St. Denis. His arrival was welcomed like a victory.

On the 6th, so soon as they were certain that the king meant to come, the troops went forward and established themselves at La Chapelle, in the dusty plain between St. Denis and Paris. But the city had taken heart of resistance and strengthened itself during the king's delay. On the very day of his arrival, there was a sharp skirmish. The Parisians were proud of holding out against Charles's army, and 'that creature in form of a woman who was with them, whom they call the Maid. Who it was, God knoweth,' says the old Burgess of Paris.

But the most serious attempt took place on the 8th of September. They fought from morning till night, the Maid leading the attack on the Porte St. Honoré. Jeanne was severely wounded by a crossbow bolt. Still she remained at her post helping to fill the ditch and cheering the soldiers on to the walls, declaring that the place would be taken.

'Once more to the breach, dear friends, once more.'

She refused to leave even when the captains suspended the attack. They removed her by force, and put her on horseback to return to La Chapelle. 'By my staff,' she cried, 'the place might have been taken!' On that same side of St. Honoré, Rue du Rampart, nearly two hundred years later, Henri Quatre established his victorious camp before Paris.

Next morning she wished to return to the charge, and internal divisions among the besieged and the confidence of the assailants made the taking of Paris appear a very likely result. But as they approached the walls, messengers arrived from the king inviting the Maid to desist, and commanding the Duke of Alençon and the other leaders to retire.

They obeyed sadly, hoping however to return by another road. There was one more chance to take the city. The Duke of Alençon had thrown a bridge across the Seine where it winds so deeply at St. Denis, thus bringing their camp much nearer the capital. By this bridge they might cross the river and attack the city at an undefended point. The king said nothing on the subject, and on the 10th of September very early the Maid set out with the Duke of Alençon and the flower of the army to pass the Seine. The bridge of St. Denis was gone! The king had had it destroyed during the night. Exasperating Charles! And all the more so that our English chroniclers say that Paris would have given way had they continued the attack a very little longer.

The king remained at St. Denis, performing some of the ceremonials of royalty and causing himself to be enthroned there. Jeanne hoped it would have been like another Rheims to see King Charles in his famous abbey church. Surely the names and tombs of the heroes of his race and their sunlit effigies emblazoned in coloured splendour on the windows would awaken this weak monarch to a sense of his belonging to that magnificent family.

This abbey, the burial-place of the kings of France from the time of Dagobert, 638, has been called one of the most sumptuous and gorgeous edifices in the world. It was rebuilt in the romanesque style by Abbé Suger in 1140-44, and this era of the building comprises the fine east end of the choir with its semicircle of chapels; but it carries its architectual history through many succeeding ages, and perhaps the greatest portion of the church belongs to the restorations of late years; for it was very nearly destroyed in the great Revolution, and has been carefully rebuilt by the succeeding sovereigns. The exterior is now mainly romanesque and early pointed, with battlemented tops to the walls, except on the north aisle, which is richly decorated with gurgoyles and a forest of flying-buttresses; a fine example of Gothic grandeur. The west front is the oldest part externally: it has two solid round-arched romanesque towers, one rearing tall its spire, like a right hand raised to heaven. In the centre a star-shaped window is set in a gabled pediment. The interior presents a harmonious mingling of decorated Gothic with the romanesque; being restored in fine white stone, it looks like a new church. To the fanciful mind it seems like a widow in bridal array.

Time, which engulfed the eleven steps forming the ancient pedestal of Notre Dame de Paris, has swept away the throne of St. Denis also. One descends four steps on entering through great bronze doors between massive clustered columns on squared plinths. Though built of fair white stone, it looks black with deep shade on entering from the dazzling out-door light, gradually growing illumined as one walks up the long nave towards the high-raised altar all white and gold, with tall candle-sticks; the bright glass in the chevetal chapels forming a glory behind the altar. It is a congregation of the dead, whose deeds do follow them. The white stone tombs of kings with clasped hands represent a silent worship. Their work is done, they are warriors taking their rest. The long aisles lined with ogival windows, headed by tracery of six-foiled rosettes, form avenues of colour leading vista-like from the entrance gloom to the clear light of the chancel. The coloured glass of the clerestory and triforium windows is absolutely dazzling in its gorgeous translucency.

The clerestory of the nave is especially luminous with figures of the kings in glory of coloured splendour. Kings arrayed in glory such as they never saw in life; they are rather pictured as in Paradise, clothed in richest green and purple, crimson, amber, deep royal-blue, in lost hues of rainbows. How different from the gaudy gaiety, or the negative greys, of pictures in the 'Salon' are these pure jewel-like hues, with the afternoon sun blazing through the glass. The windows in the choir have figure-subjects from sacred history.

It needs a catalogue to take the royal tombs in their sequence. The following are some of the most interesting tombs, not always so because they are the most elaborate:

Catherine de Courtenay in bronze, and other figures of the royal dead of 13–1400, with animals at their feet; Marie de Bourbon, 1402; Charles, Count of Anjou, King of Sicily, a child, 1285. Ermentrude, A.D., 869, and Constance of Castile, A.D., 1160, both lie beneath the great wheel window, with their feet towards the altar: this is the position of all the effigies. Here is a tomb of a princess 'dont le nom reste inconnu.' How touching, her image alone remains: with most of the noble dead, it is their name only that remains, and, with the most renowned, their works; in these we must image them for ourselves. Here is a Count of Dreux, his shield semé of fleurs-de-lys. The statues of Clovis and Clotilda stand upright as if by doors; and this is so; they were brought here from the portal of the church of Corbeil-sur-Seine at the time of the Revolution. These figures are works of the eleventh century, most probably. In the middle of the nave are three splendid monuments. The first contains the sepulchres of Louis XII. and Anne of Brittany, each under a columned canopy: the figure of Louis XII. is nude. The second covers the tombs of Henri II. and Catherine de Medicis. The third and most highly-finished monument is that of Francis I. and Queen Claude.

One ascends a flight of steps from the nave to the raised choir and the surrounding chevetal chapels. The glass in the central chapel of the Virgin is thought to be the oldest coloured glass in France. The standard of the sacred oriflamme, not used in battle since the time of Charles VII., was formerly displayed behind the high altar of St. Denis.

Two figures lie, one on a green bronze slab, in the raised chevet round the altar. Here one goes into the sacristy to see the altar treasures, passing first through a panelled room lined with modern pictures of great events that have taken place at St. Denis: the funeral of Dagobert in 638; St. Louis taking the oriflamme in 1240; Philippe le Hardi bringing the relics of his father here in 1271, and several others; but there is no picture relative to Jeanne d'Arc: the French can have no pride in Charles's deeds at St. Denis.

The same stone staircase that leads up to the chapels of the choir also leads down into the crypt, which is full of royal tombs among the solid round columns that support the church above. Here are old brasses and the (coloured) head of a king. Here is also a baby's tomb, the marble baby feet resting on a lion. Within candle-lighted gratings over small apertures, the coffins with figures of the earlier kings are seen in an inner crypt with massive round arches. Beyond these ancient effigies in a separate burial-place are those of the later Louis, with Louis XVII. in a medallion, poor hapless boy, one of the most pathetic figures in history, and fat Louis XVIII. Charlemagne, a modern sculpture but a grander figure, places in ludicrous antithesis the difference between greatness and stoutness. Neither do the colossal statutes of Louis XIV. and his family look truly great, though the wigs are bulky. The round-arched vaulting here is part of the original church.

How beautiful it is to come up and out into the coloured glow of the nave again.

Here are the effigies which more immediately concern our subject; new, or at least well-remembered in Jeanne d'Arc's time: among them the Constable of France, Jeanne de Bourbon, Charles V. and Charles VI.; Isabeau de Bavière is beside him now, then she was still living in sin within Paris yonder. Renée d'Orleans et Longueville has an unicorn at her feet. Beneath a great wheel window of violet light lie Carloman and Berthe sceptred, and four other ancient kings and queens in royal robes. There is also an Orleans chapel. It strikes one with awe to walk through past history in this way. It is a church well-calculated to raise many varied emotions. Well might Jeanne d'Arc have seen her visions here, have peopled it with visions. Poor soul, she had great need of their comfort. Her king was enthroned truly; but late events had destroyed the charm of the pageantry. It was no fresh repetition of the glory of Rheims. Ichabod—the glory was departed, the lustre dimmed. Charles had a medal struck in Jeanne's honour; on one side was her portrait, on the other a hand holding a sword with the legend ' Consilio confirmata Dei,' sustained by the counsel of God. The honour seemed a mockery now.*

The king left St. Denis on the 13th of September. His retreat had to be protected.

If Jeanne had adorned her imaginary Charles with as imaginary virtues, she must have been painfully undeceived. Charles was by nature ' à la fois aride et molle, faible et fermée;' she could not communicate to him the heroic fire of her own soul, nor persuade him that God called him to his duties. Such souls as his are deaf to the

---

* The British Museum possesses no replica of this medal, nor even a cast of it. The authorities there have no belief in the existence of such a medal. They know of no medals of Charles VII. previous to the expulsion of the English in 1451. The ' Annuaire Numismatique ' (1867) does not mention it; and Lenormant, who tells us that it is France who offers us the first example of a commemorative medal, does not give Jeanne's medal, but only the one in commemoration of the expulsion of the English in 1451; which was struck (probably) by Jacques Cœur. Were it not that every historian speaks of a medal having been struck in honour of Jeanne d'Arc, one would be disposed to seek it in the ' limbo ' of Charles's good intentions.

voice of duty. His vanity, besides, was wounded at having been made to play a secondary part in his own triumphs. The Maid eclipsed him with her heroism, and, as a French writer keenly says, 'Un dévouement si éclatant l'offusquait.' This too injured his pride. The courtiers petted him and promised to restore him by diplomacy, by Burgundian treaty, by words, not deeds. Yet, though the abbey church of St. Denis did not present the spectacle of another Rheims to Jeanne, it was the scene of a drama infinitely more touching. When words were of no avail, when arms had failed her, when she had fought and bled in vain, on Tuesday, the 13th of September, the Maid gave and left her harness complete on our Lady's altar at St. Denis and followed the king. She was still faithful to him, as a noble dog is faithful.

> 'L'Ost à Saint Denys retourna
> Où par humbles et dévotz termes
> Elle offrit, laissa et donna
> Le harnoiz dont avoit faict armes.'

She had done her utmost. She had fought and promised that Paris should be taken, *provided that they persevered*, and they would not persevere. All her prophetic promises had been of the same sort; God would help them if they helped themselves, and worked out their prayer with active will. Orleans would be delivered—but by the active efforts of men-at-arms, not by standing idly by. The Bible says, 'The effectual fervent prayer of a righteous man availeth much,' but

even here there are conditions—else where is free
will? The encouragement to work is the knowledge that God blesses work. He also blesses
rest; but rest is not idleness. Faith is an active
virtue, even hope is not always passive.

At St. Denis Louis de Contes, her page, left her;
history does not say why. Her wound received at
Paris was cured in five days, and she could now
mount her horse again and follow the king, unwearied in his service; but first she came at
evening into the Abbey of St. Denis and placed
her arms as an offering at the feet of the Virgin
and before the relics of the patron saint of the
realm. 'Because it is the cry of France,' she
said. She offered her harness complete, her
maiden white armour, with the sword, not of
Ste. Katherine, that was now broken, but the
one she had gained at the Boulevard St. Honoré.
Her offered arms were afterwards hung to a
column of the temple; even that august place
contained no more sacred relic. Her heart was
there. This was not, as has been said, an imitation of the watching of the arms of chivalry, but
an offering simply, and a beseeching to be shown
the will of God, the outward act implying the
inward reverence. Jeanne having wrought to
her utmost, could only wait on her ministry.
The tide of battle had rolled aside, the pomp of
war was moving off eastward; pageant history
again dimmed into a shade, the small suburban
town was becoming quiet again; silence would for
ages wrap round the sleep of the kings of France,

only the moon, 'kissing dead things to life,' would outline the ancient towers with silver, while it cast the more modern buildings into blackest shadow, and played in starry ripples on the waters; only the host of heaven would gather round those towers, 'a dusky empire and its diadems.'

Hear our own sweet writer upon Art and Nature describe this scene of St. Denis as pictured by our Turner. 'And then you shall hear the fainting tempest die in the hollow of the night, and you shall see a green halo kindling on the summit of the eastern hills, brighter—brighter yet, till the large white circle of the slow moon is lifted up among the barred clouds, step by step, line by line; star after star she quenches with her kindling light, setting in their stead an army of pale, penetrable, fleecy wreaths in the heaven, to give light upon the earth, which move together, hand-in-hand, company by company, troop by troop, so measured in their unity of motion that the whole heaven seems to roll with them, and the earth to reel under them.'

Within the abbey, kneeling in the moon-ray that pierces the dense darkness of that sepulchral building, see Jeanne, in her despair, offering up those arms that have failed her now. 'Pour ce que c'est le cri de la France,' and France and she still vainly cry for help to St. Denis. See her watching those arms, and still hoping, brave heart, holding up the cross-hilt of her sword before the altar, a star in the cathedral gloom: the moonlight glimmering on those old tombs and ranks of columns, those silent forms—

> 'So silent they—the place so lone—
> They seem like souls when life is gone,
> That haunt where life has been.'

Her sighs unheard through the owls hooting outside in the deep caves and gables.

The ghosts of the royal glory, revisiting these pale lunar rainbow glimpses, full of sorrowful indignation would look with pity upon Jeanne d'Arc, sunken abased on that sepulchral pavement. She has lost the proud audacity that had distinguished her; an outward, visible sign of her inward faith: that confident courage without which great actions are impossible. She sighs, and weeps, and prays that her faith and her strength may be given back to her, to be used for France and for her faithless king. These can only be sought in solitude and prayer; only by keeping off contact with all worldliness can she regain her spiritual vision. In self-abasement man is truly greatest, for then he remembers God, and recognises his own spiritual nature.

Alone, kneeling before her God, can she discern the signs and wonders that are dimmed by contact with the world, and can only be recovered by stillness and solitude in the solemnity of moonlight. She rises sad yet calm, encouraged, hopeful. More faithful to the king than the king himself, she did not quit him, but followed him full of sorrow in the bitter path of retreat. The moonlight still shines ghastly and transparent over the abbey, which has never since been aught but a sepulchre.

CHAPTER XIII.

THE KING'S RETREAT.—CAMPAIGN ON THE UPPER LOIRE.

> Et sa belle vie, par foy !
> Monstre qu'elle est de Dieu en grace,
> Par quoy on adjouste plus foy
> A son fait, car quoy qu'elle fasse,
> Tousjours a Dieu devant la face.
> *Christine de Pisan, a nun who wrote a poem on Jeanne d'Arc at the age of sixty-seven years, and finished it 31st July,* 1429.

It was a victory for the double-faced, half-hearted courtiers, only faithful to their own skin. Perhaps, too, several of them were bribed; there is a strong smell of dross about some of the chronicles; any way, their motives were ignoble. Chivalry, in the persons of Dunois and La Hire, was with Jeanne, and the love and trust of the soldiery; but selfishness and greed are stronger than chivalry, and idleness is weightier than anything in this world: these were with Charles. These were his enemies far more than the English.

Jeanne had promised the rulers that Paris should be taken—if they persevered, or even if they let her persevere for them. They did not fulfil the conditions. Her Voices told her still to remain near Paris. Jeanne felt to be going against the voice of heaven in leaving St. Denis, though she said at her trial that her Voices had afterwards given her leave to go. Her tears were as those of angels weeping for a fallen race.

It was a sorrowful day for a girl of seventeen —remember this, she was not yet eighteen. Her diminished lustre was a grief such as a woman would feel keenly, and Jeanne was sensitive on this point. The Maid's will and her army were broken. The king returned to Gien, leaving only promises behind him. He made the Duke of Bourbon his lieutenant-general and retired, his reason being that he had not money enough to carry on the war.

He returned to wrap himself in sloth; but, as Martin, who loves him little, satirically says, 'Il trouva de la célérité pour la retraite.' It took him only eight days to regain Gien, his point of departure, although he made a circuit to cross the Marne at Lagny, which the herald Berri says was reduced for him. Ah, why did he not even here make a citadel of the high-seated town of Provins, with its large-domed church, lofty for outlook, and its great tower, a curious fortress of the thirteenth century, an octagonal building, with four lesser towers grouped round it, standing on a strong round pedestal? Passing Provins (the roses over), he crossed the Seine at Bray, which this time delivered up its bridge; he forded the Yonne near Sens, still English, which refused him entry, as the English refused to be included

in the nominal truce, and, briefly halting at
Courtenay, Château Regnart, and Montargis, he
came upon the Loire on Wednesday, the 21st of
September, in time to dine at Gien ('à disner à
Gien-sur-Loire,' says the old diarist). His little
life was rounded by a dinner. I hope he had a
good appetite. To arrive at Gien in time for
dinner seems such an absurd anti-climax to his
coronation triumph.

His army dispersed. The Duke of Alençon
repaired to his viscounty of Beaumont, where his
wife awaited him, and the other captains went
home, each one to his government. La Trémouille and the Archbishop of Rheims 'thence-
forth governed the body of the king and his war
business,' as the old chronicler quaintly puts it.
While the king went 'promenant ses loisirs,' to
use Wallon's apt expression, in Touraine, Poitou,
and Berri, leaving all in confusion behind him
and open to pillage, there set in for the Maid a
period full of mental trouble and anguish, which
she proudly and bravely concealed—'a period of
transition between the splendours of victory and
of martyrdom.' The revulsion of feeling was
profound.

On Michaelmas Day the Duke of Burgundy
came to Paris, and was made lieutenant of the
kingdom by Bedford. The garrison of St. Denis
fell back on Senlis, and the English carried off as
trophies the arms the Maid had deposited in the
abbey-church. The towns were held to ransom;
it was difficult even to hold Senlis. France was

worse off than before the Maid had rescued her. It was each leader for himself; everyone ravaged his neighbour's land, and provisions rose to famine price in Paris.

Jeanne remained with the king, bearing these troubles, that he threw off so lightly in the midst of his gay, lute-thrumming court, where there was a host of gallantly-arrayed minor leaders of his disbanded army, and Alain Chartier, the poet, ready to throw the glamour of musical words over reverses of fortune. They had the luck to be light-minded, but Jeanne could not find 'repose in mere sensation,' as they all did, those rebeck-twangling courtiers and the king who lost a kingdom so gaily. They looked for repose now, having earned it, as they deemed, by their summer progress towards the capital,—and back; she only looked for rest, life's battle over.

The king remained some days resting at Gien, whence he intended to go to Tours and Chinon; but the queen, who sought to reconcile herself to her husband, came to Selles to meet him and welcome him back. The Maid, who had their reconciliation greatly at heart, saw this step with joy. She went before the king and his suite, and herself met Marie of Anjou—it seems for the first time—and paid her homage to her queen.

Instead of continuing his route towards Chinon, Charles consented to return to Bourges with the queen. Probably the two high-minded women sympathized with each other, as Jeanne seems to have been encouraged to fresh hopes, and from this time she again seems highly-strung for action. The pleasures of court life had not been able to make her lose the sense of defeat and failure, which the rest all felt so lightly, as if it were solely her affair, not theirs: she bore the burden of shame for them.

It would have been a miserable October to Jeanne but that she was soothed by womanly kindness; another of those noble ladies who all vied in paying respect to the heroine, entertained her on a visit of three weeks at her house at Bourges. This was Marguerite de la Thouroude, widow of Renaud de Bouligny, the king's treasurer. This lady paints pleasantly for us the piety of Jeanne's life and that simplicity which was unspoiled by camp life and the adulation of the crowd, who attributed miraculous powers to her, which she good-humouredly and with great good sense denied.

The Duke of Alençon had collected troops with whom he proposed to enter Normandy, attacking the English in flank by way of Brittany and Maine, provided that they permitted the Maid to accompany him. The king refused.

Even the whole of the Loire was not yet French; the enemy held La Charité and St. Pierre-le-Moustier. These strongholds threatened the safety of the royal residences—a sufficient reason for action. A council was held at Mehun-sur-Yèvre, a favourite castle of indolence of Charles, where later on he actually let himself die of starvation for fear of being poisoned by his son, afterwards Louis XI. Two ruined towers of this castle only remain. The council thought it might be for their advantage to let Jeanne act in this part of the country, so they sent her to lay siege to La Charité, preluding this conquest by that of St. Pierre-le-Moustier. Both these fortresses are on the Loire, St. Pierre the further south of the two, at the junction of the Loire and Allier.

The Maid would have preferred returning to Paris, but she set to work at once to obey her orders with good will. She went to Bourges (from Mehun) to gather the troops intended for this enterprise. It appears that the court took the opportunity of having her escort as far as Bourges, likewise a favourite residence of the king. Indeed his affections seem to have been divided out impartially among his castles. The house in the Rue de Paradis at Bourges, with the elegant staircase turret, is said to have been his palace. It is now part of the Lycée. There is a fine fireplace in the old hall still existing.

Bourges rises out of meadow-land well-stocked with grazing cattle, It is a countrified and cleanly town, peopled with clean-looking provincial folk wearing sabots. Its colossal grey cathedral stands among the lesser roofs like an elephant among mice. One walks up the hill through the picturesque and dormer-windowed town to the centre of attraction, St. Étienne, the culminating point of Berri. What a grand cathedral it is, to be sure, with its five sculptured portals and two towers, one shorter than the other. And inside, it is but a nave indeed; but what a nave! with its five aisles, all of different heights, and its outer chapels, each with triforium and clerestory complete as if they were the cathedral nave itself. The effect of this is admirably grand. Among the striking peculiarities of St. Étienne are the large lozenge-set piers of the western end, and externally, beyond the sumptuous wall-veil of the building, the massive double flying-buttresses, which by their bulky depth of shade give infinite value to the fine and lighter traceries, and to the Norman work of the older part of the church. These dark, solid arches are most fascinating to an artist, with their strange chiaroscuro and the peeps of the town-roofs lying bright in every gradation of tile-tint beneath the dark openings. The windows and portals of the west front are peculiarly deeply buttressed and embayed. This attention to strong contrast of light and shade, and the predominance of the number five in all the leading details of the church, give it an original and strongly-marked individual character, singling it out to remembrance among the numerous French cathedrals, when all these have blended in the memory as does a mountain chain in one intricate tissue of grandeur. Truly the mountains here are of man's making—under inspiration—one may say; when lifted up beyond himself.

Charles, though King of Bourges, was not the only king in Bourges: for though his famous house, now the Hôtel de Ville, was not yet built (it was begun some fifteen years later than Jeanne d'Arc's little day), yet Jacques Cœur, the goldsmith (the George Heriot of France) was the great capitalist and employer of labour of his time. 'Rich as Jacques Cœur' was a proverb. One may say almost all the gold in France passed through his hands. Jacques Cœur provided the sinews of war for Charles, as Dunois, La Hire, and Saintrailles furnished him with hands and weapons, and Jeanne d'Arc provided the brave spirit. Besides being a magnificent banker and builder of the most sumptuously florid house in France—'à vaillants Cœurs rien impossible,' Jacques Cœur favoured the disciples of Van Eyck in art. He encouraged art like a king. He was king of the arts of peace, so to speak; Charles was king of idleness.

Charles often came to Bourges to fill his purse. But at length, less wise than his prudent, crafty son, Louis XI., who made the importance of the burgesses the characteristic of his government, he killed the goose that laid the golden eggs. For in later years the courtiers envied Jacques Cœur, hated, vilified, ruined him, and the king seized his goods and drove him out into the world an aged, poor, and banished man. The courtiers declared Agnes Sorel to have been poisoned by Jacques Cœur. Agnes knew him better, knew that he was her true friend. He was appointed one of the executors to her will.

His house externally presents a range of street pictures of florid but harmonious character, while the general details would suffice to form a glossary of ornament in themselves. A new Terracottopolis might here supply itself with patterns for its gables, chimneys, roofs, and spires, and every architectural freak, without degenerating into extravagance of design.

Besides the house of Jacques Cœur, there is the picturesque gendarmerie, which is an elegant example of the spired and turreted renaissance, and there are many other old houses remarkable even in this very dormer-and-gably place, which I should call 'the French Nuremberg.' Besides the houses that Murray mentions, there is No. 44 on the road to the station, which has a moulding of lions and thistles mingled with birds feeding out of baskets, and over the door a bas-relief like a valentine; a shield resembling a heart, with two cupids as supporters, and a bust inside a crocketed Gothic arch; all laughable, but piquant withal, and not inelegant.

Even in this early November time, when also Jeanne was here, there is something fresh and bowery about the landscape. The country is still green and moist, almost too moist, and the trees are autumn-tinted, mingling their colours with the bright tile roofs and white house-fronts of the suburbs, all standing well out from the grey background, which also gives excelling brightness to yonder rainbow. The 'alize' berries are ripe, a common fruit here, growing in bunches like larger hips. I do not know them as edible fruit elsewhere than in Berri. The reddening cherry-leaves brighten the withered brown foliage round the farmsteads. This part of France is full of *homes*, from the turreted château to the dormer-windowed nests of the artisan and peasant. The dark-eyed women are fine-featured and fresh-coloured. They are handsomer here than in most parts of France; one traces a southern origin in their sometimes nearly classic outlines. I do not say the majority are beautiful, but there is a good per-centage. They wear coal-scuttle cottage bonnets, trimmed with broad black velvet, planted bolt upright on the top of their heads.

The troops and money raised, Jeanne d'Arc rode forward to besiege St. Pierre-le-Moustier, at the junction of the Loire and Allier, which from here run nearly parallel deep into the mountains of Auvergne, draining almost the whole range of the Cevennes, and all those high-peaked hills where the grey and purple rocks are set in greenest grass, for this steep country is a part of France where excellent butter is made; and now in November the densely-grown beeches changing colour, and other varied foliage of brown and yellow, relieved with scarlet leaves of the wild cherry, shelter the cattle which animate the park-like scenery of the slopes between the red-roofed and irregular towns, all busy and prosperous with their fresh-coloured, healthy-looking population.

The higher mountains are covered with brushwood mingled with beech and fir. The ascents in zigzag terraces are truly Alpine, with their viaducts and deep cuttings, fringed at the skyline with balsam pines, and rapid descents which take the breath away. Here is the infant Loire, full of stone-banks and islands from his very babyhood. He is quite a spoiled child; but when one sees where he comes from, and the sort of country he drains, one no longer wonders at the islands and shifting sandbanks at Orleans and Tours.

The Allier, too, is full of stones, islands, and sandbanks, so that art has to supplement the navigation. Near Le Guétin, close by St. Pierre-le-Moustier, is a long stone bridge, le Levé, or Pont-Canal de Guétin, carrying the lateral canal of the Loire right over the Allier: a vast work.

St. Pierre-le-Moustier lies on the boundary of the ancient provinces of Nivernois and Le Bourbonnais. It is a mere village, commanded by the ruins of the strong old donjon tower whose massy walls were held by Jeanne d'Arc's enemies. The old church still remains where the besieged had placed their goods, and which Jeanne caused to be respected. The archivolt of the north doorway has some fine remains of sculpture.

The siege of St. Pierre-le-Moustier shows that the capture of Jargeau and other places was the result of Jeanne's generalship as well as her valour, for here she was in sole command, so that one cannot attribute her success to the support of Dunois or the Duke of Alençon, for they were employing themselves in Normandy. Personally she took St. Pierre-le-Moustier, placing herself resolutely in the foremost front of danger. 'Bring faggots and hurdles, everyone, so as to make the bridge,' cried she, and a bridge was formed and the town taken by assault. The bright rainbow of Bourges had been an augury of good hope.

From here she desired to follow down the Loire and besiege La Charité. But the place was strongly fortified with its fourteenth century watch-towers, and she had not munitions sufficient to attack it. She examined La Charité from the outside, but had not the opportunity of inspecting its collegiate church, which Fergusson calls one of the most picturesque and beautiful in France. It was built 'stupenda celeritate,' and the Abbé Suger was present at its dedication in 1144. The court not furnishing her with necessaries, she addressed herself to the towns, and Bourges engaged her octrois, and Orleans also sent her succours. While waiting for these supplies she reconnoitred the country round about and followed up the Allier to Moulins, now a dull, provincial town of no special interest, except such as hangs about the moist memory of Sterne's humid Maria. Of the castle only a square tower, called 'La Mal Coiffée,' still remains. There is of course a cathedral, but this is eclipsed by the neighbouring Abbey of Souvigny, the burial-place of the Dukes of Bourbon; the St. Denis of that great family. This is one of the most remarkable buildings in the province. Jeanne wrote to Riom from Moulins on the 9th of November, which fixes the date of her visit. The avenues at Moulins were still green when she was there, notwithstanding the advanced season. In Languedoc the trees are already brown or bare by November. The climate is milder and more agreeable in the Bourbonnais. Here the cattle were not yet housed for the winter when the Maid went to La Charité on the 24th hoping speedily to capture the place. But it was hard, uphill work, and, the king still sending no supplies, the army for lack of money and provisions had to raise the siege at the end of a month, to Jeanne's great vexation. The court, as usual, asked nothing better than excuses for inaction, and was glad to disband the troops and lay up in winter quarters. La Charité was now isolated, and unlikely to disturb the king's repose.

After the failure at La Charité, they had pretext enough to prevent Jeanne from undertaking anything. They affected to console her, and heaped on her the vain favours of the court. They surrounded her with observances and honours, and her family was ennobled; but she herself kept her own name and banner.

'It is difficult,' says George Eliot, 'almost impossible for a man to pass his life amidst (court) intrigues, and yet preserve his purity intact.' Jeanne sought a higher consecration of her powers than they did, even than the best of them. Alas, it might have been hers to have redeemed France, and now the enemy had burst over and flooded the land again, and still they kept her inactive, chafing against the pettiness of their views, while following the court from Bourges to Sully, whence she visited the towns she had delivered; Orleans, for instance, and Jargeau; and she visited Montfaucon in Berri, where a soi-distant inspired person, Catherine de la Rochelle, came to seek her. Besides her foes, native and foreign, she had now a rival. This Catherine held out a more tempting bait than Jeanne, she promised gold. Jeanne only promised liberty. It has always been the case that, if the devil cannot mar any work of God, he parodies that work. The inventive or creative spirit is eminently opposed to the diabolic nature, which has no original mind, but only corrupt or perverted talents. It can only mimic scornfully what has been done, it cannot improve upon it, nor nobly copy; it can only caricature, deface, defile. This is why parody is so lowering, travesty so debasing. Everything can be made a jest of. And the humour is keenest when the highest things are brought low; the sense of contrast, of incongruity, tickles one; this is one of the elements of wit which, to be pure, must be kept within bounds of the most exquisite taste, that it may not degenerate into boisterous or vulgar fun. Attic wit is fine in its outlines as Greek sculpture, sharp cut as the intaglio on a gem; not flying fast and loose, or slipping on and off like a too easy shoe. The spirit of reverence contains the essence of beauty. Perhaps this is why the Bible warns us against levity as not convenient. It is an arm of Satan for lowering our tone of feeling and bringing all things into contempt: equalising all laws, human and divine, by crushing them into the dust and treading them underfoot. Nothing is honoured. No one can be nourished by the fragments of bread that have been flung into the gutter. The flowers are crushed, the silver broidery tarnished, all is made common by the commonest people. Travesty has none of the wholesome uses of irony and satire. Wit, which is the most exquisite zest of life, its very salt, which keeps talk from becoming corrupt and feeble, is turned to sneers and flippancy. The 'esprit moqueur' is a type which does the heart no good. George Eliot, after sad search for living truth, says, 'It is the flippant way in which the most solemn hopes of the noblest humanity are disposed of that disgusts me. It would be better (?) if they could have a false worship, with one generous emotion.' We can all understand her feeling, though we cannot endorse it altogether. In France it is said, 'To ridicule is to kill.' Are we the better for having dead bodies all around us, or dead faiths?

The clear-sighted Jeanne disbelieved in Catherine of Rochelle; this was of course attributed to jealousy of a rival. The more credulous Friar Richard was tempted to belief. His mind was so constituted that spiritual pretensions had a strange charm for him, which this time he did not care to test too closely. There is much hunger for the marvellous in this sort of people. Friar Richard was an over-credulous spiritual director for Jeanne d'Arc; it was rather she who guided him.

Catherine's offer to supply money to pay the army was the easier that the army was dispersed: the men had gone to till the ground. Protracted campaigns were impracticable before the days of standing armies. Catherine did not press for the soldiers to be recalled to their standards, she said it was too cold to pursue the siege of La Charité. In fact, no prophetess could have suited the court better, for she made no exacting demands, which are so tiresome when they come in the shape of duties. Jeanne was not in unison with their light and childish temper. As it has been said of a great employer of labour in modern times (Brassey), 'people seemed to enter into a higher atmosphere when they were in (her) presence.' And they could not bear the rarefied air. The court and she lived in two different worlds of feeling: to their world she was a stranger, their mental language was not hers. In their world she was being well-nigh driven from that sympathy with her neighbour, which is part of our communion with God, into the abstracted asceticism which is so remote from true religion. Her active, healthy physique nurtured in peasant life saved her.

She had sounded the shallows of the court in her austere young gravity, now made more serious by sorrow and by experience of a wide sort. Not long ago all choice and beautiful things had given her delight, even to fine colours, burnished steel, rich stuffs and splendour; for she was 'one of those happily constituted and well-proportioned persons who show forth a certain completeness of nature.' Jeanne had that rare personality which persuades its fellows, and attracts inferiors with reverence and superiors with admiration. But here at court no nature was so great as her own, and now she found little to admire except on looking upwards. Even when not illuminated from above, not actually in the power of immediate revelation, she was never as a lamp untrimmed. Not always carried to the third heaven, she was always prepared to be so uplifted, her imagination exalted with every other sensibility of her nature. Thus keeping her conversation in heaven, her simple nature could not be 'caught in a tangle of sophisticated' demands. She, like other prophets, was master of her own spirit, yet, as Savonarola said, who felt the like experiences, only in the different, perhaps feebler measure of a highly learned man, 'I speak as it is given me to speak—I am not master of the time when I may become the vehicle of knowledge beyond the common lights of man.' Jeanne was always ready to receive revelation, apt to perceive it: quick as light it travelled to her mind. This quicker, livelier divination makes the poet, and in fuller measure, likewise the prophet.

Catherine of Rochelle and Friar Richard more weakly allowed themselves to be ruled by those phantasies which 'govern in the place of thought.'

It has been said of Rienzi, that other character of the middle-ages who rose abnormally and suddenly from obscurity to power,—the rise seemed sudden and preternatural because the processes were hidden, the growth silent,—'Rienzi was no faultless hero of romance. In him lay strong sense, an eloquence and energy that mastered all he approached, an enthusiasm that mastered himself; luxury and abstinence, sternness and susceptibility, devoted patriotism and strong animal spirits.' All this, cast in a feminine mould and with simpler piety, might be applied to Jeanne: if indeed such opposing qualities are not distinctive of all powerful characters in whom the mingling of opposite elements effervesces in action.

In these two examples we see how little difference mere book-learning makes. Rienzi was learned, Jeanne illiterate. The ancient writings, warmed by the living fire of Petrarch, were his scriptures in which he sought the anatomy of power. The Book of God, as seen in Nature, in church teaching, and in the art and architecture of her time, was the lore she sought.

'With the sinking of high human trust, the dignity of life sinks too; we cease to believe in our own better self, since that also is part of the common nature which is degraded in our thought; and all the finer impulses of the soul are dulled.'

Even the ideal, intellectual grace of the court was dimmed and deadened unto her by the puerility of its designs. Not even Alain Chartier, the poet, could now elevate it, nor the gallantries of the courtiers enliven it, nor disarm her austerity. The falsity of it all was only too perceptible. The tinsel still glittered, but she now knew it was not real gold. She had no longer her sunny delight in life, though perhaps her angles were rounded by a higher culture.

Yet, though she could not enjoy their amusements, she neglected none of the social kindnesses. She never refused to do a favour. Many times during this lull in her active career she stood godmother for infants. The boys she was sponsor for were christened Charles, in honour of the king, the girls were named Jehanne.

With music and love-making at court ruled also the newly-invented diversion of cards. These were the three courtly graces of the time. But cards could not have contented Jeanne even as a relaxation. Her mind was not of an order to be satisfied with cards; and, as for relaxation, she only craved work whereby to relax her highly-strung soul; her free, energetic mind disdained the mimic warfare.

The king had failed France; she never said it, she resisted to her death any attacks upon her loyalty, but she knew it. She must now serve France only.

The truce with the Duke of Burgundy, which expired at Christmas, was prorogued to Easter, and instead of Compiègne, which refused to be handed over, Pont-Saint-Maxence was given up in guarantee, to the discontent of Duke Philip. Fighting was still going on in Normandy, and Château Gaillard was taken.

The Armagnacs were at the gates of Paris. On

the 23rd of March, 1430, they were again at St. Denis; on the 25th of April they were established at St. Maur. The wave of movement had begun again; as the sap rose in the trees, so rose ardour among French patriots: Jeanne glowed with hope once more.

'The breadth and grandeur of world history raised her above petty individual cares, mortifications, mischances.' Patriotism regained its predominance. Keep motives single, there lies strength of character. One needs at times to break through the tangle, the warp of life, and seek renewal alone with Nature: to bathe in open spaces of sea and sky. Jeanne felt this, and longed to be under Nature's restoring influence.

The Maid wrote on the 16th of March to reassure Rheims, which dreaded the enemy's revenge, and again on the 28th of March. This last letter is dated from Sully, probably on the eve of her departure, as she left the court in March, according to Perceval de Cagny. Jeanne now, as twice before, took her own resolution. She took no leave of the king, but went forth quietly and alone, and turned her steps towards Lagny-sur-Marne, where they were valiantly fighting, and she might aid them. Doubly orphaned, torn by destiny from her father, bereft of her hopes by her king, she left that treacherous court which only relaxed the tension of soul and nerves; where doubtless she felt she had to combat enemies within more insidious and hard to cope with than an open foe. Doubtless, too, the courtiers rejoiced at her departure, though they blamed her loudly for it. Her presence was a burden to them, now that she knew them in their true colours. No more could the court of our Charles II. have brooked the presence of a puritan. To Milton could not have been given the laurel of court favour. Jeanne was a puritan in that court of *joyeuse science*. She went out from among them, yet still to serve them.

CHAPTER XIV.

THE ROYAL IDOL BROKEN.—THE FOREST OF FONTAINEBLEAU.

'Sans la grâce de Dieu je ne ferais rien,' dit Jeanne. Le juge lui demanda si elle savait qu'elle fût dans la grâce. Elle répondit : ' Si je n'y suis, Dieu veuille m'y mettre; et si j'y suis, Dieu veuille m'y garder.' ('Without the grace of God I could do nothing,' said Jeanne. The judge asked her if she knew she was in grace. She answered, ' If I am not, may God place me therein ; and if I am, may God keep me therein.')

A GENERAL without an army—accompanied most probably by d'Aulon, her squire, as we find him with her at Compiègne, and one of her brothers, as we are told later that two men stayed with her all the time since she left the king, and one of these was her brother, young Pierre du Lys—Jeanne set forth from Sully on her chivalrous enterprise, taking her road towards Lagny-sur-Marne by way of Lorris to Montargis. The loyal Montargis, which, for its unalterable devotion to the national cause, had been freed in perpetuity from all taxes, excepting the gabelle on salt; the citizens having the right to wear a crowned M embroidered on their coats, and the town receiving the name of Montargis-le-Franc, or free. The 'Encyclopædia Britannica,' speaking of Charles as Bedford's 'vigilant enemy,' (!) says Dunois, with a thousand men, had compelled the Earl of Warwick to raise the siege of Montargis.

It is a very countrified town, whose inhabitants do not seem to take life very earnestly. In the Place, an irregular, obtuse-angled triangle, with insignificant low houses built round an accidentally shaped village green, paved as an afterthought, the dog of Montargis is chasing the pigeons, while dark-eyed, flat-capped boys play at quarterstaff with the long clubs of bread they are carrying home for breakfast. It is a flowery place. The pinks are overflowing their pots, and enlarging the boundaries of the beautiful, on the balconies belonging to the tile-floored rooms. The fathers of families are hoeing their back gardens, or busying themselves with the household offices that we English always relegate to women. The kitchen pans are full of carrots and scraped asparagus, the cook is cleaning gudgeons, while monsieur cracks up a cone of sugar, or roasts his coffee in the frying-pan. How thoroughly these good-natured Frenchmen, when they are domestic at all, enjoy their cooking and gardening; and in these country towns the meeting each other at evening church, and perhaps winding up with the unexciting dominoes over a cheerful glass of sugar and water.

The dominoes excepted, perhaps their habits were much the same in Jeanne d'Arc's time. Even then might also have been seen the women in small transparent frilled caps, lace or linen (it was before muslin was invented), washing in the river flowing below those same old wooden-fronted houses, with wooden galleries overhanging the stream, where now they kneel to wash, and chat, and laugh among the flower-pots and the many picturesque bits of out-of-door domestic life which make the less-frequented foreign towns so charming, where these things are not got up to order as part of the scenery.

High up yonder, above the pink feathery tamarisks, is what was once the extensive castle, known as 'Le Berceau des Enfans de France,' because it was used as the royal nursery. Here was formerly to be seen a fresco representing the story of the 'Dog of Montargis;' which was a tale quite recent in Jeanne d'Arc's time, as it was before the eyes of Charles VI. at Paris that the sagacious dog singled out from among a crowd the murderer of his master, indicated the spot in the Forest of Bondy where the corpse was buried, and fought the murderer and compelled him to confess his crime.

All that is left of the castle now is a tower (with traces of a portcullis) in a lofty situation commanding the town, and a few remains of walls surrounding a private house and garden, from whence there is a fine expanse of view over a featureless country.

Within the dark Gothic church, the one with the gurgoyles and flying buttresses, we might well fancy we saw Jeanne, the champion of all these simple-minded folk, her brethren. After looking on, herself unrecognised, at their innocent pursuits, once hers likewise before she was called to the path of glory, and singled out for martyrdom; we can fancy her approaching the dim taper-lighted altar, below the tall light columns and lofty pointed arches of the square-ended apse, to pray for them before fighting for them.

Her horse was rested, she must on now, her people to the northward need her.

Refreshed by her vespers, Jeanne pushed on towards the great forest of Fontainebleau in that 'quiet evening light which dissipates all unrest.' Leaving behind her the fir-fringed line of the Vernisson hills tipped with highly-charged electric clouds, and Souppes among the streams, she rode straight across the broken, irregular ground and partially reclaimed woodland descending into and then rising again across the vale, or rather ravine, of the small river Loing.

It is uneasy riding among these boulders and grey stones, and masses of yellow rock which time has aged to grey, ever cropping out among the hills. The high ground slopes broadly and insensibly off both ways, looking what it is, like the watershed of great rivers. It is now further drained by a canal. Streams meander in the purpling sunset; nightingales flood the air with melody from out the black fringe of firs against the sundown; and beyond the streams a long line of thinly-leafed poplars stands out like a border of black lace 'woven in black distinctness' upon the pale amber sky; then day entirely sinks behind the dark trees above the charcoal-burners' glimmer in the forest by Nemours, called so from the woods (nemora) which formerly surrounded it; and according to the conceit of a modern Dutch poet, translated from his quaint homely jargon, 'The slender sickle of the moon passes through the corn-field of the stars, and now and then one of the severed ears is seen to drop.'

Mingled with the trill of nightingales, the deep voices of dogs were heard baying the moon as Jeanne's small party drew up to rest for the night, under the stars possibly, the falling stars 'darting their artillery forth.' The dogs howling, an omen of death. 'The dog' (the Arabs say) 'can distinguish the awful form of Azrael, the angel of death, hovering over the doomed abode, whereas man's spiritual sight is dull and dim by reason of his sins.' Probably there was no busy bustle of an inn to welcome them; for we do not know whether Nemours would have received them or not: it may have belonged to the enemy, and Jeanne would not have been permitted to venture her person in a town where she might have been made prisoner. They three had ridden about thirty-five miles to-day.

The sun, breaking through dense masses of white-piled cloud, shone out cheerfully next morning; the air was fragrant with the scent of turpentine from the pine-trees, as, leaving to the eastward Thoméry, nestling in its vineyards, the travellers approached the forest of Fontainebleau on the St. Germain and

Franchard side. This is still a wild country (kept artificially so in some measure), though it is now crossed by good straight hunting roads in all directions, and featured hereabout by the large and lofty railway-viaduct of thirty arches over the Loing. At the landmarks, such as fountain-springs, famous trees, or the buttressed ruins of a monastery, toy-sellers with cuckoo-whistles spring out now-a-days upon the traveller, destroying all impression of the sublime, and touts drag him off to the various points of view, such as 'Maria Theresa's belvedere' and the 'Weeping Rock.' One cannot give oneself up unreservedly to the spirit of the place, which even now is only a half-reclaimed chaos.

Jeanne had the forest to herself; only the deer sprang startlingly across the bewildered path, made more confused by gleams of fitful sunshine. It was a fit scene for a struggle with mental anguish, this valley strewn with rocks and ruins. Sad and dispirited, Jeanne moved here like an outcast in a savage, gloomy land, like the land of Nod. Looking back on those days so 'prodigal of happiness,' when she was all in all to king and country, it seemed now as if the fatal charge of sorcery truly branded her brow, and she was a dread to her own party as well as a curse to the foe. There were few, very few to return her love and services with any gentle caress, and those few were the most likely to die by her side.

> 'I've heard of hearts unkind; kind deeds
>   With coldness still returning.
>   Alas! the gratitude of man
>   Has oftener left me mourning.'

X

Her check at La Charité, magnified to a phantom of failure through the mist of her own sensitiveness, was only to be retrieved by a new and more difficult attempt upon Paris. The wind music moaned through the tree stems, thrillingly, like gigantic reed-stops in a mighty organ. Among the sun blotches on the shaded forest, the great 'Pharamond' tree, a sturdy young giant in Jeanne's time, stood like a luminous sky-reaching line, surrounded by the sinuous stems of tall beeches seeking and struggling up to the light; the scented woods all vigorous in their mounting sap; the young green sprays pushing off the old shrivelled leaves. Squirrels skim from branch to branch, like shooting stars in the curve of their smooth, swift-gliding movement; ground game and feathered game peep out shyly from among the junipers, and vermin creep tortuously among the stones, while Jeanne waits, dreamily resting until her companions can discover their further way. Near where a ferruginous rill trickles from a rock set in golden genista, she gazes over the broad view of the Valley of the Solle. They had to complete another ride of thirty-five miles before they could reach Melun, and must not lose themselves in the recesses of the forest. The opportunity of asking the way of a charcoal-burner or chance forester must not be missed.

The light bursting forth in noontide strength among the tangled shadows of the stems made the scene more dazzling and difficult to comprehend than in the greyness chased away. The expanse of what is now called the Valley of William Tell must then have been a pathless labyrinth. One now climbs by a gentle ascent the ravine, half hidden by broken foregrounds. Higher up, the path joins another coming from Belle-Croix. Here one should turn to the right, following the rocky crests which command a range of ravines on the left. Advancing by the line of a rampart of rocks bristling on the right, one arrives at the Belvedere of Jeanne d'Arc, the highest point, giving a fine view over the Rocher St. Germain and the Valley of the Solle. This little-known spot, deeply sequestered in the wildest part of the forest, holds the only remaining tradition of the passage of the heroine. The winding path descends among masses of sandstone, clumps of beeches and aged junipers; the fine oak of King Robert, which is a landmark in the direction of the gorges of Franchard and Apremont, showing the direction to take in the dædalus of ravines, hills, heaps of sandstone, and coppices by those who seek this spot, named after the Maid of Orleans, which lies, least visited of any, in the very heart of the forest. Jeanne must have crossed the forest in this journey by striking across from Uri, which is on the Orleans road to Fontainebleau, passing by La Croix de Franchard, La Croix du Grand Veneur, Mont St. Père, La Croix du Beau Filleul, La Croix de la Table du Grand Maître, La Croix des Becassières, and the Plaine and Bois de la Rochette.

It was at the Croix du Grand Veneur that Henri IV. is said to have met the spectral black huntsman who haunts the forest, and who, as the legend goes, predicted the king's death shortly before his assassination by Ravaillac.

Lightning playing among the broken grandeur of these wastes gives an indescribably solemn effect. So wide a horizon illumined by flashes, revealing the destruction that is even now going on among the trees, makes it seem as if the whole wilderness had been thrown into chaos by the storm, as the lurid light, bursting forth with fierce cleaving strength, displays a shattered and a ruined world. It has a more bewildering character than a storm at sea, from the vivid revelations of blackness and contorted shapes cut dazzlingly against the momentary light. The wild birds' hooting has replaced the nightingales, the deer run tremblingly to covert, the vermin and small game to their nooks and holes; travellers seek the most frequented path as dusk closes in, for to be entangled in such a forest at night, with a storm devastating the country round, is a danger to be shunned even by the bravest warriors.

It would have been probably as evening closed on her second day's journey that Jeanne and her companions cast about them for a shelter for the night. They may have sought and found it within the town, then a hamlet, of Fontainebleau, where there was a small royal hunting castle, built in 1162 by Louis VII.; but more likely they took shelter in the monastery, whose wall alone remains.

We have no means of knowing certainly where Jeanne d'Arc halted in this unrecorded journey, but, as it is by the most direct route a ride of over seventy miles from Sully to Melun, she could not have performed it in less than two days' hard riding; and, as the country is unusually broken and difficult, she most likely found two resting-places before reaching Melun on the third day's journey.

From Sully to Montargis is twenty-four miles; from Montargis to Nemours nineteen miles; Nemours to the Belvedere of Jeanne d'Arc about seventeen; thence to Melun about ten miles. These distances are only approximately given by the modern roads, which are still not direct from point to point. At that time, of course, the paths must have been more circuitous.

The morning light again showed the scene differently. The Fontaine de Belle Eau sparkled freshly for Jeanne's morning draught (she drank nothing but water) before setting out on her ten miles' ride among the green-tasselled firs and yellow genista of the Valley of the Solle, and by the Seine winding through the woods at Bois-le-Roy, where charcoal-burners were busy at their work, and oxen were drawing loads of faggots and provisions into Melun. From far beyond where the Seine winds round under the hill-side, which casts the reflection of its undulating woods into the water, the twin towers of the town are visible. Now-a-days there is a tall spire at Melun, and a second double tower: but these Jeanne saw not.

Her object was to go to Lagny, where her friends were fighting, but she may have felt she helped the cause best by her efforts at Melun, creating a diversion in their favour, as we hear from out their camp, 'Good news arrived from Yonne and Seine. Sens "turned French," Melun revolted. Paris even felt an upstirring;' and we know from general history that at the instigation of Jeanne d'Arc the people of Melun under her leadership rose against the English and constrained them to take refuge in the castle, which was forced to capitulate after twelve days of siege.

We also know she was at Melun in the Easter week, about the 15th of April, 1430, and the truce would expire on the 17th of April, when she could legitimately begin to fight the Burgundians at Lagny. With the English there was no truce, so we are at liberty to suppose that the siege of Melun Castle was before this.

Jeanne entered Melun in the teeth of the English garrison. She had confidence in the courage of its inhabitants, who had proved themselves valiant ten years before.

In 1420, Melun, which was enclosed within strong walls, defended itself with admirable energy against the King of England, Henry V., and the Duke of Burgundy, his ally. 'Les compaignons du dedans,' says an old monkish historian, 'tiroient de grand couraige de canon et d'arbalestes, et plusieurs en tuoient. Et entre les aultres, y avoit un compaignon qu'on disoit estre réligieux de l'ordre de Sainct Augustin, donc

Simon, moyne de Jard, près Melun, très-bon arbalestrier, auquel on fit bailler une très-bonne et très-forte arbaleste. Et quand les Anglois et les Bourguignons venoient près des fossés, et qu'il les pouvait apercevoir, il ne failloit point à les tuer, et dict-on que lui tout seul, il tua bien soixante hommes d'armes sans les aultres. ('The companions inside fired cannon and crossbow with great courage, and killed several. Among the rest there was a companion that they said was a monk of the order of St. Augustin, Father Simon, monk of Jard, near Melun, a very good crossbowman, to whom they gave a very good and very strong crossbow. And when the English and the Burgundians came near the moats, and he could see them, he never failed to kill them, and they say that he alone killed fully sixty men-at-arms without the others.') The town only surrendered when there remained not a horse, nor a dog, nor a cat to eat. The monk was beheaded after the capitulation. Such a brave town deserved succour when it desired to free itself from the foreign rule, which was exercised with great severity: and this was a piece of work after Jeanne's own heart. She recovered the good town; in memory of which, in Saint Aspais, the lofty principal church of Melun, built in the fifteenth century, there is on the exterior of the chevet a bronze medallion, by Chapu, mounted in 1872, representing 'Jeanne d'Arc, deliverer of Melun, 1430.' It has been said of Mahomet that he owed his wonderful success at least as much to his intense nationality as to any other cause, whether natural or supernatural. It was the same with Jeanne d'Arc, she represented the feeling of the nation.

The restored church of Notre Dame, which dates from the tenth century, has two fine romanesque towers; one leaves this to the right in the island before crossing the principal arm of the river.

In Jeanne's time many Roman remains were visible at Melun. Some have recently been exhumed while making alterations and excavations in the Place of Notre Dame in 1864; they are chiefly fragments of sculpture, bas-reliefs, and a statuette and inscriptions of the time of Drusus Germanicus, brother of Tiberius. Of Cæsar's tower, sole vestige of the dwelling of the Frankish kings of France, only the foundation remains. The tower was destroyed in the eighteenth century.

It was while standing on the towers of Melun, looking beyond the orchards and the lines of trees by the roads which here lead the eye so far into the distance, and away to the dense woods on the ascent to the table land of La Brie, that Jeanne hearkened while her Voices told her she would be taken prisoner before St. John's Day, 24th of June. This they repeated to her every day. They announced her captivity as a thing to which she must submit, and Jeanne, though she felt death would be preferable, went on without hesitation to the accomplishment of her work. She had passed out of despondency to rekindled enthusiasm.

It was now April. The fresh spring air played about her: she was again among earnest people and not among triflers, such as those courtiers at Bourges, who had made the long winter evenings seem so terribly long by playing at cards all through them. She was roused and invigorated by the remembrance that she had a work to do, and excited rather than daunted by the near expectation of death for a noble cause.

Here upon the towers of Melun, surrounded by the music of the bells, her Voices spoke more and more clearly to her ear: and who shall say that this choice spirit did not apprehend more clearly than the duller world the messages from Heaven always ringing round us?

CHAPTER XV.

COMPIÈGNE.

'Quand j'aurai fait ce pourquoi je suis envoyée de par Dieu, je prendrai l'habit de femme.' ('When I shall have done that for which I have been sent by God, I will put on woman's dress.')
Jeanne d'Arc to her jailers.

MELUN safe, the Maid crossed the high land of Brie and pushed on to Lagny-sur-Marne, at about thirty miles distance. Here she led off by a brilliant action against some marauders, said to be English, but, as they rode under the leadership of a gentleman named Franquet d'Arras, this is very doubtful. Lagny, which had fought bravely, was relieved and made safe, and the Maid pushed on to join her friends at Senlis.

At Lagny-sur-Marne there are now vast chocolate works and a model village. The colony comprises model artisans' dwellings, schools, co-operative stores, savings' banks, reading-rooms, and other social experiments in working order; all well worth seeing.

The news of the return of the Maid to the scene of action rang through Paris, rousing the superstitious terror of the enemy. Even Bedford was alarmed, and wrote a 'proclamation against the tardy captains and soldiers, terrified by the enchantments of the Pucelle.'

The castle of Borenglise, between Compiègne and Ressons, seems to have been her headquarters at this time, as we find her often moving between Compiègne, Senlis, and other towns, to fall upon the Duke of Burgundy, who was now besieging Choisy-sur-Aisne. The leaders were delighted at her arrival, for she was worth a legion to them, and they were all of them her personal friends. Their object now was to succour Choisy. Jeanne, Saintrailles, and others attempted without success to force the passage of the Oise at Pont l'Évêque, hoping by the capture of this place to cut off the Burgundian supplies.

Monstrelet the Burgundian is the only writer of the time who speaks of the Compiègne expedition and the fruitless attack on Pont l'Évêque, a town situated at less than a mile (six hundred toises) to the south of Noyon, which was defended by a detachment of the English army. Jeanne, Chabanne, Saintrailles, and others came with two thousand men from Compiègne to attack the English. The Burgundians, running up for the defence of their allies, placed the French between two fires, and they had to fall back upon Compiègne.

They remounted the Aisne purposing to cross it at Soissons; but, the traitor Bourmel refusing them admittance within the gates of Soissons, they were compelled to take a retrograde circuit towards Compiègne, and the force gathered to rescue Choisy dispersed. Jeanne returned afflicted to Compiègne. This was very soon after the 17th of April, for the duke laid siege to Choisy-sur-Aisne immediately on the conclusion of the truce, in order to clear his path for the capture of Compiègne.

Paris, La Charité, and Pont l'Évêque were Jeanne's three failures; against which we have to place the fact that she took part in more than twenty battles, fights, sieges, or raising of sieges, without speaking of her travels. Berriat St. Prix calculates that in fifteen months she travelled over more than nine hundred leagues as the crow flies, and, allowing for obstacles, twelve or thirteen hundred leagues, in the service of the king. After it had been revealed to her at Melun that she would be taken prisoner, she ceased to act further on her own responsibility, but referred nearly everything in the war to the will of the captains. Although she was no longer acting under the direct guidance of her Voices, her presence with the army was a great moral support. She represented, only with deeper loyalty, the heart of all independent France in her time; independent either in thought or in geographical situation. Dunois and La Hire were faithful to the kingdom, Jeanne to the king. It was hard to them to see their life's work slighted, the kingdom so gaily lost. A tradition preserved in that country says that Jeanne made a pilgrimage to the church of Élaincourt St. Catherine, one of her patron saints, about the end of April, 1430. This is a romanesque church of the twelfth century.

Wallon attributes to near this date the story of Jeanne being in the church of St. Jacques at Compiègne, and standing near a pillar of the church, where many persons and children were assembled to see her. She addressed them, 'My children and dear friends, I tell you that I have been betrayed and sold, and shall soon be delivered up to death. Thus I beseech you to pray for me, for never more shall I have power to serve the king and realm of France.'

But we have no authority for any of the legends of this time, save tradition and the little book published early in the sixteenth century called the 'Mirouer des Femmes vertueuses.' Monstrelet, the only reliable historian, is too decidedly Jeanne's enemy for us to hear from him more than the barest facts, and these are coloured by his animosity. The legend seems to be a confused account of something that really happened. One can only draw from it the inference that she was much beloved.

Compiègne was the key of the kingdom on the Burgundian side, and Jeanne fully understood its value. On the 13th of May the Maid arrived at the town, and redoubled the ardour and confidence of the inhabitants by her presence. She did not shut herself up in the town, but multiplied herself, in order to revive the zeal of those who still upheld the cause of the king. She was at Crépy on the 23rd of May, whither she went to seek more men, whom she hastened to bring to Compiègne, She gathered volunteers the more anxiously that at Crépy she heard that the Duke of Burgundy and the Earl of Arundel were already come to sit down before Compiègne.

By midnight she had assembled from three to four hundred men-at-arms, and, though they told her these were very few to cross the enemy's camp, 'We are enough,' she said. 'I will go to see my good friends of Compiègne.' She rode off with them at once. At sunrise on the 24th of May she entered the town without loss or harm.

The 'Encyclopædia Britannica' (1856) says: 'The Maid threw herself into Compiègne contrary to the wishes of the governor, who desired not the company of one whose authority would be greater than his own:' but this has been shown to be a mistaken opinion.

The Maid took the sacrament in the church of St. Jacques on the 24th of May, 1430. When I was at Compiègne on last May 24th, the tall fir-trees groved round the altar of the Madonna smelt very sweet, and the steps and the whole altar elevation were a mass of white flowers. It was a beautiful sight. But the renaissance decorations on the marble facing and the modern wainscoting all over the church give it a very different aspect from what it had in Charles VII.'s reign. In the roof of the choir of St. Jacques the groined arches meet in a central starry boss, as they do in Amiens cathedral. The western tower was built for a much larger church, or else this one was never extended the full length of its plan. One sees the spring of the arches that were to have been built. The present west front is of the sixteenth century. The choir is of the thirteenth century. A double narrow triforium gallery runs round above and before the chapels of the apse, which are of the fifteenth century. In the fifth side altar to the right, on entering from the west door, a painted window represents Jeanne d'Arc receiving the sacrament on the 24th of May, 1430. Her saints, the Voices, appear above her, her standard waves in the background; she is clad in complete steel. It was in this chapel that she received the sacrament on the morning of the fight.

There is a bronze statue of the Maid in front of the picturesque Hotel de Ville, with the inscription, 'JE YRAY VOIR MES BONS AMIS DE COMPIEGNE, 1430.'

The town of Compiègne, itself defended on the Burgundian frontier by the Oise, commands the river and the valley which extends on the opposite side in low water-meadows about three-quarters of a mile broad, behind which a broken wall of hills rises on the borders of Picardy. The hills rise slightly on both sides of the river.

The Maid left the town about five in the evening to assist in dislodging the enemy from their positions. The town was far from being invested, the enemy only holding the opposite bank of the river. The Duke of Burgundy was at Coudun on the Aronde, a league away from Compiègne to the north; Jean de Luxembourg was somewhat nearer, at Clairoix, on the confluence of the Aronde and Oise. Baudon de Noyelle commanded a detached corps at Margny, a suburban village opposite Compiègne, at the issue of the road from the bridge. The English were encamped at Venette on the west.

The Maid's plan was to take the village of Margny, thence to pursue the dislodged Burgundians to Clairoix, where she hoped to be victorious, and then return to attack the English at Venette. She reckoned on the people of Compiègne stopping the English at the road beyond the bridge, in case of their falling upon her rear.

The plan was carried out at first as she intended. She fell upon Jean de Luxembourg, who was at Margny taking observations. He was surprised with the rest, and driven back on Clairoix, but, succours coming up, the battle was disputed, and the result delayed. The English moved forward to profit by the delay, but their movement was foreseen, and the archers of Compiègne were so disposed as to render their passage of the road difficult. Nevertheless, their movement alarmed the rear rank of the Maid's force. They feared to have their return cut off, and, flying towards the shelter of the town, they met with the mischance they dreaded. The English, encouraged by their flight, threw themselves more eagerly upon the road, and were there protected by the flying soldiers themselves, as their friends within Compiègne were afraid of striking them as well as the English; and, on the other hand, the Burgundians fought still more strenuously against those who remained with the Maid, who was now wounded in defence of Compiègne. Already her troops began to fall back, and insisted upon her regaining the town. They turned and fled in spite of her endeavours, and she could only cover their retreat. Friend and foe crowded together disputing the passage of the bridge, and Flavy, the governor of Compiègne, fearing the enemy might thus enter the town, raised the drawbridge and shut the gate, leaving the Maid outside. Quicherat says: 'She was pushed, with her friends, into the angle formed by the side of the boulevard and the slope of the causeway.' She was called upon by five or six men to yield herself prisoner and to give her parole. She refused to do this to the common men, and fought on until dragged from her horse by the long skirt of her tunic. An archer pulled her violently 'par sa huque (casaque) de drap d'or vermeil.' She loved the graces and elegancies of womanhood, and they proved a snare to her.

The archer was a man belonging to one of Jean de Luxembourg's knights. Her brother Pierre du Lys, D'Aulon, her squire, and Pothon de Saintrailles, who never left her, were captured at the same time. The spot of her capture, marked by the ruined tower called Tour de la Pucelle, in the Rue du Vieux Pont, is visible on the right hand in entering the town from the railway.

Thus was the Maid taken at the gates of Compiègne, abandoned by those whom she came to succour, where without her aid the governor must have succumbed. Had he attempted an energetic sortie he might have relieved the bridge and saved the Maid, who was worth a province to the French. People have cried out upon his treachery in thus abandoning her; it is his want of courage and presence of mind that they should blame; the half-heartedness of which those in highest places set the enervating example. The 'Mirouer des Femmes vertueuses' makes a long story of Flavy's purposely shutting her out of Compiègne, but it is little credible. William Caxton, born 1412, the same year as Jeanne d'Arc, prints the following concerning her: 'This mayde rode lyke a man, & was a valyaunt capitayn among them, & toke upon her many grete enterprises. After many grete featcs she was taken, & many other capitayns with her, & judged by the lawe to be brent. The othere capitayns were put to raunson, & entreated as men of warre ben accustomed.'

The 24th of May, the eve of Ascension, was that which saw her tide of fortune turn. A year, as she had foretold, was her comet path from Ascension at Orleans till now. The next 24th of May saw her condemnation to death at Rouen. Thus says Lenglet de Fresnoy, 'She, ennobled, could not surrender to the archer, but to the gentleman, le Bâtard de Vandomme. Her presence of mind pointed this out to her.'

Jeanne is supposed to have predicted her

capture, but she says plainly that, had she known she would have been taken, she would not have left Compiègne that day: and this is in accordance with her habitual good sense. She affirmed that she knew she should be captured before St. John's Day, but she knew not when or where. She was prepared for captivity and death; but she could never have believed that her friends would allow her to be sold to her enemies, and put to death without raising arm or word in her defence.

Her history while a prisoner has been told by Monstrelet, chronicler of the Burgundian faction, who was present with the Duke of Burgundy when Jeanne was taken prisoner. She was constantly watched by enemies eager to wrest every word or act to her disadvantage, to be used against her at her trial: a circumstance which proves that her conduct during the year of her imprisonment was well-nigh perfect, as good and pure as her whole life was; this year, upon her enemies' own showing, was the crowning beauty of her career. It is this which makes her looked upon as a saint and martyr. She was taken at first to the camp at Margny, and after three or four days passed in the camp, Jean de Luxembourg, from fear of rescue in keeping her so close to the besieged town, sent her to his castle at Beaulieu, near Noyon on the Vorse. She was strongly escorted, as she refused to give her word that she would not attempt to escape, holding herself always in readiness to continue her work which was thus interrupted. Her route to

Beaulieu was most probably by the right bank of the Oise to Noyon.

At Beaulieu she was parted from her faithful friend and squire, Jean d'Aulon, whose deposition in her favour is couched in terms of deepest respect and admiration.

Lebrun de Charmettes says d'Aulon had ceased to accompany her some short time after St. Pierre-le-Moustier, so that he was not with her at Fontainebleau and Lagny. I cannot find his authority for this, and it appears certain from all evidence that d'Aulon accompanied her from Sully to Compiègne. I know it is difficult to harmonise all the old historians' statements: one can only do it by dates and a good map; but I do not find one of the later historians infallible. Lenglet de Fresnoy places Jeanne's imprisonment of four months at Le Crotoy as taking place before she was taken to Beaurevoir, which is manifestly absurd, and only to be accounted for by supposing he accidentally wrote Le Crotoy for Beaulieu. Even the careful and admirable Quicherat in one place says St. Pierre-le-Moustier was taken in December, 1429, which cannot be reconciled with his other dates, and can only be explained as a slip of the pen. The lesser writers abound in mistakes. I trust I have not as often laid myself open to the same charge.

Jeanne dwelt a prisoner at Beaulieu for three months, from the end of May to August, Compiègne holding out all the while. Meanwhile whose prize was Jeanne d'Arc?

She had been taken in the diocese of Beauvais. Pierre Cauchon, the Count-bishop, came on the 14th of July to the camp near Compiègne to demand her of the Duke of Burgundy as his prisoner. The bishop, in the name of the English, offered ten thousand francs of gold for her: the price at which, according to French custom, the king had the right to ransom to himself any prisoner, even of the blood royal. The money was raised in Normandy and in the conquered provinces, and eventually paid as ten thousand livres tournois; 61,125 fcs. 69cs. of our time (£2, 445 7d. English), a large sum in the value of that period. The French had eventually to pay the money that England offered. They had better have supported Jeanne.

She said at her trial that her brothers had charge of her property, her horses, and (she believed) her sword, and effects to the value of ten or twelve thousand crowns; she adds, 'And this is not a large sum to carry on the war.' ('Ce n'est pas grand trésor à mener la guerre.') The money belonged to the king, she said. Her brothers held it in deposit. Had she possessed much money, she would have had more power, and she might have ransomed herself. When asked if the king had given her other wealth than the horse she rode when taken prisoner, she replied she had never asked anything of the king except good arms, good horses, and money to pay the people where she lodged.

At Orleans, Blois, Tours, etc., they ordered public prayers and processions for her deliverance, but Charles, King of France, offered nothing for her.

The Archbishop of Rheims, in writing to his episcopal town announcing her capture, calls it a judgment upon her because she would not take advice, but did everything according to her own pleasure. He wrote of how a young 'pastour' from the mountains had come to offer the same promises to the king as Jeanne had done, and told them that God had suffered Jeanne to be taken because she was puffed up with pride and loved rich clothing, etc. This was convenient and comfortable doctrine to those who did not wish to be further troubled with Jeanne d'Arc, nor by their own conscience. It seems to have silenced public opinion.

Jeanne very nearly escaped from Beaulieu. She was already outside the tower, and, to make her flight more secure, she was just locking her jailers inside, when the warder perceived and recaptured her. The Lord of Luxembourg, alarmed, took her to his castle of Beaurevoir, near Cambrai, where it would be safer to keep her than so near the scene of action. Leaving the neighbourhood of Noyon, formerly the residence of Charlemagne and Hugh Capet, with its exquisite cathedral, whose two tall towers were alone visible to Jeanne, the troop with their prisoner had the choice of two roads; either the one by Guiscard, thence crossing the ridge which divides the basin of the Seine from that of the Somme, and arriving at Ham, which is twelve miles from Guiscard. (The castle of Ham was not built until forty years later, that strong, dreary donjon where Napoleon III. was kept for six years a state prisoner.) Leaving Ham in its marshes on the right and the village of Nesle on the left, the road crosses the Somme by the very ford which Henry V. crossed two days before the battle of Agincourt in 1415.

Or else they followed the southern road, by which the distance from Noyon to St. Quentin, which lies on the road to Cambrai, is over forty miles.

In any case, they must have halted at some fortress on the way. The noble castle of Coucy lies most conveniently for such a purpose, causing them no great détour, if indeed they did not take the more southern road which passes directly under the walls. This vast model of a perfect feudal castle, one of the most superb in France, towers above the water-meadows of the Oise, proud as its builder's motto—

  'Roy je ne suis, Prince, ni Comte aussi,
  Je suis le Sire de Coucy.'

Coucy was then a castle of the Duke of Orleans. Saintrailles was governor of it for the duke, who was still a prisoner in England. But Saintrailles was now a prisoner himself, and the castle, being impregnable, was taken by surprise. Not at this time, we may presume; but, even if the little troop did not halt here, the castle could not now have threatened the safety of their passage.

Coucy has the loftiest tower in France, and

four lesser towers. Its proud hall was filled at that time with wonders of painting and sculptures of sacred and historical heroes in white marble, and between the two chimney-pieces was a raised tribune remarkable for the beauty of its sculptures, all the work of one hand. 'If I had not seen it with my own eyes,' says Astezan, 'I could not have believed that leaves and fruits and other minute objects could have been sculptured out of such hard stone.' The painted glass surpassed imagination. 'In one room,' says Astezan, in his piece intituled, 'De varietate fortunæ,' 'are novem mulieres probae: Semiramis, Thomyris, Deïphile, Lampeto, Menalippe, Marpesia, Orithyia, Penthesilea, and Hippolyta, admirably wrought.' The Maid of Orleans was inferior to none of them. 'The kitchen was worthy of Nero. They preserve under the lead roof fish like in a fish-pond.' There were three gradations of prisons (humanes carcer) on the ground-floor for small offences, and for crimes, a frightful cell underground. Most likely Jeanne was imprisoned in none of these, but only strongly guarded in a tower. Coucy is now the ideal ruined castle.

The road, after turning aside to Coucy, follows the sandy flats and shallows by the Somme to near St. Quentin, whose canal now connects the Somme with the Scheldt, as it joins it on the other side with the Seine, the Loire, and the Atlantic Ocean. St. Quentin is built upon a hill, a rarity in this part of the country. The greenish-grey cathedral, with its flying buttresses and high ridges of slate roof, dominates the whole district, itself overtopped by lordly Laon to the south. There is a sweet Memlingesque fresco in a side chapel of the cathedral, the second from the door. Murray calls this one of the finest, boldest, and purest Gothic buildings in this part of France, and says it is less known than it ought to be. St. Quentin is supposed to be nothing but a manufacturing place; but besides the Flemish-Gothic Hotel de Ville, which is delightful, the town is picturesquely situated. It unfortunately lies off the group of favourite Flemish towns, and people do not care to stop here (nor even at Laon, which well deserves a visit, on the longer railway journeys). There are so many places it seems better worth while to know. There is a statue in the town, a female figure with a spinning-wheel, defended by General Faidherbe with his spectacles on. The verse of inscription by Victor Hugo is as flabby as any local poet's heroics, perhaps only worthy of our own street statuary.

From St. Quentin to Busigny is eleven and a half level miles; between Busigny and Cambrai (a town whose chief interest lies in its name, which is cognate with many pleasant ideas) lay the castle of Beaurevoir, in the midst of woods. Little remains of the castle of Beaurevoir beyond the broken stone, carved with the eagle-supported shield of John of Luxembourg, charged with the two-tailed rampant lion, that forms the lintel of a door. Here resided the wife and aunt of this lord of Luxembourg, who, the younger son of a noble family, had been chosen for her heir by his aunt, the Countess of St. Pol and Ligny. These ladies were very kind to Jeanne, who won the love of all good women. The old Countess of Ligny implored her nephew not to sully by an ineffaceable stain the imperial and royal shield of Luxembourg, by delivering up the Maid of Orleans to her enemies. It was too late; he had already sold the Pucelle for a royal ransom.

She was confined in a very lofty donjon for safety, a high tower girdled by space, in which towns lay as misty islands, and in the ocean of flat country round her Jeanne must have yearned for her hills and sparkling floods of Lorraine, as moon after moon arose and shone in silver calm on this unbroken expanse. She was kindly and respectfully treated, according to the rank she had acquired, and not as a mere peasant; but she refused the women's clothes that were offered her, saying she had not yet leave from the Lord to wear them; though were she permitted to resume a woman's dress, which would imply that she renounced her mission, she had rather do so at the request of those ladies than any other ladies in France, her queen alone excepted. But her work was not yet done. Nor was it by herself, but she had roused the spirit of France, and the deliverance from a foreign yoke would be achieved in time, even though she were 'crushed by the ponderous machinery which herself had put in motion.'

Doubtless she, who said no one could teach her anything in spinning or in sewing, worked with her needle with the ladies of the castle—at embroidery, perhaps, as she had during the last fifteen months learned many of the habits of noble ladies, and she had not much clothing to make for herself. She could do these things skilfully, and she liked to do them, but when reproached at her trial for leaving alone women's work and acting like men, she remarked, 'As for women's work, there are enough women besides myself to do it.'

But her heart was far away—away with her friends at Compiègne, still holding out for France. She pined to be with them. She has herself related the spiritual combat between her wishes and her visions, to which she had hitherto been so obedient. Her Voices told her daily that God would help her and Compiègne too in their extremity, but she must be patient. The painful conflict lasted long, and when at last they told her that the town was on the eve of being taken, and the inhabitants put to the sword, she cried, in a transport of grief and reproach, 'How can God let die those good people of Compiègne, who have been so loyal to their lord!' The struggle between faith and knowledge was too strained, and, recommending herself to God, she let herself drop from the top of her tower, only aided in her endeavour to clamber down by the climbing plants that grew there. She fell to the pavement of the court, and they thought her dead; but she had only lost her senses and her memory, and they had to tell her she had leaped from the summit of the tower, which was over sixty feet high. For two or three days she could neither eat nor drink; but her Voices comforted her, reproving her gently for her imprudence, and ordering her to confess her fault and ask God's forgiveness for her impatience; they added, for her consolation, that Compiègne should be relieved before the winter. In a few days she was recovered from her fall.

The lord of Luxembourg, finding such a prisoner difficult to keep safely, delivered her over, notwithstanding his aunt's remonstrances, to the officers of the Duke of Burgundy in November, 1430.

CHAPTER XVI.

THE PRISONER OF LE CROTOY.

'Priez pour moi. Adieu.' ('Pray for me. Farewell.')
Jeanne d'Arc to the ladies of Abbeville.

FROM Beaurevoir Jeanne was taken to Arras, where it would seem she made some little stay and was not very rigorously imprisoned, as at her trial she speaks of a portrait of herself she saw at Arras, painted by a Scot (Escot), or being carried by a Scot, for the story is told both ways. It represented her, fully armed, presenting a letter to the king, kneeling on one knee. She never saw or had done any other 'ymaige or painture' of her likeness.

The three towers of Arras are visible for many miles across the plain of Picardy. This fine city has still quite a Flemish character, with its gable-fronted Gothic houses terminating like those of Ghent in scallops and scrollwork, and supported on open arcades. Picturesque as is the town in many parts, few of its public buildings remain as Jeanne saw them: the Hotel de Ville dates no earlier than 1510; the cathedral is modern renaissance; only a fragment remains of the earlier cathedral, destroyed in the time of Robespierre, born to be a dishonour to the town. The strong castle on the Scarpe, where doubtless Jeanne was confined, for she represented great commercial and political value, is now one of Vauban's fortresses with lofty ramparts masked by tall trees.

From Arras to Le Crotoy the direct route lies by Doullens, a strong fortress town on the Athie, where, nevertheless, we do not hear of her stopping, but her escort rested with her one night at the castle of Drugy, close by the town and abbey of St. Riquier, on the road to Abbeville. Of the town are now to be seen only the ruined towers of the ancient ramparts, and the Fontaine de 'Mise-en-Deuil.' But the abbey of St. Riquier is well-preserved and very splendid. It is one of the historical monuments of France. This splendid flamboyant Gothic church is, however, of the beginning of the sixteenth century; so that Jeanne saw very little of what we see in this abbey. The choir may be of her time, and there are some curious ancient frescoes on the walls of the treasury. The provost, townspeople, and two of the old monks of St. Riquier came to pay Jeanne a visit of respect at Drugy.

Drugy is about six miles east of Abbeville, which it appears they avoided, possibly not wishing to encounter the expression of public feeling which we may imagine to have been very strongly in Jeanne's favour, from the circumstance of the ladies of Abbeville having come to visit her at Le Crotoy. The present farm of

Drugy is built on the site of the castle where Jeanne d'Arc halted on the road from Arras to Le Crotoy. The chapel-like portion of the building, with the pointed roof, is part of the former castle. It contains a vaulted room, in which it is said Jeanne d'Arc was imprisoned. They passed close by the battlefield of Crécy. It is curious that Jeanne should have made such a near acquaintance with the most famous battle-fields of the English in France, those nearest her own time, too : Poitiers, Agincourt, and Crécy, while all the traditions of the fights were still hovering warm about the localities. Of course the objects of interest would have been pointed out to her in taunt and triumph, if not otherwise, or in mere curiosity to see how she would like the recital. She would naturally have felt deep interest in these scenes patriotically, if not professionally, for arms were her profession ; she too had been a soldier.

Perhaps, although a prisoner, she was yet among sympathisers in this journey, for her escort, though Burgundians, were yet Frenchmen, whose homes were not so very far from hers ; therefore they may have felt some sparks of national jealousy against the victorious foreigner, as she was only finally given up to the English on reaching Le Crotoy about the 21st of November. According to local traditions, says Henri Martin, she received lively expressions of sympathy from the populations of Ponthieu.

The woods which remain here now are part of

the renowned forest of Crécy. These are a
change from the soothing monotony of the scenery from Arras to Drugy, a landscape of a gauzy,
shimmering sort, a symphony in green and grey-
ish white, reminding one of the best French
etchings, white sky, white water written on by
rushes and branches, not painted with flowers
nor bathed in blue: a sombre scene laid in a
minor key, not rich, nor young, nor smiling:
with distance purpled down by memory's sad
sweetness, all full of easily-read and sympathetic
poetry; but few people and not much wealth of
cattle; perhaps one goat to be seen browsing on
the rough ridge of a common. On the direct
road to Crotoy, at about two leagues from Crécy,
is Rue, on the river Maie, where we find another
certain trace of the passage of Jeanne d'Arc.
She must have passed through this small place,
a station on the Boulogne railway, which Murray
calls 'a poor and hitherto out-of-the-way town,
with an old church.' It is near the ford of
Blachetaque, where Edward III. crossed the
Somme with his army before the battle of
Crécy. Rue is scarcely more than a village,
yet it boasts a pretty Hotel de Ville, with four
round turrets adorned with spires and pinnacles,
all of an early period, and its church is one of the
curious old 'Monuments Historiques,' that they
preserve with so much care in France. This
chapelle du St. Esprit dates from the thirteenth
century, with additions in the fifteenth and sixteenth centuries.

As the church at Rue was a famous pilgrimage, Jeanne's captors probably halted here, the more especially as it lies about midway between Drugy and Le Crotoy, and they may have let her visit the chapel of the famous crucifix, which floated here from Jerusalem (?) ! on the first Sunday in August, 1109, when Rue was much more of a seaport than it was even in Jeanne d'Arc's time, as it stood on the tidal waters of the Maie, which came up much higher than they flow now. The Maie opens out into the embouchere of the Somme at St. Firmin.

Though Louis XI. and Isabel de Portugal had not yet enriched the chapel, it was even then a sumptuous place of worship for so small a town.. The legend of the miraculous cross is painted on the walls; the pierced screen to the chapel is elegant, and the vaulting very fine and rich. The stalls of the church, adjoining the shrine-like chapel, are of fine old carving and the exterior façade is elaborately enriched. The chapel is now only used for the neuvaines of Pentecost.

It is a good four miles from Rue to Le Crotoy, on the Somme, where Jeanne was being taken, on a white, winding road, with a blue level distance. The irregular lines of trees are bent back with the sea-wind, for it is a bleak country. This journey gave Jeanne her first sight of the sea in its grey, gloomy November aspect, cold and cruel as the English over yonder. She arrived about the 21st of November at Le Crotoy, and was imprisoned within the castle, which no longer

z

exists, but which formerly, with its heavy mass and frowning aspect, presented, we are told, great resemblance to the Bastille at Paris. The castle of Le Crotoy, according to an old drawing, was an oblong, battlemented fortress with round towers at the four corners, mounted on a fortified pedestal with round bastions guarded by cannons. Here Jeanne's friend, the Duke of Alençon, had formerly been kept prisoner. This old castle has entirely vanished, melted, they say, in the sand of the sea; but the name Rue de la Tour indicates its position.

The church is plain and strong like a fortress, with a strong tower heavily buttressed, and having long stone shoots to carry off the rain. The body of the church is modern, of rubble-work rough-cast with brick dressings; but there are elsewhere, and in its immediate neighbourhood, remains of walls built of pebbles with brick-string courses. The church stands on the rising ground at the further verge of the town, or rather village, of Le Crotoy. (It is a town because it has a mayor, but it looks like a village.)

Beyond the town lies a long stretch of sandy coast.

The view from the shingly beach is a curious scene of mingled sands and river channels, which are crossed on foot at low tide, with the assistance of two ferries across the two larger streams, by those who wish to reach St. Valéry, nestling among the wooded hills on the opposite side of the Somme.

Down by the port, where the boats are drawn up, is a bronze statue of Jeanne d'Arc in peasant's dress with bare arms, gazing sadly across the Somme towards St. Valéry; an image full of a noble melancholy, more touching than many a more famous statue. It was erected by the Maire du Crotoy in 1881.

The inscription runs thus: 'A Jeanne d'Arc. A cette fille du peuple, qui, pleine de foi dans les destinées de la France quand tous désespéraient, délivra notre patrie en laissant un nom sans égal dans l'histoire.

'Ici la libératrice de la France, abandonnée par ceux qu'elle avait sauvés est restée plusieurs mois prisonnière avant d'être conduite à Rouen où s'acheva son martyre.

'Elle aima tant la France; souvenons-nous toujours, Français, que la patrie chez nous est née du cœur d'une femme, de sa tendresse et de ses larmes, du sang qu'elle à donné pour nous.'*

The idea that Jeanne passed some months at Le Crotoy seems incorrect, as the surest data we possess name the time of her arrival here as the 21st of November, and state that she left here for

---

* 'To Joan of Arc. To this daughter of the people, who, full of faith in the destinies of France when all despaired, delivered our country while leaving a name unequalled in history.

'Here the liberator of France, abandoned by those she had saved, stayed several months prisoner before being conducted to Rouen, where her martyrdom was completed.

'She loved France so much; may we French always remember that our country is born from the heart of a woman, from her enderness and from her tears, from the blood which she shed for us.'

Rouen the second fortnight in December. Her trial began January 9th, 1431, three days after her nineteenth birthday.

But Jeanne spent some weeks here, a peaceful time, a rest for her, though sad, yet calm; beautified, like the whole of her life, with lovely thoughts. She received great consolation from her Voices: as when examined on this subject at the trial, and especially concerning her visions of St. Michael, she says, 'I never saw him often, and I have not seen him at all since I left the castle of Crotoy.' But the female Voices often visited her there and comforted her.

Her captivity was not rigorous: she was allowed to go to church and to confession. A priest from Amiens cathedral, who was staying in the castle, administered the communion to her and heard her in confession. Five ladies of Abbeville, who came down in a boat to see the heroine and bring her the sympathy of their town, were admitted to visit her. She thanked these noble visitors, and kissed them affectionately, recommending herself to their prayers as she said, 'A Dieu.' Never again was she to hear human words of love and sympathy; never again on this side of the resurrection. Wallon bears witness to the kindness felt for her by women. That among all the injuries to which she was subjected, not one came from women. From them instances of admiration alone are cited, and esteem for her whom they justly felt caused no dishonour to their sex by the dress which so scandalised the modesty of men: a most absurd mock-modesty, when the circumstances of her life are considered.

Besides these sources of comfort to the heart, she was strengthened in her faith. The glad news had pierced her prison that before St. Martin (October 24th) Compiègne was succoured, according to the promise of her Voices. 'Jeanne's spirit had led her friends of Compiègne to victory,' says Henri Martin.

Perhaps she was allowed to walk, under guard of course, in the neighbouring roads and fields. The country is pleasant hereabout.

I was much reminded of Jeanne's shepherd life in Lorraine when, in returning from a ramble by the fields of barley in blossom, three little lambs scampered after me bleating. By-and-by a tall, strong girl came to untether her cow; the lambs knew her, and ran gladly after her, leaving off their doubtful, imploring gaze on me. Here they were certain of a friend, as she fondled them with her hand before striking in the tethering peg again with her heavy mallet. Jeanne the prisoner had once been just like this girl.

It was not the season for lambs while Jeanne was at Le Crotoy, but the ways and works of these simple people must often have carried her back, far back into that peaceful past, so far off in seeming, so little while ago in reality, blotting out the brilliant scenes of her glory, and bringing before her her peasant life once more, her mother, father, kind uncle Durand Laxart, and her home.

How sweet the views are hereabout. The wet

sands, lustrous with the sheeny reflection of the sun, the crumpled elms and oaks, the history of their battle with the wind told by every writhing limb, the golden grass before that aërial blue distance of far-off shores and low peninsulas, so out of the world, so remote from any book-learnt geography, dotted with amphibious hamlets, only to be reached barefoot twice in the twenty-four hours.

A stranger marvels how it is possible to cross even to St. Valéry, which is some miles nearer, the river seems to wind so among the sands. One hears of a ferry, and one expects the tide to rise that boats may cross the waste of ribbed sands intersected by water channels to St. Valéry, set in the woods opposite.

Jeanne could hear its bells as their music floated over the waters, which then came higher up than now : only at neap-tide then could the river have presented its now peculiar appearance.

The mystery of the passage is solved on hearing one has to walk across barefoot to St. Valéry. Every man (comme-il-faut) has a pair of high boots, coming half-way up the thigh, in which he can wade conveniently. Persons of inferior position carry a net in which they put their shoes, and, it may be, stockings. It is a refreshing novelty in travel to cross these sands barefoot, by turns wading in pretty deep water, and walking over sands sometimes ribbed and firm, and hard to the feet, sometimes softer and studded with delicate shells, lilac, pink, or brimstone-coloured bivalves opening like butterflies, and crabs at play in the little channels of the tide.

The manners of the people are simple and primitive as those of children. Crossing the river barefoot is taken as a matter of course. They would never themselves think of walking (or getting somehow) to Rue and going round to St. Valéry by train.

There is first a narrow ferry, then, about a mile off, (for the estuary is upwards of a mile wide) there is another ferry across the main stream of the Somme, whence once sailed the fleet of William of Normandy bound for the conquest of England. This tradition was of course well-known to Jeanne d'Arc.

Le Crotoy is really more on the sea-board than St. Valéry, for on this western side of the Somme there are outlying lands, or islands, beyond the sands seaward where the red roofs of Le Hourdel can just be distinguished from the end of the digue, built up of hurdle work and large pebbles, at St. Valéry, or from the highest outlooks of Le Crotoy; and the inhabitants may be seen wading across to the more in-world parts for the business or gaiety of shopping and visiting.

The fishing-boats are beached, all but a few in the river channel, which are spreading their light gauzy wings of large prawning-nets, bigger than sails, to the breeze. These are stretched on wide, slender, curved yards borne on a long pole at the bows. Flood-tide alters the aspect of the scene. Then one is truly at the sea-side, whether at Le Crotoy or St. Valéry. Standing on the firm rising land by the Tower of Harold, one can watch the flotilla of fishing smacks come in, about fifty of them, all marked St. V.SS., sweeping up the river channel in single file, their sails dark against the evening sky, all laden with prawns and various fish. A flock of eager women with creels, nets, and baskets hurry down the pebble bank to secure the wriggling, multi-coloured prize. The fisher-boys, with red trowsers, carry nets full of fish slung on long poles over their shoulders.

Did Jeanne, in watching this harvest of the sea, think of that so different harvest, the grapes and corn of her own sweet, sunny land? Bishop Cauchon had also woven his net, and was spreading it to catch her in his toils.

Now at flood-tide the Somme looks like a fine river, and if one saw it first like this one would not believe that one would ever walk or wade across it. A few hours hence and the expanse is all sand again.

For long Jeanne's eyes must have strained themselves across to the church of St. Valéry, high-set upon its round-towered platform, yet embowered in trees, and traced its low, square spire, its walls diapered with patterns in black flint, its five gables standing seaward to the north, and others east and west in this church of many aisles, as the sound of its bells was wafted by the south-west wind across the sands to the weary prisoner at Le Crotoy, whom all had forgotten save her enemies, as St. Valéry's fleet of boats set sail and returned daily, bringing no message of deliverance or love to her; and the sun set like a shield of flame illumining the waste of sands that spread like the wide stretch of a lasting captivity before her young life, which was indeed to set like that sun in a blaze of fire—dying gloriously.

I have tried to give a plain, truthful narrative of Jeanne's travels, her mission, and her achievements as they seemed to her, whose unsophisticated faith knew nothing of politics, of pro and con, and disturbing coils of diplomacy, the froth of statesmanship more often than its oil.

She held in view the simple right, as she was shown it, and went to her task direct as the crow flies, knowing no refinements of sophistry. Vanquishing her own womanly weakness, she could not overcome the weakness, the vacillation of others, their indifference, their sloth, their—perhaps pretended—unbelief. She could conquer the strength of the foe, but these cushiony weaknesses are always the greatest obstacles in the way of a purpose. They exhaust more than action, they wear more than friction, being like the deep ruts of a heavy road.

These weaknesses (of others) were her real enemies, as they always are enemies of the simple right.

Jeanne knew little or nothing of the history of Europe, even of her time, but she knew and held sacred her duty to her country and her king. For a time she was the only one who brought opinion to the test of action, until the eloquence of her deeds roused the French nation from its lethargy and the fatalistic doctrine of laissez-faire.

CHAPTER XVII.

JOURNEY TO ROUEN.

' Rouen, Rouen, mourrai-je ici !   Oh, Rouen, j'ai grand'peur que
tu n'aies à souffrir de ma mort.'
Jeanne d'Arc's soliloquy.

ONE more journey remains for us to take with Jeanne, it is the last. The order came at length for the prisoner to be brought to Rouen there to await her trial for sorcery, heresy, and rebellion.

This was in the second fortnight of December, 1430.

Jeanne was carried across the Somme at flood-tide in a boat. This was more practicable then than now, as the river was navigable, perhaps, at all times. She was then taken to Rouen on horseback by way of Eu and Dieppe. Notwithstanding her presentiment that Rouen would see her death, perhaps the change was not unwelcome to her. Oh, how the return to horseback must have revived her longing to escape! The road lay, as now, up by the wall-flowered ramparts of St. Valéry (gay in spring with song-birds whose nests are in the ivy), up through an archway to the chequer-built Norman church with its strong rectangular tower and deeply projecting buttresses. A covered stairway leads from here to the higher ramparts, towering above the platform of the church, whence the view of Le Crotoy, with the site of its former castle, is only a soft grey silhouette in the distance.

St. Valéry abounds in picturesque objects, ruined fortifications with crenellated round towers and machicolated archways, as well as pretty children and stately young women with fine hair, and elder women with quaint coifs and caps.

The church, which looks like an outwork of the fortress, stands on a broad pedestal of the ramparts that formerly extended far along the heights. The lower bastions are built of pebbles with string courses of hewn stone. The names of Harold and William the Conqueror are household words among the dwellings niched and nestled in these ruined walls, notwithstanding that French history insists that it was St Valéry-en-Caux which saw the mighty gathering of the Conqueror's fleet. It is a steady ascent out of St. Valéry, branching off into pretty walks and avenues; but the road to Eu descends soon after to the level of the shore, where one can make out somewhat better the puzzling geography of the sea and river.

Among the wild-fowl found in the low grounds here is the Canard Sarcelle d'été: (Ana querquedula, Linn.)—a pretty little brown mottled duck with black bill and feet.

It is about sixteen miles from St. Valéry

to Eu, twenty-five kilometres by the measuring stones. It is a rather monotonous road, exposed to the full violence of the sea-breeze, between St. Valéry and Eu, pleasant enough in spring-time, when the barley is in ear, when the larks and thrushes, warbling above the fields powdered on their banks with a short-stemmed stitchwort, fill the stimulating breeze with gladness, and the nooks and valleys are filled with wild-flowers rejoicing in the clear blue sky of France. But it had not this pleasant aspect to the sad little cortége that followed this bleak road in December, 1430.

At between five and six kilometres from St. Valéry begins the long, straggling village of Sallenelle, set between exposed banks with trees bare almost up to midsummer with the bleakness of the situation, and bent by struggling with the wind.

Sallenelle is almost continuous with Lanchères and Brutelles, a half-way village between St. Valéry and Eu. The long continuity of farms and detached houses along the main road gives this part of Picardy the appearance of being well-peopled; but this populousness is confined to the borders of the good high-road. The land is well-cultivated, but of poor quality. Few strangers pass this road; there is no public conveyance. St. Valéry once left behind, one must needs walk to Brutelles, whence it is sometimes possible to hire a cart to Eu. Past Brutelles the roads grows absolutely dreary and still more bleak, with stunted, leafless trees struggling against the biting wind in a poor soil alternately composed of chalk and beds of clay, peopled only by shepherds in long woollen cloaks with crooks (and pipes) before the road turns off to Ault St. Charles, a brand-new watering-place, dismal enough in winter.

From the heights at length one looks down upon Eu, a town, they say, of eleven thousand inhabitants, and Tréport, with three or four thousand, a local calculation which Murray upsets in stating it as three thousand seven hundred and thirty for Eu. But Tréport is a populous place, and Eu gives the idea of a larger town than Murray's calculation warrants. Eu lies on the Bresle, which forms the boundary of Normandy, at the foot of a steep hill clothed in green woods, snug as in a nest in the valley, which looks all the richer in contrast with the bare table-lands above. The town has some groups of street architecture and wooden crossbar-fronted houses that would please an artist. Its picturesque church in the early-pointed style is raised on a height in the centre of the town, a rich brown church that they like to speak of as 'the cathedral,' to which its apse, surrounded with decorated flying buttresses, gives much the appearance of one. Not far from this is the red-brick château of the Comte de Paris, where Louis Philippe once received our queen. His well-kept park and plantations stretch nearly to the white cliffs of Tréport, whose dashing blue sea, like sapphire fringed with silver, is visible in peeps between the woods.

Jeanne d'Arc halted in Eu, she most probably slept there, as it is thirty-two kilometres (about twenty miles) further to Dieppe, and there is no place of security for a prisoner on the road, unless it may be at Criel. The days were short, besides, and darkness might favour a rescue. The way to Dieppe is up the steep hill beyond the present barracks, and out on the Roman road which extends straight as an arrow flight for about five miles before it turns off at an obtuse angle straight out again. The trees that line the roads grow rather more freely here than on last evening's length of road, as the soil is better. Colza and barley are the principal crops. Public vehicles ply (frequently in summer) between Eu and Dieppe. The new road, marked by the kilometre stones, branches off to the right from the straight old Roman road, avoiding the more abrupt hill. The old road was, of course, the one followed by Jeanne d'Arc and her guard.

Descending the hill (on the old road) one comes in sight of the small town, or village, of Criel. The country is more varied here, with broken chalk-hills pierced by caves, and a triangular dip of the blue sea visible beyond the red roofs and slates and spire of the village. Caravans of gipsies halt in the warm sheltered nook where the hawthorn comes early into bloom, in quite another climate from the piercing winter and scorching summer on the exposed Roman road. The church, on the nearer side of the bridge, was the same in Jeanne's time. It has an irregular chancel with stone gurgoyles, crockets, and carved abutments, and a low square tower. The churches seem always especially connected with Jeanne d'Arc. Where there was a church Jeanne found a friend, and she entered it to worship whenever she could do so. The carved image of our Saviour signified a sympathy with her. Her escort may have halted here, human nature is much the same in all ages; men liked a cup of cider and horses required a feed then pretty much as they do now, and the church and the inn lie near together.

Up a long pull of hill between banks of chalk imbedded with flints. The country is very like Wiltshire or Sussex. We gain the high ground and the straight road again to Tocqueville (a name one knows). How clearly and how far one can hear the sound of distant footsteps before the people are in sight, as Indians hear the trail. The lark soars and sings above the waving barley crops; the sun-warmed breeze, the coolness of mother-earth with her daisies, make all one luxury as one rests upon the wayside banks. A shepherd with his flock are near, and men are ploughing.

The Roman road passes Biville-sur-mer, another oasis set in orchards and fertility; another half-way house from time pre-historical. It is a long way from the beach, notwithstanding its name of Biville-sur-mer.

The inn is of the most homely kind, but from its first-floor windows one can participate in the life of the place, such as it has ever existed since the iron age. A young countryman on a dapple-grey horse, bedight with crimson woollen trappings, rides up and shakes hands with the inn-keeper, and everyone gives him a hearty greeting. It is quite the country inn and rider of olden time. An animated picture, with human interest in it. The inn-keeper, just the man known to novel-readers as the jolly host, is the fixed centre of a changing circle. All are cheery, genial, glad to see and note the traveller on the route and mutually detail the news. All are glad to pass and repass, sure of a welcome and God-speed. Within doors the hostess prepares the 'cutlets of bacon,' broiled on the gridiron, for the guests, and hangs the basket of washed salad out to strain. The children of the hamlet play wholesomely outside, learning to be carters and horsemen in their turn. The full-cropped ducks waddle by, gobbling upwards to the oats that may chance to fall as the horse feeds at his trough yonder. The very game-cock, for all his gaudy feathers, lives at peace with the other stag-birds and the hens. The fields beyond the orchard are sunshiny with yellow colza, whose golden ground is a setting for silvery abeles and grey-powdered willows. The other village children, who have gabbled their catechism to the curé in the church, rush out to play likewise, and learn, incidentally and in playing, their duty to their neighbour after having learnt their duty towards God in the church.

Oh, that our poor little creatures in London—whom people, who do not pity and respect their childhood, call 'gutter-snipes'—had the roses and happiness of these really wealthy children, who will never become rich and wretched; and, likewise, their simple piety and love towards each other. A big boy has just taken his little brother a ride in a large toy-wheelbarrow; another boy attends to pick up the pieces. Laughter and chat pervade all ages; they seem so happy with each other. Their happiness contrasts with our luxury in cities, wrongly so named: this sort of life is the real luxury; if enjoyment of sweet air, perfumes, birds' songs, and laughter are pleasures. To be able to sit at this open window, by the rising moon, enjoying the balmy air of early May is bliss indeed! But we are free to go and come, the sense of liberty and repose adds to the enjoyment of this halt by the wayside; while every step took poor Jeanne d'Arc further from rescue, further from her country, and riveted her chains more firmly.

Off next morning early, driving 'unicorn' on the Roman road with the bare trees on each side, and the blue belt of sea to the right. Again the road makes an obtuse angle at St. Martin, at twelve kilometres from Dieppe, and darts off straight towards the sea: another angle and another, but the lines between them all straight as arrows'-flights, each of several kilometres long. Still we are on Jeanne's road, travelling with her phantom. Look out well, Jeanne, on the distant cliffs beyond the sunny colza; poor Jeanne! you will never see the glad country again. Here, just below us, is the castle of Dieppe, fresh built

A A

and terrible in Jeanne's time, with its cone-headed towers and its bridge and drawbridge over a chasm extending to the sea; then all new and hard; not picturesque as we now see it, softened by time and age. The road descends into Dieppe, broad and smooth from the table-land that breaks off abruptly in white cliffs, keen-edged against the blue. The smell of the sea wafts up through the dirty fishing-port beyond the weather-beaten brown church tower. The river Arques with its tidal-harbour, is filled with fishing-vessels. The road from Dieppe to Rouen lies in lower ground, where the climate is more tender, and the vegetation is never wholly asleep.

At St. Aubin there are larch and fir plantations rising straight from the earth skywards, no longer beaten back by the winds. This soft, well-wooded, pretty country, with meadows and mill-streams, must have smiled at Jeanne and seemed homely to her. It was a treacherous welcoming. The bleak Roman road above was like the English; hard, stern foes who never pretended to be otherwise; this softer path leading to Rouen, and to death, is like the cruel priests who seemed to be her friends, to bear love for her soul, and yet who tried to entangle her in her talk; mostly too her own countrymen, for the Bishop of Winchester was the only English prelate present at her trial; like these and the gay, faithless king and court who abandoned her to her fate so soon as she had served their turn.

This is a land of plenty; mill-streams and orchards and tall, graceful, slender avenues deck this part of the pleasant land of France, that Jeanne, more than anybody else, won back for her own people. These perhaps loved her still, but the populace are ever fickle, besides, they dared not uplift their voice. Black was their rulers' ingratitude, for, after all, the benefit at that time was theirs.

Longueville, Auffay, St. Victor, each greener, sweeter than the last. There is a taste of spring here even in the depth of winter; even in the dismal time, so near to Christmas, too, when Jeanne d'Arc passed by here, so close on her nineteenth birthday. But she saw not the full gladness of the land: that was left for her judges and captors to behold, the priests and great rich foreign lords who swept by here proudly, on war-horses and caparisoned mules, in spring, when the fields were golden green, shading into blue in the wheatlands on the borders of the new-ploughed earth, pinky like the under-side of a mushroom, changing to foxy red, then to chalk again, with sweeps of wood and moorland which are now being brought under cultivation. They saw it clothed in Nature's sweet young soft May green, shot with golden fires of planta-genista. The breeze that fanned their faces lifted the broad soft young green horse-chestnut leaves with no sound, neither did the not yet crisp twigs of the apricot cause a rustling. They might have felt Nature interceding with them for Jeanne d'Arc, so young and brave; but when did hard-hearted men ever read Nature to learn charity?

It is such a graceful country, elegant, if one may so call it. And yet people say France is ugly; generalising in a narrow-minded way from the strip they may have seen and carped at just outside the railway.

This sweet tender country in May did not soften the hearts of Jeanne's judges, riding through it with grim purpose, gathering like eagles to the slaughter of this one poor ewe-lamb. And yet they looked and prayed for mercy for themselves.

Malaunay and the busy manufactories existed not then, nor was Rouen pierced by the fine broad street that now proudly bears the name of Rue Jeanne d'Arc. But the tangled ribbon of the Seine wound then as deliciously among its wooded islands as in this year of grace, 1885, and, when moonlighted and exquisite with stars, the fair scene bears much the same aspect as it presented in Jeanne's time to a spectator standing on the slopes outside the city. A few minutes later, and the electric blaze is lighted, and everything is brought forward into the glare of modernness; reflections from the lamp-clusters on the bridge make even the water, the satiny Seine, appear turbulent.

It was a mercy that poor Jeanne d'Arc could not see this view from her prison windows at Rouen; it would have recalled too painfully the poplared islands on the Meuse. Few dungeon windows admit of much study of the scenery from their cellar-like openings, and Jeanne was caged and strongly chained in her tower in the castle, with irons on her feet, and bound by a chain to a great block of wood. Nature neither mocked nor soothed the Maid's sorrow with this year's spring beauty.

Though much of Rouen's former picturesqueness has crumbled into dust and has been swept away as lumber, still it can never quite lose its fifteenth-century aspect while its close, busy streets and thronged markets lead to its glorious cathedral, where there is so much to be forgiven (architecturally), and which is yet so beautiful: entrancing as a dream as one enters its cool shades from the scorching streets and mingles with its devotion—in feeling, if not in fact.

Neither St. Maclou, nor the picturesque Hotel Bergtheroude, which the common people wrongly call Maison de la Pucelle, then existed; they rose into beauty a very little later. But go further up the town, through wider, newer streets, and behold St. Ouen that had just then begun to be lovely, the rose and crown of decorated Gothic architecture. Standing in its gardens, a thing of beauty, behind the dense shade of horse-chestnut avenues, all in flower and leaf, the lilac and the may, exquisite in colours of white and crimson and freshness, with busy gardeners carting huge orange-trees beyond the beds of pinks, now one mass of glaucous grass, enhancing all surrounding hues. This was the scene of the abjuration which has caused righteous indignation in so many hearts, by the mental torture here inflicted on the Maid. The two scaffolds that we read of, one for the judges and one for the falsely-accused, were erected in the burial-ground of the abbey of St. Ouen, between the central tower and the west end of the church. This site was only discovered in 1871, when the abbey cemetery was unearthed in the course of the works then going forward. Stand in the Place and gaze in at the wide open doorway right through the church. It looks such a sacred shade viewed in this way, the shadowed altar seen thus from the busy street, with the coloured windows above the shrine. Surely one would say that the reign of a milder justice had set in when that transcendant choir was built.

Yet no, the choir was already perfect, and the nave and tower of St. Ouen were still in building when the Marché aux Veaux, not far beyond the shadow of its sacred stones, saw the cruel death of the youngest of Christian martyrs, after a barbarous imprisonment and a trial in which they allowed her no advocate, although she was a minor (quoiquelle fût mineure d'age); and Rouen thought it honoured God by building rather than by mercy. May her blood still plead for France to the King of kings, whose faithful servant she was, and may England be forgiven her share in the patriot's cruel fate.

St. Ouen was commenced in 1318, and the choir and transepts were completed twenty-one years after. The English wars delayed the progress of the building, which was resumed about 1490. St. Maclou was later, 1432—1500.

The cathedral at Rouen, which has been called a 'romance in stone,' possesses parts belonging to all ages. 'It was created with a total disregard to all rule, yet so splendid and picturesque that we are almost driven to the wild luxuriance of nature to find anything with which we can compare it.' The ghastly iron skeleton, called a spire, is a modern atrocity.

Jeanne d'Arc was immured in the great tower of Rouen Castle. It was the only tower of the castle which existed in Lebrun's time when he wrote: 'It has always borne the name of the heroine, sometimes also that of " Donjon Tower." For a long time it was thought that a little tower, since destroyed, was Jeanne's prison, but it has been shown that this could not have been the case.' Eight steps led up to Jeanne d'Arc's prison from the castle court, and the room looked out on the country. This old tower was destroyed soon afterwards, in 1780.

The details of the trial, and her rehabilitation, are foreign to the intention of this book, though our knowledge of most of the actual circumstances of Jeanne's life are gathered from the trial, with its collateral inquiries. It is from these that the Maid of Orleans emerges heroic, victorious, and saintly, yet a woman still. The facts are more wonderful than the legends that have overlaid and obscured her history.

Her resignation at the last is as remarkable as her obedience from the first. After months of neglect, Jeanne, still loyal at her trial, only fired up when they dared to touch her king. He was sacred to her: she might be condemned, but he, at least, she said, had done no wrong. The wrong, if any, she maintained, was hers, and hers alone. Contrast this nobleness with his indifference. Charles, who held so many prisoners in his hands, proposed not to exchange one of note for her to whom he owed them all. L'Averdy says that the history of the Maid of Orleans has been exhausted by a great number of writers who have lightly read the original sources without enough attention to the nature of the case and to the forms which were followed.

L'Averdy's work, which fills a thick quarto volume, is styled, 'Historical and Critical Reflections on the Conduct of Charles VII. with regard to Jeanne d'Arc after she was taken Prisoner by the English at the Siege of Compiègne.' The title reads still more ponderously in the original. Vainly trying to excuse Charles, he tacitly accuses him. 'They say' (? who say) 'that she had ceased to have the rights of a prisoner of war, and could not consequently be ransomed.' 'Il est prouvé qu'il (le roi d'Angleterre) en a fait *l'achat*, et non pas le *rachat*.' 'Jean of Luxembourg and the Bastard of Wandonne were forced to abandon her to Henry VI. The English were enraged at seeing France escape from their hands by means of a young peasant who declared herself minister of the will of Heaven.'

If Charles had burnt his prisoners in revenge, the English might have done the same to the Duke of Orleans. Reprisals once begun, there would have been a perpetual blood-feud. Then also her judges were French, having at their head the University of Paris.

L'Averdy makes this very important admission, that not one Englishman took part in the case. 'Il n'y pas un seul Anglais qui ait agi dans les procédures!' He admits at last that however powerful the reasons, and however difficult it is to answer them, 'there remains however at the bottom of the heart a secret dissatisfaction against the inaction of Charles VII.' He speaks mildly.

So marvelling at this inaction, he dives again for motives and brings up this pearl for his trouble: that Charles believed she was a sorceress. Then Charles was an accomplice of the pretended crime of Jeanne, of which he reaped the fruit: which was what the English wished to prove. Jeanne felt this danger for her king, and defended him nobly, interrupting the orator to cry, 'By my faith, with due reverence, I dare say and swear to you, under peril of death, that he is the most noble of Christians, who best loves the faith and the church, and he is not such as you say of him.'

'Silence her,' said the orator to the usher. Noble, generous girl.

Her trials prove that Jeanne was sincere, that

she died convinced of the truth and reality of her visions and revelations. 'The supposition of pure chance appears to me wholly inadmissible,' says L'Averdy, in speaking of the remarkable fulfilment of her words and predictions on many occasions, and the success which attended her measures when she asserted them to be of heavenly command.

On January 9th, 1431, Jeanne's public trial began, when she was just nineteen years of age: on the 9th of May, after a searching and inquisitorial examination and a cruel and rigorous captivity, she was threatened with torture in order to force her into admissions against herself: her judges having failed during these four months of cross-examination to find justification for a capital sentence against her.

Although the Duchess of Bedford (after being assured by a jury of matrons of the virginity of Jeanne) gave orders to the wardens of the prison, and others, to do her no species of violence, yet they kept her strongly fettered. 'They took her from her cage (for trial) and drew off from her three pairs of irons. After the session, they replaced the irons on her feet.' It does not appear that she was imprisoned in a cage after this first examination: naturally the French historians place her imprisonment at Rouen in its worst light, and the customs of the time were indeed very cruel; especially would they be so to a person of the lower orders, suspected, with such show of reason, of witchcraft.

The 24th of May, a year from the date of her capture at Compiègne, saw Jeanne's abjuration and release, both so-called: the 30th of May saw her cruel death.

The whole sad tale of this young girl's grievous captivity is beyond the scope of this book; those pathetic scenes of her trial, when Cardinal Winchester and even Bishop Cauchon, most cruel inquisitor of all, wept; and one of the English lords, a spectator, cried out, 'She is really a good woman. If she were but English!' I am obliged to leave out her own touching and beautiful answers and conduct at her trial.

She was of those young souls early culled, while flowers, for Heaven, their fruit to ripen in Paradise. Many aged saints have borne their fruit here on earth. 'Heaven was made for those who have failed in this world,' says Lord Carlisle, and the word has consoled many. Jeanne seemed to have failed here; as many who have worked in God's way seem to have failed, and their failure is better than the worldly man's success. The ardent spirit is at rest. There is no more work for her on this side the resurrection.

But her work was done, so far as it was given to her to do. She showed France the way of liberty, of body and soul, and she won it for her people through suffering: without which no real blessing is ever obtained. Jeanne suffered, but her country gained freedom. Her last care was for her friends' safety. Her last word, amid the flames, was Jesus. Round what was left of her—a heap of ashes—the residue of a being—rose her monument, Circumspice. Look round—on France, a free nation.

Faithful unto death, to her is given a crown of life.

APPENDIX.

BIBLIOGRAPHY OF JEANNE D'ARC.

'It is by means of such works' (bibliographies) 'that the student comes to know what has been written on every part of learning, that he avoids the hazard of encountering difficulties which have already been cleared ; of discussing questions which have already been decided ; and of digging in mines of literature which have already been exhausted.'
—Dr. Johnson.

Early in life I possessed a chap-book with spirited cuts, full of battles, with exciting sword-play of Talbot and Dunois, of the Maid of Orleans with her banner, and her king standing with ermine mantle à la George IV. at Madame Tussaud's, with his best leg foremost. The accompanying verses were at least as much founded on fact as other poems that have been written on the heroine. The final lines (with the picture) fulfilled the mission of tragic poetry and brought tears to my childish eyes. I was no great critic at eight years old.

> ' "Twas Rouen saw the closing scene,
>   Courageous died the guiltless fair ;
> Her look, undaunted and serene,
>   Made England blush that brought her there.'

Later on, I read Lord Mahon's essay (from the 'Quarterly Review'), which contained the sum of all that England then knew about the Maid of Orleans. Indeed, at the present day, one may ask many persons of fair average reading, ' What is your opinion of Jeanne d'Arc ?' ' Of whom ?' ' Of Joan of Arc ?' ' Well, h'm, ha, I really know next to nothing about her ;' and then they cast about to remember what Shakespeare has written on the subject.

Even the great Duke of Marlborough said, 'Shakespeare's historical plays are the only (English) history I ever read in my life.' Some of us are in like case. For many of us Joan of Arc is a name, or at most the heading of a pathetic fable.

The histories of England contain little beyond the bare facts that she fought us and we burnt her, and in this humanitarian age we are ashamed of ourselves for so doing.

Bastien Lepage's picture of Jeanne d'Arc gave the finishing touch to my longing to learn all I could of her myself, and now I wish to make other people know her too.

This book is the product of many journeys in France, some two or three especially devoted to this end. I have spared no trouble to examine things I hoped would be interesting. and what I have set aside as being less closely cognate with my subject would fill a book twice as large.

Half being sometimes more than the whole, I have refrained from anecdote and such of the Maid's personal history and feats as have often been told before. Applying to my heroine the realism of the present day, I have given prominence to the scenery of her actions; as this often illustrates her deeds and gives them a solidarity to our minds such as no narrative, save that of a poet—a Walter Scott, for instance—or the vigorous verisimilitude of an eye-witness can convey. In trying to put together collateral matters bearing directly on the subject and in themselves interesting, I hope I have not made it too much of a 'sausage-book,' which is my abhorrence; though I fear I may be called a 'Grangerite.'*

There are French histories of Jeanne in abundance. They have multiplied since Lebrun de Charmettes made a good road through a mass of fragments of histories in a

---

* The 'Grangerites' are the people who enlarge a book, in itself of little value, by inserting into its pages plates, playbills, letters, libels, street ballads, pamphlets, newspaper clippings, and anything bearing on the subject matter of the original volume. The excuse for the Grangerite is that he thus accumulates data for the future chronicler. The horror of h m is that his work may multiply the sources of error.

complete and regular history of the heroine, published in 1817 : but in England we had nothing but what I have mentioned, beyond the short and incorrect accounts in the biographical dictionaries—except G. Ann Grave's much-abridged translation of Lenglet du Fresnoy, published in 1812—until Miss Parr, sitting down in 1865 before the four volumes of Lebrun de Charmettes and the five volumes of Quicherat, did for England something the same as Wallon has done for France (allowing for the natural ignorance of an Englishwoman as to French topography and customs). She has sifted the evidence, shortened the accounts of conflicting authorities, and given us in a readable summary the life and death of perhaps the most interesting woman who ever lived; of a figure, at all events, unique in history.

I have taken a totally different line of inquiry, and, setting aside the bulky volumes of evidence, I take it for granted that English people have read (or will read) Miss Parr, or at least Lord Mahon, as most French people have read Wallon; therefore I need not go over that ground again. Though I have found amply sufficient data to make, I hope, an interesting story of the heroine's life, mine must rather be viewed as a supplementary volume to Wallon, or in English to Miss Parr, as I leave out almost all that they have treated of; not by utilizing their leavings, but by looking elsewhere for material. Theirs is the indoor, mine the outdoor history. There is no similarity between them

Among authorities I may not include the imaginative writers, ranging from Shakespeare to the rhapsodists, whose so-called biographies are ebullitions of the enthusiasm of 1820, when Monsieur Jollois, superintending engineer in the Vosges, gratified the public with a glorification (in folio) of the tasteless little monument at Domremy, then 'inaugurated;' a word appropriately consecrated to such themes. He gives a view of the long since dried-up fountain, miscalled Greek, whose shelving roof shelters the bust of the Maid of Orleans in plumed toque and costume of the time of the Restoration (in France), surrounded by the throng of fashionable people who waved their tear-bedewed handkerchiefs dry at the 'inauguration.'

Southey set the example of honouring Joan of Arc in

England. His volume is in verse, and it is kindly, complimentarily meant; but it lacks the poetry of truth. It rings false throughout and leaden: as a book it is a creditable rather than a delightful possession. Southey found a picturesque subject and dressed it up in fancy costume of classic flow, like the then fashionable statues; taking his fanciful history from Caze, the worst guide he could have had. Caze's pretended royal parentage of Jeanne is nonsense, as is the whole of his history. It is founded on sand.

One cannot expect real value from an epic poem written at nineteen and published at twenty-one, and Southey's verse is very boyish and high-flown. Like Schiller he evolved a Jeanne from his moral consciousness, and from reading a poem of Chapelain's called, 'La France délivrée,' which he analysed, and his epic grew out of a shorter chimera of his own which he called 'The Vision of the Maid of Orleans.' Southey learnt better as he grew older and read Lebrun de Charmettes, who quotes Caze only to refute him. I read Lebrun de Charmettes from Southey's own well-marked copy, dated Keswick, 1837.

For Schiller there is less excuse for having given us a fictitious Jeanne, in that he had greater genius and riper years. In thus painting the lily, gilding the violet, he has shown what is less pardonable than error of judgment in a poet—to wit, want of taste. He also had read L'Averdy and knew the truth, therefore was not privileged to go wrong. He has not improved his play by his aberrations, else some might have forgiven him in the interests of art. He has wilfully defaced one of the loveliest stories the world has ever known; one which is poetry itself even when unadorned by verse. The poem has become a common-place German legend. In his glowing commentary on Schiller's drama, Carlyle, who does not believe in Jeanne's pretensions, shows far deeper appreciation of the beauty of her character than Schiller, who believes too much.

The poets have each and all overstepped the boundaries of the most ample poetical license. Our Shakespeare is the least to blame in this, as he uttered the belief of his time and nation; but for Voltaire, we can only do to him as the Jews to the tomb of Absalom, take up a stone and throw it behind our backs.

L'Averdy's work was already written and talked of when Southey wrote. He was occupied with it in 1791, but the publication was delayed, and no wonder, considering the condition of France at that time. L'Averdy brings forward all the letters and MSS. relative to Jeanne's pretended marriage and life after the scene at Rouen, where, like a new Iphigenia or another Isaac, a substitute is supposed to have been provided. Polluche, commenting on the recital of the doyen of St. Thiebaut, says, 'The Maid after escaping from the hands of the English, it matters little how,' (il importe peu comment). Yet this is the most necessary thing to know. The misplaced credulity of that age averred that by her sanctity Jeanne escaped the fire, and they burnt another believing it to be herself. Two persons are known to have passed for the escaped Pucelle.

Quicherat has cleared up these things for France, but the damage of a fable is its tendency to be perpetuated by oral tradition till it seems to have become a truth, or, at least, to be a respectable opinion. England owes Jeanne too much reparation to prolong these errors.

Setting aside the poets, the over-credulous, and the unbelievers, who maintain that the real Jeanne was an impostor, I find the historians all follow each other like sheep, until, like counting an imaginary flock in a wakeful night, one wearies of the vain repetitions and re-discussions of settled points; the question of Jeanne's inspiration emptying itself into each writer's preconceived idea, leaving each unconvinced reader still of his own opinion. I seem to know Petitot, who devotes to Jeanne d'Arc more than half of the eighth volume of his 'Memoirs relating to French history,' word for word; he has copied, and he has so often been re-copied. It is one of a chain of similar links.

Many of these writers, among others Berriat St. Prix (highly complimented in his time), attach to a rhapsody beginning, 'Femme illustre et infortunée! Voilà donc la récompense de tant de services et de vertus!' &c. &c., a list of authors and quotations from their opinions, making as pleasant reading as any other unclassified dictionary.

Half of everybody's book is filled with the trial,

oftener this is two-thirds; half of the remainder is made up of rhapsodies and apostrophes.

The information on collateral points of Jeanne's history is voluminous. Besides Quicherat's five octavo volumes of the two trials, there are five volumes by A. Renard on the name of Jeanne d'Arc and if she was French, besides many smaller works on the history of her family. The dissertations on the particle and apostrophe (D'Arc, Darc) would fill a large volume. There are six printed columns of works on Jeanne d'Arc in the British Museum catalogue, mostly French and Latin, next most Italian, some German, few English.

Quicherat's important work, 'The Trial and Rehabilitation,' with notes, was judged worthy of being published by the Société de l'Histoire de France, 1st of August, 1841. This is in five volumes; one on the condemnation, four on the rehabilitation. Concerning Jeanne d'Arc's life, history is nowhere built on better evidence. She was the subject of four trials, of which the two last great trials (procès) were one for her and the other against her; arraying the powers of both church and state for her condemnation and rehabilitation. Better evidence cannot exist; it was gathered from every source with most careful (or malicious) minuteness. This was written in the old law Latin for the trials; Quicherat (in 1841) has digested the Latin text and added elucidatory notes. Each brick is well laid, and the reader possesses herein not only the evidence, but also the original text of every contemporaneous author, and can collate them easily; that is, presuming he can read the Latin, the old French, and old English. The notes are pleasant reading.

Lebrun de Charmettes, in 1817, had already condensed and translated many of these documents into French; yet, such is the upsetting power of legend, in almost every record of Jeanne written of late years, we find inexactitude, on every inscribed tablet a wrong date, and succeeding writers have always followed the wrong indications. Lebrun and Quicherat would seem to have laboured in vain.

Even our 'Encyclopædia Brittanica' of 1856 was weak enough to follow word for word a trashy biography compiled for the newspapers, when it would have been almost as easy to copy authentic documents. The very short notice of Jeanne d'Arc in the ninth edition (1879) has few or no errors, it has been shortened by having the errors cut out, while little or nothing has been added or altered. Hume, who follows at second-hand the text of Monstrelet, the Burgundian, is wrong in every date he gives.

Walcknaer, in his 'Biographic Universelle,' says no history rests upon such authentic materials as that of Jeanne d'Arc, because of the juridical testimony of the two trials. He does not include the trial at Poitiers, which I consider highly important. It would be unnatural if authors, even of the period in question, agreed in each particular. The writings of the holy evangelists themselves do not tally—whereby we get a wider truth. The sacred historians do not always speak in unison. The result is a harmony, a complete chord: or, if an apparent discord should occur, remember, a resolved discord is the most exquisite of musical effects. I doubt if the special correspondents of our newspapers would agree in the same features of the self-same campaign; yet each one would give his individual quota of fact, and we should gain the broad general impression of the truth.

When Lebrun de Charmettes wrote (in 1817) France possessed no complete and regular history of the heroine, for we cannot call such the Latin work (incomplete) of Hordal, nor Richer's unpublished MSS. which had been pillaged by Lenglet du Fresnoy. L'Averdy's immense work, drawn from the MSS. in the Bibliothèque du Roi, was written; but if already published, which is doubtful, Lebrun de Charmettes does not seem to have referred to it; nor to the 'Recueil Historique,' published in 1806, by Monsieur Chassard, which is but the maimed verbal copy of L'Averdy's work, in which positive documents were for the first time brought to light. As Lebrun de Charmettes says, 'After all, it is Jeanne d'Arc herself who seems to relate her life and plead her own cause,' so carefully were her answers taken down at the trials. Her own words are her best history, and her monument. She wrote nothing, but she lived, spoke, and worked, and died for her faith, which she believed in to the point of martyrdom. How few of us can plead one quarter as much!

Other books on Jeanne d'Arc are as difficult reading as swallowing a wineglass-full of sand. All authors are short on the subject of her journey to Chinon; even Wallon only devotes two pages to it; most of them skip over the one hundred and fifty leagues like grasshoppers, the rest clear them at a bound. Cuvier-like, one can often construct a chain of story on the evidence of *what must have been*, as he constructed an organised animal from one authentic bone. This journey is a case in point, as indeed are many of Jeanne's journeys, for she travelled much and kept her eyes open. No one has hitherto followed her in her journey from Sully to Melun. She is here completely lost to history. This is a point that proves the value of the geographical treatment of history. Monsieur Jollois, in his 'Abridged History,' calls Monsieur Berriat St. Prix remarkable for the science and scope of his researches. One is disappointed on reading his work, which has been over-praised by the polite flattery of a contemporary. I thought I was the first to trace the heroine's route and follow her step by step through her career: but there is nothing new under the sun, and my book was nearly finished, the rough copy complete, when I discovered Berriat St. Prix was my forerunner in this line.

I flew to consult his work, for instruction, of course, yet hoping in my inmost soul he had not preoccupied my ground. He had given a map, a poor one, few places were marked on it and the rivers ran wrong, meandering in lines of beauty at their own sweet will. I picked him to pieces. In Berriat St. Prix's map Coudray Tower is a long way off in the wrong direction, southward of Chinon, and in his text he sends this luckless castle flying three leagues to the north, beyond even a Château de Coudrai which has nothing to do with Jeanne's history. This Tower of Coudray has already been a stumbling-block to me with several authors, the father of whose errors I had now found. He had also mistaken St. Florent-le-Vieil, between Angers and Nantes, for St. Florent-les-Saumur, another pitfall for succeeding historians. From this I opined that Monsieur Berriat St. Prix did not know the country, that he chiefly travelled in his arm-chair, or slept in the coupé of the diligence.

In high glee I still further worried my author and confirmed my opinion that his intention was better than his work of the Itinerary: of which he daringly exclaims, 'Voilà un ouvrage entièrement neuf!'

He had the thought of it, I admit, so had I—some sixty years later. I think I am the first to walk in Jeanne's actual paths, and I can fairly say that my book was not hatched in a museum library. Berriat St. Prix takes the materialistic view of Jeanne's character, while Lebrun de Charmettes looks upon her entirely as an inspired warrior.

The plates are the most important part of Monsieur Jollois' work. He gathered up the current traditions of the department of the Meuse, where he superintended the erection of Jeanne's monument.

Mrs. Bray's book is an abridged translation of Henri Martin's 'History of France,' flavoured with extracts from the 'Chronique de la Pucelle.'

One might make a genealogical chapter of the writers on Jeanne d'Arc something in this manner: Lenglet du Fresnoy, son of Richer; Petitot, son of Denis Godefroy; Lebrun de Charmettes and Quicherat are parents of Wallon, their son and heir, and a daughter, Miss Parr, &c., &c.

My intention has not been to write the life of Jeanne d'Arc at all, but to give a general view of the country through which she passed, in its present condition; dwelling most on the objects upon which her eyes rested, and which helped in their measure to form her character, as the geographical and strategical features of the country moulded the plan of her campaigns. I do not pretend, nor propose to describe the sieges which have been so often written of before, and I give no account of the great trials which form the bulk of literature concerning the Maid of Orleans. Does anyone care to see what she saw, and share the thoughts that may, or must, have passed through her mind in viewing so large a portion of the fair land she fought and died for? If so, let them follow the route traced in my map, and they will find as much varied enjoyment as in any other line of travel, with health and the pleasures of sympathy.

GENEALOGICAL TABLE OF WRITERS.

'Books do contain a progeny of life, as do those who bring them forth.'—MILTON.

Perceval de Cagny, 1428; Gui de Laval, 1428; Jean Chartier, 1429; and most of the other writers of the fifteenth century are given in full in Quicherat's valuable work. Lebrun de Charmettes gives Astezan (1435).

1429.—Jacques Gelu, Archbishop of Tours, and in 1427 of Embrun, wrote his treatise on the Maid in 1429. It is MS. in the library of the late King of France (1812) Bibliothèque Nationale.

1431.—Monstrelet lived at Cambrai. Hume copies Monstrelet through Rapin Thoyras. Shakespeare follows current tradition inimical to the Maid.

1661.—Denis Godefroy, historiographe de France.

1714—78.—Voltaire follows a vicious fancy.

1753.—Richer's unpublished life of Jeanne d'Arc is the first composed from authentic sources; from him comes Lenglet du Fresnoy. He says of Rapin Thoyras, the most esteemed historian of Jeanne d'Arc in England, that he had not seen the procès of justification, but only Monstrelet and not the other historians of Jeanne's time.

1791.—L'Averdy, Academician, declares Lenglet du Fresnoy's work très médiocre.

1798.—A vision of the Maid of Orleans. Southey.

1801.—Schiller's drama of the Maid of Orleans. Entirely fictitious, though he had read L'Averdy.

1806.—R. Southey published his epic poem of Joan of Arc.

1812.—G. Ann Grave abridged and partially translated Lenglet du Fresnoy.

1815.—Chalmers' 'Biographical Dictionary.' The article might then have been better written.

1817.—Berriat St. Prix follows Tripaut and L'Averdy, whose work he calls 'très précieux.'

1817.—Lebrun de Charmettes published his fine work.

1819.—Petitot (published 1825), follows J. Chartier, Denis Godefroy, &c. He devotes more than half of the eighth volume of his 'Memoirs relating to the History of France from Philip Augustus to the beginning of the seventeenth century,' to Jeanne d'Arc.

1821.—Jollois' 'Abridged History of Jeanne d'Arc.' He follows L'Averdy and Lebrun de Charmettes. He says Chaussard's 'Recueil historique et complet' is only an extract of L'Averdy's work.

1825.—Carlyle's 'Life of Schiller,' first edition 1825, second edition 1845, third edition 1872: treats at some length of Joan of Arc.

1841.—Quicherat's great work published. He prints the writers of the fifteenth century in the original text with notes.

1848.—Henri Martin devotes a great part of the seventh volume of his 'Histoire de France' to Jeanne d'Arc. He follows Lebrun de Charmettes and his own fevered brain. He has written a valuable history of France, however.

1851.—Gorton's 'Biographical Dictionary' follows Chalmers in its calm, its errors, and its impartial views; though the earliest writer is (naturally) the longest and wrongest.

1860.—Wallon's work crowned by the French Academy. The edition of 1876 is beautifully embellished.

1866.—Miss Parr's 'Life and Death of Joan of Arc,' compiled from Quicherat, Lebrun de Charmettes, and Wallon. Other writers are mere romancers or rhapsodists; nobody's children.

1882.—Joseph Fabre. His thin duodecimo 'Life of Jeanne d'Arc' is one of a series of small books called, 'Ecole de l'homme et du Citoyen.' This book is a familiarised Wallon without the religious feeling. Though an ardent admirer of Jeanne, he shows her in black and white, politically and patriotically only. Religion coloured Jeanne's whole life; thus it is a false view, a pen and ink sketch of a person whose chief beauty lies in her colour.

1885.—Florence Caddy follows object lessons and the cross-country roads. Which is her apology for putting forward the hundredth work on Joan of Arc.

This list and my sheaf of British Museum tickets represent a considerable amount of reading (much of it is in old French with antiquated type), besides a number of books read in France at the recommendation of the Abbé Bourgaut and others. Yet I trust my book will be found to smell of the hayfields rather than of the reading-room. I have sought my building materials in their native quarries, in museums only the mortar that holds them together.

'The gradual building-up of primitive history is, in my eyes, to the full as interesting and as fruitful a process as the extension of physical sciences which attracts a thousandfold more attention.'—W. E. GLADSTONE.

THE END.

www.ingramcontent.com/pod-product-compliance
Lightning Source LLC
Chambersburg PA
CBHW032021220426
43664CB00006B/325